Microsoft® Official Academic Course

Windows Server® Administration Fundamentals, Exam 98-365

WILEY

Credits

EDITOR	Bryan Gambrel
DIRECTOR OF SALES	Mitchell Beaton
DIRECTOR OF MARKETING	Chris Ruel
MICROSOFT SENIOR PRODUCT MANAGER	Merrick Van Dongen of Microsoft Learning
EDITORIAL PROGRAM ASSISTANT	Jennifer Lartz
CONTENT MANAGER	Micheline Frederick
SENIOR PRODUCTION EDITOR	Kerry Weinstein
CREATIVE DIRECTOR	Harry Nolan
COVER DESIGNER	Jim O'Shea
TECHNOLOGY AND MEDIA	Tom Kulesa/Wendy Ashenberg

Cover photo: Credit: © Aimin Tang/iStockphoto

This book was set in Garamond by Aptara, Inc. and printed and bound by Bind Rite Graphics.
The cover was printed by Phoenix Color.

Microsoft, ActiveX, Excel, InfoPath, Microsoft Press, MSDN, OneNote, Outlook, PivotChart, PivotTable, PowerPoint, SharePoint, SQL Server, Visio, Visual Basic, Visual C#, Visual Studio, Windows, Windows 7, Windows Mobile, Windows Server, and Windows Vista are either registered trademarks or trademarks of Microsoft Corporation in the United States and/or other countries. Other product and company names mentioned herein may be the trademarks of their respective owners.

The example companies, organizations, products, domain names, e-mail addresses, logos, people, places, and events depicted herein are fictitious. No association with any real company, organization, product, domain name, e-mail address, logo, person, place, or event is intended or should be inferred.

The book expresses the author's views and opinions. The information contained in this book is provided without any express, statutory, or implied warranties. Neither the authors, John Wiley & Sons, Inc., Microsoft Corporation, nor their resellers or distributors will be held liable for any damages caused or alleged to be caused either directly or indirectly by this book.

ISBN 978-0-470-90182-3

Printed in the United States of America

10 9 8 7 6 5 4

Foreword from the Publisher

Wiley's publishing vision for the Microsoft Official Academic Course series is to provide students and instructors with the skills and knowledge they need to use Microsoft technology effectively in all aspects of their personal and professional lives. Quality instruction is required to help both educators and students get the most from Microsoft's software tools and to become more productive. Thus our mission is to make our instructional programs trusted educational companions for life.

To accomplish this mission, Wiley and Microsoft have partnered to develop the highest quality educational programs for Information Workers, IT Professionals, and Developers. Materials created by this partnership carry the brand name "Microsoft Official Academic Course," assuring instructors and students alike that the content of these textbooks is fully endorsed by Microsoft, and that they provide the highest quality information and instruction on Microsoft products. The Microsoft Official Academic Course textbooks are "Official" in still one more way—they are the officially sanctioned courseware for Microsoft IT Academy members.

The Microsoft Official Academic Course series focuses on *workforce development*. These programs are aimed at those students seeking to enter the workforce, change jobs, or embark on new careers as information workers, IT professionals, and developers. Microsoft Official Academic Course programs address their needs by emphasizing authentic workplace scenarios with an abundance of projects, exercises, cases, and assessments.

The Microsoft Official Academic Courses are mapped to Microsoft's extensive research and job-task analysis, the same research and analysis used to create the Microsoft Technology Associate (MTA) and Microsoft Certified Information Technology Professional (MCITP) exams. The textbooks focus on real skills for real jobs. As students work through the projects and exercises in the textbooks they enhance their level of knowledge and their ability to apply the latest Microsoft technology to everyday tasks. These students also gain resume-building credentials that can assist them in finding a job, keeping their current job, or in furthering their education.

The concept of life-long learning is today an utmost necessity. Job roles, and even whole job categories, are changing so quickly that none of us can stay competitive and productive without continuously updating our skills and capabilities. The Microsoft Official Academic Course offerings, and their focus on Microsoft certification exam preparation, provide a means for people to acquire and effectively update their skills and knowledge. Wiley supports students in this endeavor through the development and distribution of these courses as Microsoft's official academic publisher.

Today educational publishing requires attention to providing quality print and robust electronic content. By integrating Microsoft Official Academic Course products, *WileyPLUS*, and Microsoft certifications, we are better able to deliver efficient learning solutions for students and teachers alike.

Bonnie Lieberman

General Manager and Senior Vice President

Welcome to the Microsoft Official Academic Course (MOAC) program for Windows Server Administration Fundamentals. MOAC represents the collaboration between Microsoft Learning and John Wiley & Sons, Inc. publishing company. Microsoft and Wiley teamed up to produce a series of textbooks that deliver compelling and innovative teaching solutions to instructors and superior learning experiences for students. Infused and informed by in-depth knowledge from the creators of Microsoft products, and crafted by a publisher known world-wide for the pedagogical quality of its products, these textbooks maximize skills transfer in minimum time. Students are challenged to reach their potential by using their new technical skills as highly productive members of the workforce.

Because this knowledge base comes directly from Microsoft, creator of the Microsoft Certified IT Professional, Microsoft Certified Technology Specialist (MCTS), and Microsoft Certified Professional exams (www.microsoft.com/learning/certification), you are sure to receive the topical coverage that is most relevant to students' personal and professional success. Microsoft's direct participation not only assures you that MOAC textbook content is accurate and current; it also means that students will receive the best instruction possible to enable their success on certification exams and in the workplace.

■ The Microsoft Official Academic Course Program

The *Microsoft Official Academic Course* series is a complete program for instructors and institutions to prepare and deliver great courses on Microsoft software technologies. With MOAC, we recognize that, because of the rapid pace of change in the technology and curriculum developed by Microsoft, there is an ongoing set of needs beyond classroom instruction tools for an instructor to be ready to teach the course. The MOAC program endeavors to provide solutions for all these needs in a sys-tematic manner in order to ensure a successful and rewarding course experience for both instructor and student—technical and curriculum training for instructor readiness with new software releases; the software itself for student use at home for building hands-on skills, assessment, and validation of skill development; and a great set of tools for delivering instruction in the classroom and lab. All are important to the smooth delivery of an interesting course on Microsoft software, and all are pro-vided with the MOAC program. We think about the model below as a gauge for ensuring that we completely support you in your goal of teaching a great course. As you evaluate your instructional materials options, you may wish to use the model for comparison purposes with available products.

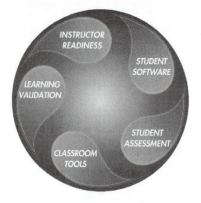

■ Pedagogical Features

The MOAC textbook for Windows Server Administration Fundamentals is designed to cover all the learning objectives for that MTA exam 98-365, which is referred to as its "objective domain." The Microsoft Technology Associate (MTA) exam objectives are highlighted throughout the textbook. Many pedagogical features have been developed specifically for *Microsoft Official Academic Course* programs.

Presenting the extensive procedural information and technical concepts woven throughout the textbook raises challenges for the student and instructor alike. The Illustrated Book Tour that follows provides a guide to the rich features contributing to *Microsoft Official Academic Course* program's pedagogical plan. Following is a list of key features in each lesson designed to prepare students for success as they continue in their IT education, on the certification exams, and in the workplace:

- Each lesson begins with a **Lesson Skill Matrix**. More than a standard list of learning objectives, the Domain Matrix correlates each software skill covered in the lesson to the specific exam objective domain.

- Concise and frequent **Step-by-Step** instructions teach students new features and provide an opportunity for hands-on practice. Numbered steps give detailed, step-by-step instructions to help students learn software skills.

- **Illustrations:** Screen images provide visual feedback as students work through the exercises. The images reinforce key concepts, provide visual clues about the steps, and allow students to check their progress.

- **Key Terms:** Important technical vocabulary is listed with definitions at the beginning of the lesson. When these terms are used later in the lesson, they appear in bold italic type and are defined. The Glossary contains all of the key terms and their definitions.

- Engaging point-of-use **Reader Aids**, located throughout the lessons, tell students why this topic is relevant (*The Bottom Line*), provide students with helpful hints (*Take Note*). Reader Aids also provide additional relevant or background information that adds value to the lesson.

- **Certification Ready** features throughout the text signal students where a specific certification objective is covered. They provide students with a chance to check their understanding of that particular MTA objective and, if necessary, review the section of the lesson where it is covered. MOAC offers complete preparation for MTA certification.

- **End-of-Lesson Questions:** The Knowledge Assessment section provides a variety of multiple-choice, true-false, matching, and fill-in-the-blank questions.

- **End-of-Lesson Exercises:** Competency Assessment case scenarios, Proficiency Assessment case scenarios, and Workplace Ready exercises are projects that test students' ability to apply what they've learned in the lesson.

■ Lesson Features

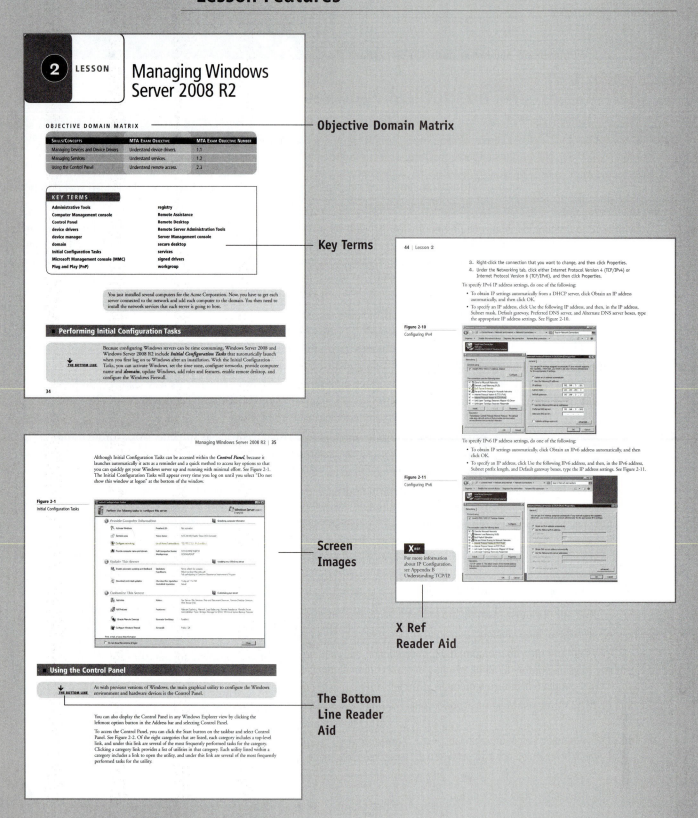

Objective Domain Matrix

Key Terms

Screen Images

X Ref Reader Aid

The Bottom Line Reader Aid

206 | Lesson 7

3. Under Create virtual network, select the type of network you want to create.
4. Click Add. The New Virtual Network page appears.
5. Type a name for the new network. Review the other properties and modify them if necessary.
6. Click OK to save the virtual network and close Virtual Network Manager, or click Apply to save the virtual network and continue using Virtual Network Manager.

MODIFY A VIRTUAL NETWORK

GET READY. To modify a virtual network:

1. Open Hyper-V Manager.
2. From the Actions menu, click Virtual Network Manager.
3. Under Virtual Networks, click the name of the network you want to modify.
4. Under Virtual Network Properties, edit the appropriate properties to modify the virtual network.
5. Click OK to save the changes and close Virtual Network Manager, or click Apply to save the changes and continue using Virtual Network Manager.

REMOVE A VIRTUAL NETWORK

GET READY. To remove a virtual network:

1. Open Hyper-V Manager.
2. From the Actions menu, click Virtual Network Manager.
3. Under Virtual Networks, click the name of the network you want to remove.
4. Under Virtual Network Properties, click Remove.
5. Click OK to save the changes and close Virtual Network Manager, or click Apply to save the changes and continue using Virtual Network Manager.

ADD A NETWORK ADAPTER

GET READY. To add a network adapter:

1. Open Hyper-V Manager. Click Start, point to Administrative Tools, and click Hyper-V Manager.
2. In the results pane under Virtual Machines, select the virtual machine that you want to configure.
3. In the Action pane under the virtual machine name, click Settings.
4. In the navigation pane, click Add Hardware.
5. On the Add Hardware page, choose a network adapter or a legacy network adapter.
6. Click Add. The Network Adapter or Legacy Network Adapter page appears.
7. Under Network, select the virtual network you want to connect to.
8. If you want to configure a static MAC address or virtual LAN identifier, specify the numbers you want to use.
9. Click OK.

✦ MORE INFORMATION
For more information about Hyper-V, visit the following Web site: http://technet.microsoft.com/en-us/virtualization/default.aspx

More Information Reader Aid

Certification Ready Alert

Take Note Reader Aid

Managing Windows Server 2008 R2 | 41

CERTIFICATION READY
How do you manage a server from your desk?
2.3

Configuring Remote Settings

As with most enterprise versions of Windows including Windows Server 2008 and Windows Server 2008 R2, you can remotely connect to a server using *Remote Assistance* and *Remote Desktop*.

With Remote Assistance and Remote Desktop, you can access a computer running Windows with another computer that is connected to the same network or over the Internet just as if you were sitting in front of the server. You will be able to use your mouse and keyboard to access the desktop, taskbar, and Start menu. You will be able to run programs and access all of the configuration tools.

Remote Assistance is designed for support personnel to connect to an active login session to assist or troubleshoot a problem. Unlike Remote Desktop, Remote Assistance allows the user to interact with the current session including seeing the same computer screen. If you decide to share control of your computer with your remote user, you both will be able to control the mouse cursor.

To keep the system secure and to make sure you want the option available, you must first install Remote Assistant as a feature. It must also be enabled in the Remote tab of the System properties dialog box. Next, you will have to invite the person using email or an instant message. You can also reuse an invitation that you sent before. After the person accepts the invitation, a two-way encrypted connection will be created.

To start a Remote Assistance session and to create an invitation, open the Start Menu, click All Programs, Select Maintenance, and click Windows Remote Assistance. See Figure 2-7.

Figure 2-7
Windows Remote Assistance

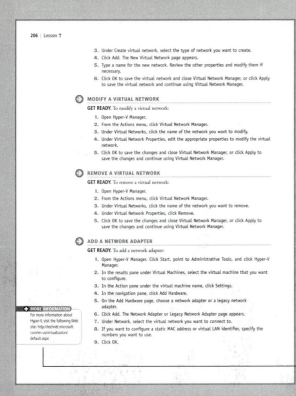

TAKE NOTE
Before you can use Remote Assistance with Windows Server 2008 R2, you must first install the Remote Assistance feature.

TAKE NOTE
Before you can use Remote Desktop, you must first enable it using System Properties. In addition, by default, administrators and users are members of the Remote Desktop users group and have access to Remote Desktop.

Remote Desktop allows a user running the Remote Desktop program to access a server remotely. By default, Windows Server 2008 R2 supports two remote desktop connections (three if you also count the console mode, which is the active connection as if you were actually sitting in front of the server keyboard and monitor).

Unlike Remote Assistance, Remote Desktop is installed but must be enabled before you connect to the server. To enable Remote Desktop, open the System Properties and select one of the following settings:

• Allow connections from computer running any version of Remote Desktop (less secure).
• Allow connections running Remote Desktop with Network Level Authentication (more secure).

Easy-to-Read Tables

38 | Lesson 2

Table 2-1
UAC Settings

SETTING	DESCRIPTION	SECURITY IMPACT
Always notify	You will be notified before programs make changes to your computer or to Windows settings that require the permission of an administrator. When you're notified, your desktop will be dimmed, and you must either approve or deny the request in the UAC dialog box before you can do anything else on your computer. The dimming of your desktop is referred to as the *secure desktop* because other programs can't run while it's dimmed.	This is the most secure setting. When you are notified, you should carefully read the contents of each dialog box before allowing changes to be made to your computer.
Notify me only when programs try to make changes to my computer	You will be notified before programs make changes to your computer that require the permission of an administrator. You will not be notified if you try to make changes to Windows settings that require the permission of an administrator. You will be notified if a program outside of Windows tries to make changes to a Windows setting.	It's usually safe to allow changes to be made to Windows settings without you being notified. However, certain programs that come with Windows can have commands or data passed to them, and malicious software can take advantage of this by using these programs to install files or change settings on your computer. You should always be careful about which programs you allow to run on your computer.
Notify me only when programs try to make changes to my computer (do not dim my desktop)	You will be notified before programs make changes to your computer that require the permission of an administrator. You will not be notified if you try to make changes to Windows settings that require the permission of an administrator. You will be notified if a program outside of Windows tries to make changes to a Windows setting.	This setting is the same as "Notify only when programs try to make changes to my computer," but you are not notified on the secure desktop. Because the UAC dialog box isn't on the secure desktop with this setting, other programs might be able to interfere with the dialog's visual appearance. This is a small security risk if you already have a malicious program running on your computer.
Never notify	You will not be notified before any changes are made to your computer. If you are logged on as an administrator, programs can make changes to your computer without you knowing about it. If you are logged on as a standard user, any changes that require the permission of an administrator will automatically be denied. If you select this setting, you will need to restart the computer to complete the process of turning off UAC. Once UAC is off, people that log on as administrator will always have the permission of an administrator.	This is the least secure setting. When you set UAC to never notify, you open up your computer to potential security risks. If you set UAC to never notify, you should be careful about which programs you run, because they will have the same access to the computer as you do. This includes reading and making changes to protected system areas, your personal data, saved files, and anything else stored on the computer. Programs will also be able to communicate and transfer information to and from anything that your computer connects with, including the Internet.

www.wiley.com/college/microsoft *or*
call the MOAC Toll-Free Number: 1+(888) 764-7001 (U.S. & Canada only)

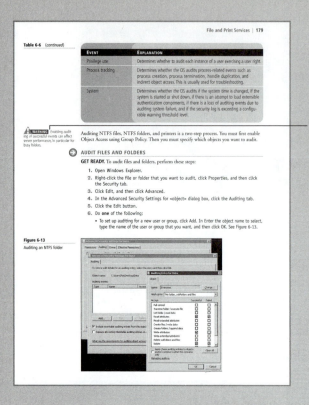

Warning Reader Aid

Photos

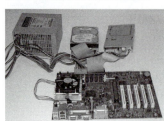

Step-by-Step Exercises

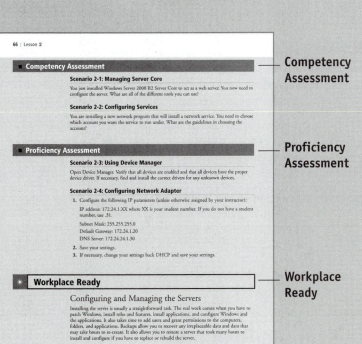

Skill Summary

Knowledge Assessment

Competency Assessment

Proficiency Assessment

Workplace Ready

Conventions and Features Used in This Book

This book uses particular fonts, symbols, and heading conventions to highlight important information or to call your attention to special steps. For more information about the features in each lesson, refer to the Illustrated Book Tour section.

CONVENTION	MEANING
↓ THE BOTTOM LINE	This feature provides a brief summary of the material to be covered in the section that follows.
CLOSE	Words in all capital letters indicate instructions for opening, saving, or closing files or programs. They also point out items you should check or actions you should take.
CERTIFICATION READY	This feature signals the point in the text where a specific certification objective is covered. It provides you with a chance to check your understanding of that particular MTA objective and, if necessary, review the section of the lesson where it is covered.
TAKE NOTE*	Reader aids appear in shaded boxes found in your text. *Take Note* provides helpful hints related to particular tasks or topics.
X REF	These notes provide pointers to information discussed elsewhere in the textbook or describe interesting features of Windows Server that are not directly addressed in the current topic or exercise.
Alt + Tab	A plus sign (+) between two key names means that you must press both keys at the same time. Keys that you are instructed to press in an exercise will appear in the font shown here.
Example	Key terms appear in bold italic.

The *Microsoft Official Academic Course* programs are accompanied by a rich array of resources that incorporate the extensive textbook visuals to form a pedagogically cohesive package. These resources provide all the materials instructors need to deploy and deliver their courses. Resources available online for download include:

- The **MSDN Academic Alliance** is designed to provide the easiest and most inexpensive developer tools, products, and technologies available to faculty and students in labs, classrooms, and on student PCs. A free 3-year membership is available to qualified MOAC adopters.

  Note: Microsoft Windows 2008 Server, Microsoft Windows 7, and Microsoft Visual Studio can be downloaded from MSDN AA for use by students in this course.

- The **Instructor's Guide** contains Solutions to all the textbook exercises and Syllabi for various term lengths. The Instructor's Guide also includes chapter summaries and lecture notes. The Instructor's Guide is available from the Book Companion site (http://www.wiley.com/college/microsoft).

- The **Test Bank** contains hundreds of questions in multiple-choice, true-false, short answer, and essay formats, and is available to download from the Instructor's Book Companion site (www.wiley.com/college/microsoft). A complete answer key is provided.

- A complete set of **PowerPoint presentations and images** are available on the Instructor's Book Companion site (http://www.wiley.com/college/microsoft) to enhance classroom presentations. Approximately 50 PowerPoint slides are provided for each lesson. Tailored to the text's topical coverage and Skills Matrix, these presentations are designed to convey key concepts addressed in the text. All images from the text are on the Instructor's Book Companion site (http://www.wiley.com/college/microsoft). You can incorporate them into your PowerPoint presentations, or create your own overhead transparencies and handouts. By using these visuals in class discussions, you can help focus students' attention on key elements of technologies covered and help them understand how to use it effectively in the workplace.

- When it comes to improving the classroom experience, there is no better source of ideas and inspiration than your fellow colleagues. The **Wiley Faculty Network** connects teachers with technology, facilitates the exchange of best practices, and helps to enhance instructional efficiency and effectiveness. Faculty Network activities include technology training and tutorials, virtual seminars, peer-to-peer exchanges of experiences and ideas, personal consulting, and sharing of resources. For details visit www.WhereFacultyConnect.com.

MSDN ACADEMIC ALLIANCE—FREE 3-YEAR MEMBERSHIP AVAILABLE TO QUALIFIED ADOPTERS!

The Microsoft Developer Network Academic Alliance (MSDN AA) is designed to provide the easiest and most inexpensive way for universities to make the latest Microsoft developer tools, products, and technologies available in labs, classrooms, and on student PCs. MSDN AA is an annual membership program for departments teaching Science, Technology, Engineering, and Mathematics (STEM) courses. The membership provides a complete solution to keep academic labs, faculty, and students on the leading edge of technology.

Software available in the MSDN AA program is provided at no charge to adopting departments through the Wiley and Microsoft publishing partnership.

As a bonus to this free offer, faculty will be introduced to Microsoft's Faculty Connection and Academic Resource Center. It takes time and preparation to keep students engaged while giving them a fundamental understanding of theory, and the Microsoft Faculty Connection is designed to help STEM professors with this preparation by providing articles, curriculum, and tools that professors can use to engage and inspire today's technology students.

*Contact your Wiley rep for details.

For more information about the MSDN Academic Alliance program, go to:

http://msdn.microsoft.com/academic/

Note: Windows Server 2008, Windows 7, and Visual Studio can be downloaded from MSDN AA for use by students in this course.

■ Important Web Addresses and Phone Numbers

To locate the Wiley Higher Education Rep in your area, go to http://www.wiley.com/college and click on the "*Who's My Rep?*" link at the top of the page, or call the MOAC Toll Free Number: 1 + (888) 764-7001 (U.S. & Canada only).

To learn more about becoming a Microsoft Certified Technology Specialist and exam availability, visit www.microsoft.com/learning/mcp/mcp.

▪ Additional Resources

Book Companion Web Site (www.wiley.com/college/microsoft)

The students' book companion site for the MOAC series includes any resources, exercise files, and Web links that will be used in conjunction with this course.

Wiley Desktop Editions

Wiley MOAC Desktop Editions are innovative, electronic versions of printed textbooks. Students buy the desktop version for up to 50% off the U.S. price of the printed text, and get the added value of permanence and portability. Wiley Desktop Editions provide students with numerous additional benefits that are not available with other e-text solutions.

Wiley Desktop Editions are NOT subscriptions; students download the Wiley Desktop Edition to their computer desktops. Students own the content they buy to keep for as long as they want. Once a Wiley Desktop Edition is downloaded to the computer desktop, students have instant access to all of the content without being online. Students can also print out the sections they prefer to read in hard copy. Students also have access to fully integrated resources within their Wiley Desktop Edition. From highlighting their e-text to taking and sharing notes, students can easily personalize their Wiley Desktop Edition as they are reading or following along in class.

▪ About the Microsoft Technology Associate (MTA) Certification

Preparing Tomorrow's Technology Workforce

Technology plays a role in virtually every business around the world. Possessing the fundamental knowledge of how technology works and understanding its impact on today's academic and workplace environment is increasingly important—particularly for students interested in exploring professions involving technology. That's why Microsoft created the Microsoft Technology Associate (MTA) certification—a new entry-level credential that validates fundamental technology knowledge among students seeking to build a career in technology.

The Microsoft Technology Associate (MTA) certification is the ideal and preferred path to Microsoft's world-renowned technology certification programs, such as Microsoft Certified Technology Specialist (MCTS) and Microsoft Certified IT Professional (MCITP). MTA is positioned to become the premier credential for individuals seeking to explore and pursue a career in technology, or augment related pursuits such as business or any other field where technology is pervasive.

MTA Candidate Profile

The MTA certification program is designed specifically for secondary and post-secondary students interested in exploring academic and career options in a technology field. It offers students a certification in basic IT and development. As the new recommended entry point for Microsoft technology certifications, MTA is designed especially for students new to IT and software development. It is available exclusively in educational settings and easily integrates into the curricula of existing computer classes.

MTA Empowers Educators and Motivates Students

MTA provides a new standard for measuring and validating fundamental technology knowledge right in the classroom while keeping your budget and teaching resources intact. MTA helps institutions stand out as innovative providers of high-demand industry credentials and is easily deployed with a simple, convenient, and affordable suite of entry-level technology certification exams. MTA enables students to explore career paths in technology without requiring a big investment of time and resources, while providing a career foundation and the confidence to succeed in advanced studies and future vocational endeavors.

In addition to giving students an entry-level Microsoft certification, MTA is designed to be a stepping stone to other, more advanced Microsoft technology certifications, like the Microsoft Certified Technology Specialist (MCTS) certification.

Delivering MTA Exams: The MTA Campus License

Implementing a new certification program in your classroom has never been so easy with the MTA Campus License. Through the one-time purchase of the 12-month, 1,000-exam MTA Campus License, there's no more need for ad hoc budget requests and recurrent purchases of exam vouchers. Now you can budget for one low cost for the entire year, and then administer MTA exams to your students and other faculty across your entire campus where and when you want.

The MTA Campus License provides a convenient and affordable suite of entry-level technology certifications designed to empower educators and motivate students as they build a foundation for their careers.

The MTA Campus License is administered by Certiport, Microsoft's exclusive MTA exam provider.

To learn more about becoming a Microsoft Technology Associate and exam availability, visit www.microsoft.com/learning/mta.

▪ Activate Your FREE MTA Practice Test!

Your purchase of this book entitles you to a free MTA practice test from GMetrix (a $30 value). Please go to www.gmetrix.com/mtatests and use the following validation code to redeem your free test: **MTA98-365-2851EC249E8C.**

The **GMetrix Skills Management System** provides everything you need to practice for the Microsoft Technology Associate (MTA) Certification.

Overview of Test features:

- Practice tests map to the Microsoft Technology Associate (MTA) exam objectives
- GMetrix MTA practice tests simulate the actual MTA testing environment
- 50+ questions per test covering all objectives
- Progress at own pace, save test to resume later, return to skipped questions
- Detailed, printable score report highlighting areas requiring further review

To get the most from your MTA preparation, take advantage of your free GMetrix MTA Practice Test today!

For technical support issues on installation or code activation, please email support@gmetrix.com.

Acknowledgments

■ MOAC MTA Technology Fundamentals Reviewers

We'd like to thank the many reviewers who pored over the manuscript and provided invaluable feedback in the service of quality instructional materials:

Yuke Wang, University of Texas at Dallas

Palaniappan Vairavan, Bellevue College

Harold "Buz" Lamson, ITT Technical Institute

Colin Archibald, Valencia Community College

Catherine Bradfield, DeVry University Online

Robert Nelson, Blinn College

Kalpana Viswanathan, Bellevue College

Bob Becker, Vatterott College

Carol Torkko, Bellevue College

Bharat Kandel, Missouri Tech

Linda Cohen, Forsyth Technical Community College

Candice Lambert, Metro Technology Centers

Susan Mahon, Collin College

Mark Aruda, Hillsborough Community College

Claude Russo, Brevard Community College

David Koppy, Baker College

Sharon Moran, Hillsborough Community College

Keith Hoell, Briarcliffe College and Queens College— CUNY

Mark Hufnagel, Lee County School District

Rachelle Hall, Glendale Community College

Scott Elliott, Christie Digital Systems, Inc.

Gralan Gilliam, Kaplan

Steve Strom, Butler Community College

John Crowley, Bucks County Community College

Margaret Leary, Northern Virginia Community College

Sue Miner, Lehigh Carbon Community College

Gary Rollinson, Cabrillo College

Al Kelly, University of Advancing Technology

Katherine James, Seneca College

Contents

www.wiley.com/college/microsoft *or*
call the MOAC Toll-Free Number: 1+(888) 764-7001 (U.S. & Canada only)

Server Overview

OBJECTIVE DOMAIN MATRIX

SKILLS/CONCEPTS	MTA EXAM OBJECTIVE	MTA EXAM OBJECTIVE NUMBER
Installing Windows Server 2008 R2	Understand server installation options.	1.3
Introducing Server Roles	Identify application servers.	2.1
Comparing Physical Servers and Virtual Servers	Understand server virtualization.	2.5
Selecting Server Hardware	Identify major server hardware components.	5.1
Identifying Methods to Install Windows Servers	Understand Windows updates.	6.3

KEY TERMS

BIOS

clean installation

disk cloning

drives

firmware

motherboard

network connections

ports

power supply

processor

RAM

server

Server Core

server features

server role

system preparation tool

unattended installation

upgrade installation

virtual server

Windows activation

Windows Deployment Services (WDS)

Windows updates

You just got hired at the Acme Corporation. They have several Windows Server 2003 and Windows Server 2003 R2 Servers and a Windows Server 2008 Server. While talking to your management team, you determine that you need to upgrade all of the servers to Windows Server 2008 R2 and you need to create a web farm consisting of three new web servers and a single back end SQL server, also running Windows Server 2008 R2. You need to figure out the best way to accomplish your goal.

■ Understanding What a Server Does

THE BOTTOM LINE

With today's computers, any computer on the network can provide services or request services depending on how the network is set up. A *server* is a computer that is meant to be a dedicated service provider, and a client is a computer that requests services. A network that is made up of dedicated servers and clients is known as a client/server network. A server-based network is the best network for sharing resources and data, while providing centralized network security for those resources and data. Networks with Windows Server 2003 and Windows Server 2008 are usually client/server networks.

If you have been using Windows XP, Windows Vista, or Windows 7 for a significant amount of time, you should realize that your computer is providing services and requesting services (although it is most likely requesting services more than it is providing services). When you access a web page over the Internet, access your email, access a data file on another computer, or access a printer that is connected to the network, you are requesting services. While Windows servers are designed to provide a wide range of network services, Windows XP, Windows Vista, and Windows 7 can provide printer and file sharing and web pages (although you are limited by the number of concurrent connections, especially when compared to Windows servers, and are not optimized for multiuser access). Therefore, while these versions of Windows are designed as clients, they can also be utilized to provide services.

While computers with Windows Server 2003 and Windows Server 2008 are designed to provide services, they can also request services from other computers. For example, they can access a web server locally or over the Internet, access a software repository, or print to a network printer.

When you are determining hardware and software needs, look at the role the computer needs to fill and the load the computer will be placed under. You can then start researching the hardware (including the number of computers, number of processors, amount of RAM, and amount of disk storage) and software requirements to reach those goals. Remember that you will also need to look at disaster recovery including the steps you will need to take if a server fails and you lose data.

TAKE NOTE*

Don't forget to plan your server for growth. Most servers should be designed for three to five years of service. Be sure to envision what your landscape may look like three to five years from deployment of the server. This will help you avoid purchasing and reinstalling the server several months later. It should also be noted that the bare basic server leaves little room for growth.

Introducing Server Roles

CERTIFICATION READY
Can you list and describe the basic server roles?
2.1

Before selecting server hardware and software components, you must first understand what your server is supposed to do. First identify the server roles and network services that the server will need to provide. Then examine how many people will be accessing the server at one time to help determine the load the server needs to fulfill.

A *server role* is a primary duty that a server performs. You should note that a server could have multiple roles. Some of the more common server roles include:

- File services
- Print services
- Web services

- Remote access
- Application servers
- Email server
- Database server
- Monitoring servers
- Threat management servers

A file server allows you to centrally locate files to be accessed by multiple people. Because the files are centrally located, it is easier for multiple users to access and find files (assuming they are organized well) and it is easier to back up these files. When using Microsoft Windows to provide file sharing, you will usually be using Server Message Block (SMB) to access Microsoft Shares or shared folders. Windows Servers can also provide NFS shares for Unix/Linux users.

Multiple users can access a centrally located printer using print services, which means that you may share an expensive heavy-duty, or fast, printer that supports advanced options such as color. Printers can be accessed as a network printer that is connected directly to the network or through a Microsoft Windows server (again using SMB).

Because the Internet has become more prevalent in today's business applications, so has the use of web services. Using a web server to provide web services means that users can access web pages using their browsers. These web services may be used to do research, provide leads for sales, allow customers to purchase goods and services, and provide customer support over the Internet. Web services may also be used to provide an easy method to access databases, run reports, track sales leads, provide customer support, and even help you with payroll and human resources. Because you are using a standard browser such as Internet Explorer, you will be using the Hypertext Transfer Protocol (HTTP) or HTTP Secure (HTTPS) protocols. Microsoft provides web services using Internet Information Services (IIS).

Remote access is a service that supports multiple inbound requests in connecting to the server or network. It can provide terminal services so that multiple users can log on to a server remotely and access a desktop, start menu, and programs as if they were sitting in front of the server. On the other hand, remote access can also provide network access over the Internet using a virtual private network (VPN), which allows a user to be at home and yet have full access to their internal network resources such as email and data files.

Finally, the application server role provides an integrated environment for deploying and running server-based business applications. In other words, the server delivers networked applications. When you access a file from a shared folder, your PC does all of the work; in this case, the server will also do some of the processing.

When talking about servers and server applications, you may hear the terms front end and back end. In client/server applications, the client part of the program is often called the front end, and the server part is called the back end. The front end is the interface that is provided to a user or another program. It may be accessed via a web page or a customized application that runs on the client PC. The back end will often contain a database that is used to store, organize, query, and retrieve data.

One commonly used application server that is essential for most corporations is the mail server. The mail server is a server that stores and manages electronic messages (email) among users. If you are using Microsoft email products, you will be using Microsoft Exchange to act as your mail server, and you would most likely access the email using Microsoft Outlook or a web browser.

Two additional examples of application servers are sales tracking or inventory control applications. You would access this type of server on your company network by using a customized program or using your browser. You would then request information or input some data, which would then be retrieved from or sent to the back end server running a database such as Microsoft SQL server.

The last two types of servers, monitoring servers and threat management servers, are not commonly known servers but are essential within any organization. Since many organizations have large or complex networks and multiple servers, you will most likely need one or more monitoring servers to help you monitor servers that provide the necessary services to your users and customers. With monitoring servers, you should use threat management servers to monitor your network and servers for intruders or other security breaches.

Selecting Server Hardware

When choosing the server to use and the hardware components that make up the server, keep the following in mind. First, the server is designed to provide network services. Since a server is designed to be used by multiple users at the same time, the server is usually much more powerful than most client PCs. Remember, if the server fails or becomes inaccessible, the problem will affect multiple people. Therefore, you need to choose hardware that is less prone to failure than a normal client PC and that has some redundancy built in. You also need to plan so you know how to deal with these problems when they occur.

These are the primary subsystems that make up a server:

- Processor
- Memory
- Storage
- Network

If any of these fails, the entire system can fail. In addition, if any one of these is asked to do more than what it was designed for, it can cause a bottleneck that may affect performance of the entire system.

TAKE NOTE*

Even if you strive for 100% uptime, it is next to impossible to get it over a long enough period of time. However, by anticipating the type of failure that could occur; adding additional servers, components, or technology that will make the system more fault tolerant; and developing good plans so that you can react quickly when a failure occurs, you can alleviate much of this to reduce your chances of a failure and the impact that failure would have when it occurs. In addition, while you need to spend money to make a system more fault tolerant, just about every organization has a limit on how much money it can put toward a server or network service.

The subsystems just listed are not the only components that make up the server but they are the primary factors that are examined when determining what a server can handle. Servers may also include sound cards, but they normally do not provide sound to multiple users using that sound card. Instead, data is sent over the network to an individual client and the client sound card produces the sound. The same is true for video. You won't have 20 monitors connected to a single computer providing graphics. Therefore, you do not normally need a high-performance video system for the server.

UNDERSTANDING THE PROCESSOR

The computer, including servers, is built around one or more integrated chips called the *processor*. It is considered the brain of the computer since all of the instructions it performs are mathematical calculations and logical comparisons. Intel and AMD produce most of today's processors.

The clock speed of a processor is usually expressed in gigahertz (GHz). A gigahertz is 1 billion (1,000,000,000) cycles per second. During each cycle, a circuit reacts in a predictable way—it brings in a value, performs a calculation, or performs a comparison. It is these reactions that make the computer do what it does. Of course, if a processor runs at a faster speed, it would be safe to assume that it could do more in a shorter amount of time.

Over the last several years though, speed is not the only factor that determines processor performance. Most of the processors sold today are multi-core processors, which is like having two or more processing cores packaged as one. In addition, they use other technologies to keep the processor working at peak efficiency, like using an assembly line approach or trying to anticipate what needs to be done first so that the pipelines are always clear for new tasks.

TAKE NOTE *

Having additional cores doesn't always mean a linear increase in performance. For example, having two cores doesn't always mean that you get double the performance. In these cases, performance is limited by how well the software is optimized to use both cores.

Another factor is how much data a processor can process. Today, the newer processors are 64-bit, which work faster than the older 32-bit processors. A 64-bit processor has a default word size of 64 bits and a 64-bit external data bus. Most people don't realize that today's processors can already handle 64-bit calculations. (Remember every value, small and large numbers, and numbers with decimal points are broken down into 0s and 1s or bits. Most processors can process 128, 256, and maybe even larger numbers internally. But one of the main benefits of 64-bit processors is that they can process significantly more memory than 32-bit processors (4 GB with a 32-bit address bus and 64 GB with a 36-bit address bus). Technically a 64-bit processor can access up to 16.3 billion gigabytes (16 exabytes). The AMD64 architecture currently has a 52-bit limit on physical memory (which supports up to 4 petabytes or 4048 terabytes) and only supports a 48-bit virtual address space (256 terabytes). Usually, you reach the limit of the motherboard or memory chips before you reach the limit of the processor.

With more data in memory, a 64-bit processor can work faster because it can access larger amounts of RAM instead of swapping data back and forth with the much slower disks. In addition, with the larger internal registry, it can process larger numbers without breaking them into several smaller numbers, and it can even take several smaller numbers and do some mathematical calculation or comparison of these numbers at the same time. Today, just about every computer processor sold is a 64-bit processor.

Today's 64-bit processors include virtualization technology (VT), which lets a processor act as if it were several processors working in parallel, so that several operating systems may run at the same time on the same machine. As of this writing, to run Microsoft's Hyper-V, which is Microsoft's virtualization software, you need to have processors and basic input/output systems (BIOS) that support virtualization technology.

If an operating system and programs are written to use the larger 64-bit calculations and use the additional accessible memory, the processing power of a computer can be significantly increased. Most programs designed for a computer running a 32-bit version of Windows will work on a computer running 64-bit versions of Windows. Notable exceptions are some antivirus programs and some hardware drivers. The biggest problem that you may encounter is finding 64-bit drivers for some of your older hardware devices.

RAM

RAM, which stands for random access memory, is the computer's short-term or temporary memory. It stores instructions and data that the processor accesses directly. If you have more RAM, you can load more instructions and data from the disks. In addition, having sufficient RAM can be one of the main factors in your computer's overall performance. Unfortunately, when power is cut to the RAM, like when you shut off your PC, the contents of the RAM disappear. This is the reason you use disks rather than RAM for long-term storage.

STORAGE

Traditionally, hard *drives* are half electronic/half mechanical devices that store magnetic fields on rotating platters. Today, some hard drives, known as solid-state drives, are electronic devices with no mechanical components. While most personal computers have only local storage consisting of internal hard drives, servers may connect to external storage through a network-attached storage (NAS) or storage area network (SAN).

Most systems today have some form of optical drive. Older systems will have compact disk drives, which use disks similar to a music CD player. Newer systems have either a DVD or Blu-ray drive. In either case, the optical drives store information using laser light. Traditionally, optical disks were considered read-only devices, but now many systems have burning capabilities that allow the user to write data to special optical disks.

NETWORK CONNECTIONS

The last primary component that makes up a server is the ***network connection***. Without a network connection, the server is not able to communicate with other servers or the clients. Most servers include one or more network interface cards or NICs. Because servers are designed to support many network connections, you must have the available bandwidth from the server. The minimum speed of today's network cards is 100 Mbit/second, while the minimum speed for servers is 1 Gbit/second or faster.

THE MOTHERBOARD

The component that brings these four subsystems together is the ***motherboard***. For the processor to communicate with the rest of the system, the processor plugs in or connects to a large circuit board called the motherboard or system board. The motherboard allows the processor to branch out and communicate with all of the other computer components. Although everything is made around the processor, the motherboard is considered the nervous system of the PC. Motherboard capabilities have been greatly expanded (most include sound and network connectivity), and you can further expand the capabilities of the system by installing expansion cards, sometimes referred to as daughter boards. See Figure 1-1.

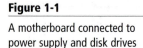

Figure 1-1

A motherboard connected to power supply and disk drives

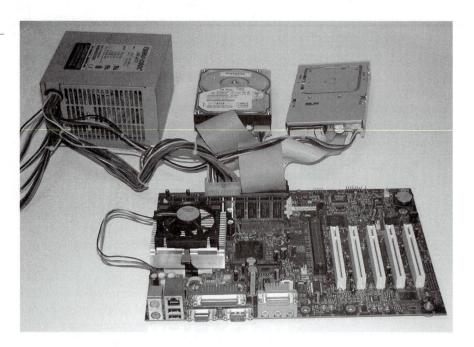

You can find processors, RAM, the motherboard chipset, and motherboard BIOS on the motherboard. The chipset represents the nerve clusters that connect your various components including the keyboard, disk drives, and RAM. Depending on the design of the motherboard, one chipset may run faster than another chipset or have more redundant features. Of course, these types of systems usually cost more.

On the motherboard and expansion cards, you may find firmware. *Firmware* is software contained in read-only memory (ROM) chips. Unlike RAM, ROM instructions are permanent and can't be changed or erased except with special software. When you shut off your computer, ROM instructions remain so that when you turn your computer on again, it knows how to boot the system, test the system, and find a boot device such as your hard drive.

Instructions that control most of the computer's input/output functions, such as communicating with disks, RAM, and the monitor kept in the System ROM chips, are known as the ***BIOS*** (basic input/output system). You can think of the BIOS as the instincts of the computer. By having instructions (software) written on the BIOS, the system already knows how to communicate with some basic components such as a keyboard and how to read some basic disks such as IDE drives. It also looks for additional ROM chips that may be on the motherboard or on expansion cards that you add to the system. These additional ROM chips will have instructions to operate other devices such as SCSI or RAID drives.

If you have not realized it by now, instructions written on the BIOS is software. Unlike the normal software you purchase at a store or order off the Internet, it is not written on a disk. Unfortunately like any software, the BIOS may need to have a bug fixed or may need to be expanded to support a new type of hardware that did not exist when the BIOS was written. Sometimes a newer BIOS version can lead to better system performance. To overcome some problems, you should check with your system or motherboard manufacturer to see if they have a new version of the BIOS that you can download and apply to your system. The process of updating your system ROM BIOS, is called flashing the BIOS.

Unfortunately, flashing the BIOS is a delicate process. If the process gets interrupted in the middle or you install the wrong version, your system may not become accessible and you may have to replace your motherboard to overcome the problem.

Therefore, if it is your first time to flash a system, you should do it a couple of times with someone who has done it before. In addition, you should enter your BIOS or CMOS Setup program and write down all of your current settings in case you have to restore your previous settings. Last, be sure to thoroughly review the system or motherboard manufacturer's documentation to determine your system's BIOS version and the correct version to download and install. You can then download the BIOS image and an executable program to flash the BIOS.

To enter the BIOS or CMOS setup program, you can press a key or combination of keys early during the boot process before the operating system loads. Common keys are usually the Del key or F10 key. To find out which key or keys, you should look at the screen during boot up or access the server or motherboard manual.

POWER SUPPLIES AND CASES

WARNING Make sure you don't have any mishaps such as power failures or someone tripping over the power cord while you are upgrading the BIOS. Remember if the process stops halfway through, the system may become unusable.

A case provides an enclosure that helps protect the system components that are inside. A case with the power supplies and additional fans are usually designed to provide a fair amount of airflow through the system to keep the system cool. Typically if you have items that are designed for performance, they can produce a good amount of heat and too much heat is always bad for electronic and mechanical devices.

You can think of the ***power supply*** as the blood of the computer. The computer runs on electricity. Without it, the computer is just a box. Since power supplies are half electronic and half mechanical devices, they are considered high-failure items when you compare them to pure electronic devices such as memory chips or processors. Mechanical devices tend to wear out over a period of time. Therefore, servers may have redundant power supplies. In addition, to resist power outages or even power fluctuations, the server or server room may be connected to one or more uninterruptible power supplies (UPSs) and/or power generators.

PORTS

Servers are computers. As with any computer, you need to be able to add external devices to the server. *Ports* are plug sockets that enable you to connect an external device, such as a printer, keyboard, mouse, or external drive, to your computer. You can usually identify these ports by the shape of the plug socket, the number of pins, the number of rows of pins, and the orientation of the pins (male or female). These are the most popular ports:

- **Parallel port:** 2-row, 25-pin female D port—Considered a legacy port that is used to connect printers.
- **Serial port:** 2-row, 9-pin male D port—While considered a legacy port, this port is often used to connect to switches and routers to configure them. It can also be used to connect legacy keyboards, mice, and printers.
- **VGA port:** 3-row, 15-pin female D connector—Used to connect a monitor to the computer.
- **Universal Serial Bus (USB) port:** A popular device that can be used to connect keyboards, mice, printers, modems, and external disk drives.
- **PS/2 mouse or keyboard port:** 6-pin Mouse mini-DIN—Used to connect a legacy mouse.
- **RJ-45 connector:** Also Known as an Ethernet connector, used to connect a 10Base-T/ 100Base-T/1000Base-T network cable.
- **DVI-I port:** A high-quality video interface designed to replace VGA ports.

See Figure 1-2.

Figure 1-2

Common ports (PS/2 keyboard and mouse ports, serial port, parallel port, 1394 port, USB port, Ethernet port, DVI-I port, and VGA port)

COMPARING SERVERS AND WORKSTATIONS

When you purchase any computer, you can usually choose between a mobile computer, a personal computer, a workstation, or a server. Mobile computers are not designed to be stand-alone servers. A personal computer and workstation are designed for a single user. Workstations usually contain components for faster performance over a standard inexpensive personal computer so that they can perform heavy graphics or extensive mathematical calculations. But again, a workstation is designed for only one person.

A server, on the other hand, has two goals. First since servers are designed to support many users, they often have an increased load compared to a single user computer. Second, because

CERTIFICATION READY
What can virtual servers do for a corporation?
2.5

many users access a server, the server needs to be reliable. Therefore, servers often contain components that are fault tolerant and reliable (such as redundant power supplies, redundant hard drives, and redundant network cards). Therefore, systems designated as servers often contain additional circuitry to detect problems with the system including conditions like when the system overheats, when a fan has failed, and even when a system has been physically opened. Of course, the system being opened is more of a security feature than a fault-tolerant component.

COMPARING PHYSICAL SERVERS AND VIRTUAL SERVERS

So far, our discussion has been focused mostly on physical servers. Over the last few years, virtualization has become more popular. Virtual machines or *virtual server* technology enables multiple operating systems to run concurrently on a single machine. This allows for a separation of services so that changes on one virtual server do not affect the other virtual servers. In addition, it offers a way to better utilize hardware since most hardware is sitting idle most of the time. By placing several virtual servers on a powerful server, you can better utilize the hardware while keeping cost to a minimum. In addition, it can easily and quickly create Windows test environments in a safe, self-contained environment.

One leader of virtualization is VMware. To compete against VMware, Microsoft includes Hyper-V, which is a replacement to Microsoft's Virtual Server and Virtual PC.

LOCATING THE SERVER

After you select and purchase the server and its components, you also need to figure out where it should go. The server room is the work area of the Information Technology (IT) department that contains the servers and most of the communication devices including switches and routers. The room should be secure, with only a handful of people allowed to have access to it. Of course, the room should be secured and locked when not in use and possibly include some type of biometric access that also provides a log of who enters the server room. The server room should also be provided with clean uninterruptible power and proper cooling. It should also contain equipment to perform proper backups.

When you purchase a server, you can choose from numerous sizes and form factors. Larger server rooms with lots of servers typically contain servers that fit horizontally into a rack. Since these servers are the same width, you can stack 10 to 20 servers within a rack or server cage. The size of a piece of rack-mounted equipment is frequently described as a number in "U." For example, one rack unit is often referred to as "1U," 2 rack units as "2U," and so on. One rack unit is 1.75 inches (44.45 mm) high.

Other servers stand upright and are usually not made to be stacked on top of each other. Of course, servers that stand upright typically take up more room than a stackable server, especially when you have multiple servers.

Selecting the Software

Software contains the instructions that the hardware follows, which make the computer do what it does. It also provides us with an interface that we can use to configure and manage the computer. With a server, you would first choose the operating system, choose the roles that the operating system provides, and then install any additional software to make the server do what you want. Fortunately, Microsoft includes a wide range of network programs and servers with their Windows Server products and also has a wide range of additional products to expand what a server can do.

Windows NT (first released in 1993) is a family of operating systems produced by Microsoft. Since then, Microsoft has built on the previous version and has released Windows 2000 Server, Windows Server 2003, Windows Server 2003 R2, Windows Server 2008, and Windows Server 2008 R2.

Windows Server 2008 R2 builds on Windows Server 2008, expanding existing technology and adding new features to enable IT professionals to increase the reliability and flexibility of their server infrastructures. New virtualization tools, web resources, management enhancements, and exciting Windows 7 integration help save time, reduce costs, and provide a platform for a dynamic and efficiently managed data center and provide security enhancements. Powerful tools such as Internet Information Services (IIS) version 7.5, updated Server Manager and Hyper-V platforms, and Windows PowerShell version 2.0 combine to give customers greater control, increased efficiency, and the ability to react to frontline business needs faster than ever before.

Similar to previous Windows Servers, Windows Server 2008 R2 will be released with six editions. These are the most common editions:

- **Windows Server 2008 R2 Foundation** is an entry-level cost-effective technology foundation for your business designed for small business owners with less than 15 users. Foundation is an inexpensive, easy-to-deploy, proven and reliable technology that provides organizations with the foundation to run the most prevalent business applications as well as share information and resources.

- **Windows Server 2008 R2 Standard** is an advanced server platform that provides more cost-effective and reliable support for business workloads. It offers innovative features for virtualization, power savings, and manageability and helps make it easier for mobile workers to access company resources.

- **Windows Server 2008 R2 Enterprise** is an advanced server platform that provides more cost-effective and reliable support for mission-critical workloads by offering an increased amount of RAM and number of processors supported and failover clustering. It offers innovative features for virtualization, power savings, and manageability and helps make it easier for mobile workers to access company resources.

- **Windows Server 2008 R2 Datacenter** delivers an enterprise-class platform for deploying business-critical applications and large-scale virtualization on small and large servers. It offers improved availability, enhanced power management, and integrated solutions for mobile and branch workers. It enables you to reduce infrastructure costs by consolidating applications with unlimited virtualization licensing rights. Compared to other editions, the Windows Server 2008 R2 Datacenter offers the maximum amount of processors and memory recognized under Windows.

- **Windows Web Server 2008 R2** is a powerful web application and services platform. Featuring Internet Information Services (IIS) 7.5 and designed exclusively as an Internet-facing server, it offers improved administration and diagnostic tools to help reduce infra-structure costs when used with a variety of popular development platforms. With included web server and DNS server roles, as well as improved reliability and scalability, this platform allows you to manage the most demanding environments—from a dedicated web server to an entire web server farm.

See Table 1-1 for the features included in the common editions of Windows Server 2008 R2. The sixth edition of Windows Server 2008 R2 is Windows Server 2008 R2 for Itanium-Based Systems.

Table 1-1

Features of Windows Server 2008 R2 by edition

FEATURE	ENTERPRISE	DATACENTER	STANDARD	WEB	FOUNDATION
.NET 3.0	X	X	X	X	X
.NET Framework 3.5.1 Features	X	X	X	X	X
Administration Tools	X	X	X	X	X
BitLocker Drive Encryption	X	X	X	X	X
BITS Server Extensions	X	X	X		X
BranchCache Content Server	X	X	X	X	X
BranchCache Hosted Server	X	X			
Desktop Experience	X	X	X	X	X
DirectAccess Management	X	X	X		
Failover Clustering	X	X			
Group Policy Management Console	X	X	X	X	X
Ink and Handwriting Services	X	X	X	X	X
Internet Printing Client	X	X	X		X
LPR Port Monitor	X	X	X	X	X
Microsoft Message Queuing (MSMQ)	X	X	X		X
Multipath I/O	X	X	X	X	X
Peer Name Resolution Protocol	X	X	X	X	X
Quality Windows Audio Video Experience	X	X	X		X
RAS Connection Manager Administrator Kit	X	X	X		X
RDC	X	X	X		X
Remote Assistance	X	X	X	X	X
Remote Differential Compression	X	X	X		X
Remote Server Admin Tools	X	X	X	X	X
RPC Over HTTP Proxy	X	X	X		X
Simple TCP/IP Services	X	X	X	X	X
SMTP	X	X	X	X	X
SNMP	X	X	X	X	X
Storage SAN Manager for SANS	X	X	X		X
Subsystem for Unix-Based Applications (SUA)	X	X	X		X
Telnet Client	X	X	X	X	X
Telnet Server	X	X	X	X	X

Table 1-1 (*continued*)

FEATURE	ENTERPRISE	DATACENTER	STANDARD	WEB	FOUNDATION
TFTP Client	X	X	X		X
Windows Biometric Framework	X	X	X	X	X
Windows Internal Database	X	X	X	X	X
Windows Internet Naming Service (WINS)	X	X	X		X
Windows Network Load Balancing (WNLB)	X	X	X	X	X
Windows PowerShell Integrated Scripting Environment (ISE)	X	X	X	X	X
Windows PowerShell	X	X	X	X	X
Windows Process Activation Server	X	X	X	X	X
Windows Server Backup	X	X	X	X	X
Windows Server Backup Features	X	X	X	X	X
Windows Server Migration Tools	X	X	X		X
Windows System Resource Manager (WSRM)	X	X	X	X	X
Windows TIFF IFilter	X	X	X	X	X
WINS Server	X	X	X		X
Wireless Client	X	X	X	X	X
Wireless LAN Service	X	X	X	X	X
XPS Viewer	X	X	X	X	X

Since 64-bit processors have become the industry standard for systems ranging from the most scalable servers to desktop PCs, Windows Server 2008 R2 is only available in the 64-bit version. This is different from Windows Server 2003, Windows Server 2003 R2, and Windows Server 2008. Like Windows Server 2003 and Windows Server 2008, Windows Server 2008 R2 will provide for 32-bit applications with Windows on Windows 64 or WOW64. Both 32-bit and 64-bit applications can run natively on x64 processors, with Windows Server managing the transitions—resulting in excellent performance for both. The end result is a platform that utilizes the existing wealth of 32-bit applications while also providing a smooth migration path to 64-bit computing.

INTRODUCING SERVER ROLES IN WINDOWS SERVER 2008 R2

A server is designed to provide services. Therefore, Windows Server 2008 R2 has organized the most common services into server roles, thus a server role describes the function of the server. When you define a server role in Windows Server 2008 R2 (see Table 1-2), you are installing and configuring a set of software programs that allow a computer to perform a specific function for multiple users or other computers within a network.

Table 1-2

Available roles in Windows Server 2008 R2

ROLE NAME	DESCRIPTION
Active Directory Certificate Services	Provides service for creating and managing public key certificates used in software security systems that employ public key technologies to prove the identity of person, device, or service, which can be used by secure mail, secure wireless networks, virtual private networks (VPN), Internet Protocol Security (IPSec), Encrypting File System (EFS), smart card logon, and others. For ease of use, the digital certificates interface with Microsoft's Active Directory.
Active Directory Domain Services	Transforms a server into a domain controller to provide a directory service via Microsoft's Active Directory (AD), which stores information about users, computers, and other devices on the network. Active Directory helps administrators securely manage this information and facilitates resource sharing and collaboration between users. Active Directory is required for directory-enabled applications such as Microsoft Exchange Server (email server) and to apply other Windows Server technologies such as Group Policy.
Active Directory Federation Services	Provides web single-sign-on (SSO) technologies to authenticate a user to multiple web applications using a single user account.
Active Directory Lightweight Directory Services (ADLDS)	For applications that require a directory to store application data as a data store without installing Active Directory domain services. Since this runs as a non-operating-system service, it allows multiple instances of ADLDS to run concurrently on a single server, and each instance can be configured independently for servicing multiple applications.
Active Directory Rights Management Services (AD RMS)	Technology that works with Active Directory RMS enables applications to help safeguard digital information from unauthorized use by specifying who can use the information and what they can do with it (open, modify, print, forward, and/or take other actions).
Application Server	Provides a complete solution for hosting and managing high-performance distributed business applications built around Microsoft.NET Framework 3.0, COM+, Message Queuing, Web services, and Distributed Transactions.
Dynamic Host Configuration Protocol (DHCP) Server	Allows servers to assign, or lease, IP addresses to computers and other devices that are enabled as DHCP clients.
Domain Name System (DNS) Server	Provides a naming service that associates names with numeric Internet addresses. This makes it possible for users to refer to network computers by using easy-to-remember names instead of a long series of numbers. Windows DNS services can be integrated with Dynamic Host Configuration Protocol (DHCP) services on Windows, eliminating the need to add DNS records as computers are added to the network.
Fax Server	Sends and receives faxes, and allows management of fax resources such as jobs, settings, reports, and fax devices on this computer or on the network.

(continued)

Table 1-2 (*continued*)

ROLE NAME	DESCRIPTION
File Services	Provides technologies for storage management, file replication, distributed namespace management, fast file searching, and streamlined client access to files.
Network Policy and Access Services	Delivers a variety of methods (including using VPN servers, dial-up servers, routers, and 802.11 protected wireless access points) to provide users with local and remote network connectivity, to connect network segments, and to allow network administrators to centrally manage network access and client health policies.
Print Services	Enables users to print to and manage centralized printers that are connected directly or indirectly to print servers.
Terminal Services	Allows users to connect to a terminal server to remotely run programs, use network resources and access the Windows desktop on that server.
Universal Description, Discovery, and Integration (UDDI) Services	Provides capabilities to share information about Web services within an organization's intranet, between business partners on an extranet, or on the Internet.
Web Server (IIS)	Enables sharing of information on the Internet, an intranet, or an extranet via a unified web platform that integrates Internet Information Server (IIS) 7.5 to provide web pages, File Transfer Protocol (FTP) services or newsgroups, ASP.NET, Windows Communication Foundation, and Windows SharePoint Services.
Windows Deployment Services	Used to install and configure Microsoft Windows operating systems remotely on computers with Pre-boot Execution Environment (PXE) boot ROMs.
Windows SharePoint Services	Helps organizations increase productivity by creating Web sites where users can collaborate on documents, tasks, and events and easily share contacts and other information. The environment is designed for flexible deployment, administration, and application development.
Windows Server Virtualization	Provides the services that can be used to create and manage virtual machines (virtualized computer systems that operate in an isolated execution environment that allows the user to run multiple operating systems simultaneously) and their resources.

INTRODUCING SERVER FEATURES IN WINDOWS SERVER 2008 R2

Windows Server 2008 R2 *server features* are software programs that are not directly part of a role. Instead, they are often used to augment the functionality of one or more roles or to enhance the functionality of the entire server. The features that are included in Windows Server 2008 are shown in Table 1-3. To install Windows Features, you would use the Initial Configuration Tasks window or the Server Manager console.

Table 1-3

Features available in Windows Server 2008 R2

FEATURE NAME	DESCRIPTION
.NET Framework 3.0 Features	Combines .NET Framework 2.0 Application Programming Interface (APIs) to build applications with appealing user interfaces and to provide various forms of security for those services.
BitLocker Drive Encryption	Helps protect data on disks by encrypting the entire volume.
BITS Server Extension	Short for Background Intelligence Service, allows a client computer to transfer files in the foreground or background asynchronously so that the responsiveness of other network applications is preserved.
Connection Manager Administration	Customizes the remote connection experience for users on your network by creating pre-defined connections to remote servers and networks via a Virtual Private Network (VPN) server.
Desktop Experience	Includes features of Windows Vista such as Windows Media Player, desktop themes, and photo management.
Failover Clustering	Allows multiple servers to work together to provide high availability of services and applications. If one server fails, a second server is available to take over its work.
Group Policy Management	A Microsoft Management Console snap-in that allows easy management of Active Directory Group Policies to secure or standardize a network environment.
Internet Printing Client	Enables clients to use Internet Printing Protocol (IPP) to connect and print to printers on the network or Internet.
Internet Storage Name Server	Provides discovery services for Internet Small Computer System Interface (iSCSI) storage area networks.
LPR Port Monitor	Enables the computer to print to printers that are shared using a Line Printer Daemon (LPD) service. LPD service is commonly used by UNIX-based computers and printer-sharing devices.
Message Queuing	Provides guaranteed message delivery, efficient routing, security, and priority-based messaging between applications.
Multipath I/O	Along with the Microsoft Device Specific Module (DSM) or a third-party DSM, provides support for using multiple data paths to a storage device on Windows.
Network Load Balancing (NLB)	Distributes traffic across several servers, using the TCP/IP networking protocol. NLB is particularly useful for ensuring that stateless applications such as web servers running IIS are scalable by adding additional servers as the load increases.
Peer Name Resolution Protocol	Allows applications to register and resolve names on your computer so that other computers communicate with these applications.
Quality Windows Audio Video Experience	A networking platform for audio and video streaming applications on IP home networks.
Remote Assistance	Enables you or a support person to offer assistance to users with computer issues or questions.
Remote Differential Compression	Computes and transfers the differences between two objects over a network using minimal bandwidth.

(continued)

Table 1-3 (*continued*)

FEATURE NAME	DESCRIPTION
Remote Server Administration Tools	Includes an MMC snap-in and a command-line tool to remotely manage roles and features.
Removable Storage Manager	Manages and catalogs removable media and operates automated removable media devices.
RPC over HTTP Proxy	Relays RPC traffic from client applications over HTTP to the server as an alternative to clients accessing the server over a VPN connection.
Simple TCP/IP Services	Supports Character Generator, Daytime, Discard, Echo, and Quote of the Day TCP/IP services.
SMTP Server	Supports the transfer of email messages between email systems. SMTP is short for Simple Mail Transfer Protocol.
SNMP Services	Includes the SNMP service and SNMP WMI provider. SNMP is short for Simple Network Management Protocol. SNMP is used in network management systems to monitor network-attached devices for conditions that warrant administrative attention.
Storage Manager for SANs	Helps create and manage logical unit numbers (LUNs) on Fibre Channel and iSCSI disk drive subsystems that support Virtual Disk Service (VDS)
Subsystem for UNIX-based Applications	Allows the user to run UNIX-based programs and compile and run custom UNIX-based applications in the Windows environment.
Telnet Client	Uses the Telnet protocol to connect to a remote Telnet server and run applications on that server.
Telnet Server	Allows remote users to perform command-line administration and run programs using a Telnet client, including UNIX-based clients.
TFTP Client	Allows users to read files or write files to a remote Trivial FTP (TFTP) server.
Windows Internal Database	A relational data store that can be used only by Windows roles and features.
Windows PowerShell	A command-line shell and scripting language.
Windows Process Activation Service	Generalizes the IIS process model, removing the dependency on HTTP.
Windows Recovery Disc	Allows users to restore their computer using the system recovery options if they do not have a Windows installation disc or cannot access recovery options provided by their computer's manufacturer.
Windows Server Backup Features	Allows users to back up and recover their operating system, applications, and data.
Windows System Resource Manager	An administrative tool that can control how CPU and memory resources are allocated.
Windows Internet Naming Service (WINS) Server	Provides a distributed database for registering and querying dynamic mappings of NetBIOS names for computers and groups used on the user's network.
Wireless LAN Service	Configures and starts the WLAN AutoConfig service, regardless of whether the computer has any wireless adapters.

COMPARING FULL VERSION AND SERVER CORE

Starting with Windows Server 2008, you can install Windows in one of two modes: Full Version or Server Core, both of which are provided on the installation DVD.

The full version is the normal version that you would expect from Windows with a fully functional GUI interface.

Server Core installation provides a minimal environment with no Windows Explorer shell for running specific server roles and no Start button. See Figure 1-3. Just about the only thing that you can see is a command prompt window to type in commands. Since the system has a minimal environment, the system runs more efficiently, focusing on what it needs to provide instead of processing fancy graphics for you to manage the system. It also reduces the attack surface for those server roles that could be exploited by a hacker because not all of the components that Windows has will be running.

Figure 1-3

A server running Server Core

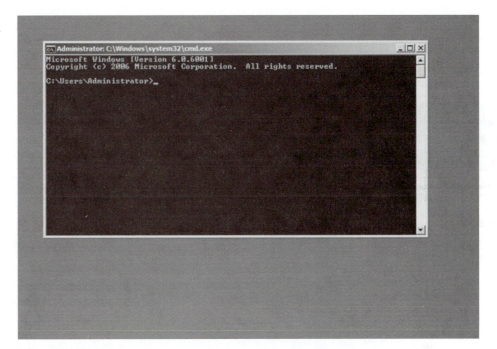

A Server Core machine can be configured for the following roles:

- Active Directory Lightweight Directory Services (ADLDS)
- DHCP Server
- DNS Server
- Domain controller/Active Directory Domain Services
- File Services (including DFSR and NFS)
- IIS 7 web server (but does not include ASPNET, .Net Framework, IIS Management Console, IIS Legacy Snap-In, and IIS FTP Management)
- Print Services
- Streaming Media Services
- Terminal Services including Easy Print, TS Remote Programs, and TS Gateway
- Windows Server Virtualization

A Server Core machine can be configured for the following features:

- Backup
- Bitlocker Drive Encryption

- Failover Clustering
- Multipath IO
- Network Load Balancing
- Removable Storage
- Simple Network Management Protocol (SNMP)
- Subsystem for UNIX-based applications
- Telnet client
- Windows Internet Name Service (WINS)

■ Installing Windows Server 2008 R2

↓ THE BOTTOM LINE

Before you can start using, managing, or configuring an operating system, you will need to first install the operating system.

CERTIFICATION READY
Can you list all of the methods used to install Windows?
1.3

Before installing Windows Server 2008 R2 software, you should look at the system requirements shown in Table 1-4. Of course, the values shown in Table 1-4 are minimum requirements and will usually require additional resources if you want acceptable performance for the load that the server must handle. Therefore, for a simple production system, you should not have less than dual core processors and 2 GB of memory. For a heavier load, four dual-core physical processors and 64 GB of memory would not be unheard of, particularly for large Microsoft Exchange or Microsoft SQL Server installations.

Table 1-4

System requirements for Windows Server 2008 R2

COMPONENT	REQUIREMENT
Processor	Minimum: 1.4 GHz (x64 processor)
	Maximum number of physical sockets: 1 (Foundation) 4 (Web and Standard), 8 (Enterprise), 64 (Datacenter)
Memory	Minimum: 512 MB RAM
	Maximum: 8 GB (Foundation) or 32 GB (Web and Standard) or 2 TB (Enterprise and Datacenter)
Disk Space Requirements	Minimum: 32 GB or greater
	Note: Computers with more than 16 GB of RAM will require more disk space for paging, hibernation, and dump files.
Display	Super VGA (800 × 600) or higher resolution monitor
Other	DVD drive, keyboard and Microsoft mouse (or compatible pointing device), and Internet access

TAKE NOTE ✱

Remember, the amount of RAM and disk space is not the place to skimp.

Performing Clean Installations

A ***clean installation*** is installing the software from scratch on a new drive or on a newly reformatted drive. Many people find that doing a clean install of an operating system is the best way to go because you are starting fresh. The disadvantage is that the system and all of its software needs to be reinstalled, patched, and configured and data copied over, something that may take hours or even days.

Server Overview | 19

 PERFORM A CLEAN INSTALLATION

GET READY. To install Windows Server 2008 R2, you would use the following steps:

1. Insert the appropriate Windows Server 2008 R2 installation media into your DVD drive.

2. Reboot the computer and boot from the installation media.

3. When prompted for an installation language and other regional options, make your selection and press Next.

4. Next, press Install Now.

5. Enter your Product ID in the next window. If you want the computer to automatically activate when the installation is complete, select the appropriate option. Click Next. If you do not have the Product ID available right now, you can leave the box empty and click Next. You will need to provide the Product ID later, after the server installation is over.

6. Select the edition of Windows Server 2008 R2 that you own (see Figure 1-4) and click the Next button.

Figure 1-4

Select the Windows Server 2008 R2 edition

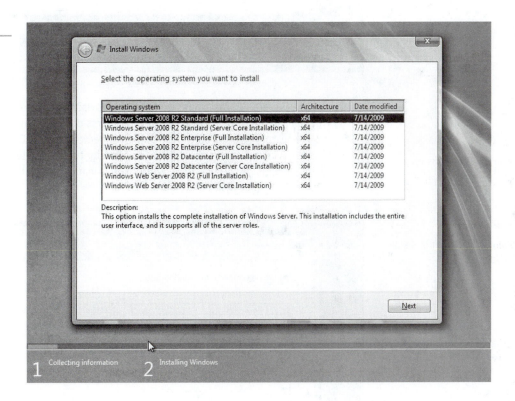

7. Read and accept the license terms by clicking to select the check box and pressing Next.

8. In the "Which type of installation do you want?" window, click the only available option—Custom (advanced). See Figure 1-5.

Figure 1-5

Select the type of installation

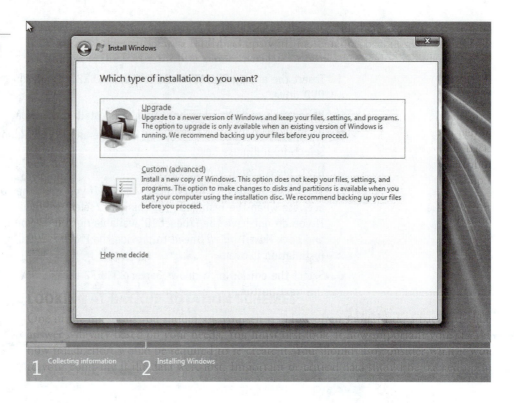

9. In the "Where do you want to install Windows?", if you're installing the server on a regular IDE hard disk, click to select the first disk, usually Disk 0, and click Next. If you're installing on a hard disk that's connected to a SCSI or RAID controller, click Load Driver and insert the media provided by the controller's manufacturer. If you want, you can also click Drive Options and manually create a partition on the destination hard disk. See Figure 1-6.

Figure 1-6

Where do you want to install Windows?

10. When the installation begins, it will first copy the setup files from the DVD to the hard drive. It will then extract and uncompress the files and then install Windows. Depending on the speed of your system, this may take 20 minutes or longer. When the installation is complete, the computer will reboot.

11. When the server reboots, you'll be prompted with the new Windows Server 2008 R2 type of login screen. Press CTRL+ALT+DEL to log in.

12. Click on Other User. The default Administrator is blank, so just type Administrator and press Enter.

13. You will be prompted to change the user's password. In the password changing dialog box, leave the default password blank and enter a new, complex password that is at least 7 characters long. Of course, make sure you remember the password.

14. When the password is changed, click OK.

15. When the log on process is complete, the initial server configuration box will appear.

When you buy proprietary servers such as HP, IBM, or Dell, often the servers include a disk (typically a CD or DVD) with drivers and a guided install program that configures hardware. Since the Windows installation program may not know how to access some SCSI or RAID drives, you will have to click the Load Driver disk during the installation to specify the driver. In other instances, you will boot the disk that comes with the server, run the associated program on the disk, configure the RAID controller and associated drives, partition the drives, and specify which operating system you want to install. It will then copy the drivers to a folder on the drive and either install the operating system from the disk or prompt you to insert the operating system installation disk. If you don't use this disk, the operating system will not load the proper disk drivers, and the drives will not be recognized.

Performing an Upgrade

In some instances, you will want to take a current system and upgrade from an older version of Windows to Windows Server 2008 R2. You can upgrade (using an *upgrade installation*) from the previous versions of Windows to Windows Server 2008 R2 as shown in Table 1-5. Unfortunately, you cannot perform an in-place upgrade from 32-bit to 64-bit architecture since all editions of Windows Server 2008 R2 are 64-bit only. You also cannot upgrade from one language to another.

Table 1-5

Upgrading to Windows Server 2008 R2

IF YOU ARE RUNNING:	YOU CAN UPGRADE TO THIS EDITION:
Windows Server 2003 Standard Edition with Service Pack 2 (SP2) or Windows Server 2003 R2 Standard Edition	Windows Server 2008 R2 Standard, Windows Server 2008 R2 Enterprise
Windows Server 2003 Enterprise Edition with SP2 or Windows Server 2003 R2 Enterprise Edition	Windows Server 2008 R2 Enterprise, Windows Server 2008 R2 Datacenter
Windows Server 2003 Datacenter Edition with SP2 or Windows Server 2003 R2 Datacenter Edition	Windows Server 2008 R2 Datacenter
Server Core installation of Windows Server 2008 Standard with or without SP2	Server Core installation of either Windows Server 2008 R2 Standard or Windows Server 2008 R2 Enterprise

(continued)

Table 1-5 (*continued*)

IF YOU ARE RUNNING:	YOU CAN UPGRADE TO THIS EDITION:
Server Core installation of Windows Server 2008 Enterprise with or without SP2	Server Core installation of either Windows Server 2008 R2 Enterprise or Windows Server 2008 R2 Datacenter
Server Core installation of Windows Server 2008 Datacenter	Server Core installation of Windows Server 2008 R2 Datacenter
Server Core installation of Windows Web Server 2008 with or without SP2	Server Core installation of either Windows Server 2008 R2 Standard or Windows Web Server 2008 R2
Full installation of Windows Server 2008 Standard with or without SP2	Full installation of either Windows Server 2008 R2 Standard or Windows Server 2008 R2 Enterprise
Full installation of Windows Server 2008 Enterprise with or without SP2	Full installation of either Windows Server 2008 R2 Enterprise or Windows Server 2008 R2 Datacenter
Full installation of Windows Server 2008 Datacenter with or without SP2	Full installation of either Windows Server 2008 R2 Datacenter
Full installation of Windows Web Server 2008 with or without SP2	Full installation of either Windows Server 2008 R2 Standard or Windows Web Server 2008 R2
Server Core installation of Windows Server 2008 R2 Standard	Server Core installation of either Windows Server 2008 R2 Standard (repair in place) or Windows Server 2008 R2 Enterprise
Server Core installation of Windows Server 2008 R2 Enterprise	Server Core installation of either Windows Server 2008 R2 Enterprise (repair in place) or Windows Server 2008 R2 Datacenter
Server Core installation of Windows Server 2008 R2 Datacenter	Server Core installation of either Windows Server 2008 R2 Datacenter (repair in place)
Server Core installation of Windows Web Server 2008 R2	Server Core installation of either Windows Web Server 2008 R2 (repair in place) or Windows Server 2008 R2 Standard
Full installation of Windows Server 2008 R2 Standard	Full installation of either Windows Server 2008 R2 Standard (repair in place) or Windows Server 2008 R2 Enterprise
Full installation of Windows Server 2008 R2 Enterprise	Full installation of either Windows Server 2008 R2 Enterprise (repair in place) or Windows Server 2008 R2 Datacenter
Full installation of Windows Server 2008 R2 Datacenter	Full installation of either Windows Server 2008 R2 Datacenter (repair in place)
Full installation of Windows Web Server 2008 R2	Full installation of either Windows Web Server 2008 R2 (repair in place) or Windows Server 2008 R2 Standard

When you want to upgrade to Windows Server 2008 R2, you should follow these guidelines:

- Verify that the current server will support Windows Server 2008 R2. In addition, make sure you have the appropriate drivers before installation.
- Update your antivirus program, run it, and then disable it. After you install Windows, remember to re-enable the antivirus program, or install new antivirus software that works with Windows Server 2008 R2.
- Back up your files. You can back up files to an external hard disk, a DVD or CD, or a network folder.

- Connect to the Internet. Make sure your Internet connection is working so that you can get the latest installation updates. These updates include security updates and hardware driver updates that can help with installation. If you don't have an Internet connection, you can still upgrade or install Windows.

If your system is a production system, verify and/or test all applications to make sure they are compatible with Windows Server 2008 R2.

UPGRADE WINDOWS SERVER 2008 R2

GET READY. To upgrade to Windows Server 2008 R2, you would use the following steps:

1. Start the old version of Windows that you want to upgrade and log on using an account with administrative privileges.
2. Insert the Windows Server 2008 R2 installation DVD.
3. Click the Install Now button and the computer will begin the installation. See Figure 1-7.

Figure 1-7

Starting the upgrade process

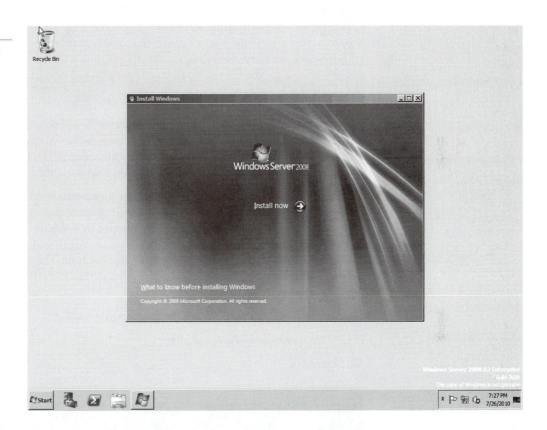

4. After some files are copied, choose the Install option.
5. When it asks to get important updates for installation, click the Go online to get the latest updates for installation option.
6. When it asks to accept the license term, click the appropriate check box, and click the Next button.
7. Toward the end of the installation process, specify a Windows login name and password.
8. Set the time and date.

In the past, Microsoft has provided tools to check whether your system is ready for the operating system. Today, you would use the Microsoft Assessment and Planning (MAP) Toolkit, which is designed to give you essential infrastructure knowledge for planning your migration to Windows Server 2008 R2. The MAP Toolkit takes inventory of your current server environment, determines hardware and device compatibility and readiness, and then generates actionable reports of recommended upgrades for migration. Power savings benefits are calculated with MAP's Power Savings Assessment tool, enabling you to quickly determine potential savings with Windows Server 2008 R2 prior to deployment.

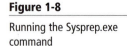

The Microsoft Assessment and Planning (MAP) Toolkit for Windows Server 2008 R2 is located at:

http://technet.microsoft.com/en-us/solutionaccelerators/dd537573.aspx?ca=NOT&su=
WINSVR&sa=MAP&ct=WEBS&cn=MSCOMWEBS&au=BDM&go=MAPTN&dt=
04012009.

Disk Cloning and System Preparation Tool

One way to install Windows Server 2008 R2 is to use *disk cloning* software such as Norton Ghost to create an image file, which is a sector-by-sector copy stored in a large file. To use the disk cloning software, you use the installation disk to install Windows onto a master computer (also called reference computer), update and patch the computer, customize Windows, and install any additional software. You then use the cloning software to copy the contents of a hard drive to a file. You use the disk cloning software to copy the contents of the image to a target computer.

If you create a cloned copy of Windows and apply the cloned copy to multiple computers, each copy of Windows cloned to a target computer using the same image has the same parameters, including the same computer name and security identifier (SID). Unfortunately, for these computers to operate properly without conflict on a network, these parameters have to be unique.

To overcome this problem, you run the *system preparation* tool (Sysprep), which removes the security identifiers and all other user-specific or computer-specific information from the computer before you run the disk cloning software to make the cloned disk image. When you copy the cloned image to the disk image, a small wizard runs that enables you to specify the computer name and other computer specific information. The SID and other information is recreated automatically. The Sysprep utility is located in the c:\Windows\System32\sysprep or the c:\Windows\SysWOW64\sysprep folder.

Most of the time, you will execute the following command:

Sysprep.exe /oobe /generalize

See Figure 1-8.

Figure 1-8

Running the Sysprep.exe command

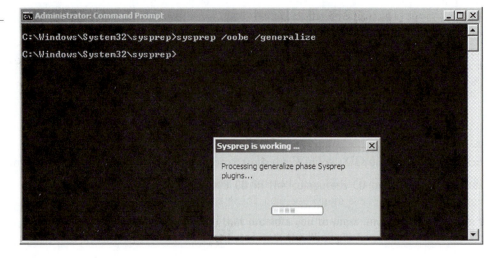

The /generalize prepares the Windows installation to be imaged. If this option is specified, all unique system information is removed from the Windows installation. The security ID (SID) resets, any system restore points are cleared, and event logs are deleted. The next time the computer starts, a specialized configuration pass runs. A new security ID (SID) is created, and the clock for Windows activation resets, if the clock has not already been reset three times.

The /oobe (oobe stands for Out of the Box Experience) restarts the computer into Windows Welcome mode. Windows Welcome enables end users to customize their Windows operating system, create user accounts, name the computer, and other tasks. Any settings in the oobe system configuration pass in an answer file are processed immediately before Windows Welcome starts.

Performing an Unattended Installation

An **unattended installation** is an installation that requires little interaction to install. To perform an unattended installation of Windows, you would use an answer file. An answer file is an XML file that stores the answers for a series of graphical user interface (GUI) dialog boxes. The answer file for Windows Setup is commonly called autounattend.xml. Since the answer file is an XML file, you can use any text editor such as notepad to create and modify the answer file.

A sample answer file can be found at http://technet.microsoft.com/en-us/library/cc732280(WS.10).aspx. However, you will find it much easier if you use the Windows System Image Manager (SIM) to create the answer file. It can also be used to validate the answer file.

To install Windows SIM, you first need to download and install Windows Automated Installation Kit (AIK) for Windows 7 from the Microsoft Web site (http://www.microsoft.com/downloads/details.aspx?FamilyID=696dd665-9f76-4177-a811-39c26d3b3b34&displaylang=en). To start Windows SIM, you then click the Start button, select Microsoft Windows AIK, and select Windows System Image Manager (see Figure 1-9).

Figure 1-9

Windows Server Image Manager

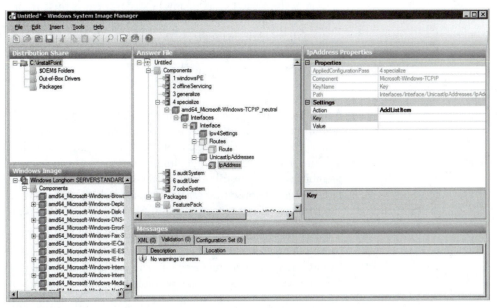

After you create an answer file called autounattend.xml, you place the file on removable media, such as a USB flash device, CD/DVD drive, or floppy disk. You then insert the removable media into the destination computer and boot the destination computer from DVD. Setup automatically searches for autounattend.xml and performs the installation with the parameters specified without any interaction from you.

Using Windows Deployment Services

Windows Deployment Services (WDS) is a technology from Microsoft for network-based installation of Windows operating system including Windows XP, Windows Vista, Windows Server 2003, and Windows Server 2008. The deployment of Windows can be fully automated and customized through the use of unattended installation scripting files.

The Windows installation files can be distributed within a Windows Imaging Format (WIM) file. WIM is the file-based imaging format that Windows Server uses for rapid installation on a new computer. WIM files store copies (known as images) of the operating systems, such as Windows PE, Windows 7, or Windows Server 2008. Maintaining an operating system in a WIM file is easy because you can add and remove drivers, updates, and Windows components offline, without ever starting the operating system.

Windows Deployment Services uses the WIM files to install Windows. If set up properly, you need to boot a computer with Windows PE 2.0 or 3.0 or perform a PXE boot. Windows Preinstallation Environment (Windows PE) 2.0 is a minimal Win32 operating system with limited services, built on the Windows kernel. It is used to prepare a computer for Windows installation, to copy disk images from a network file server, and to initiate Windows Setup.

+ MORE INFORMATION

For more information on Windows Deployment Services, visit the following Web site: http://technet.microsoft.com/en-us/library/cc733011.aspx

You then, connect to the WDS server and install Windows from a configured image. A configuration script is executed that verifies the computer's configuration and hardware requirements. It can also be used to run the Diskpart tool to partition and format the disk. If necessary, the script can back up the user's data to a shared folder on another computer. Eventually, the script connects to a shared folder containing the Windows Setup files and runs the Windows Setup program to install the operating system fully unattended.

Understanding Windows Licensing

One of the biggest costs to any IT department is the cost of software. When you add the client copies of Windows and Office, the cost of the server operating system, and the cost of additional enterprise software such as Exchange or SQL, it can easily add up to thousands of dollars. Therefore, you need to look at your available options to get the best price for what you need to do.

A software license is given to you from a software company like Microsoft that gives you permission to use a specific software package and usually comes with many restrictions. Most licenses from corporations such as Microsoft work more like a lease rather than a purchase of the actual software. The typical restriction limits you to use only one copy of the software per license and prohibits you from distributing or copying the license in any way (except for backup purposes). Licenses for enterprise-class server software (such as Microsoft Exchange or Microsoft SQL) could also require a Client Access License (CAL) for each user that is to access the server software.

The least inexpensive license to obtain is the OEM (Original Equipment Manufacturer) license, which can only be purchased with a new computer from a system builder such as HP or IBM. Unfortunately, these licenses are tied to a specific machine and cannot be transferred later to a new machine. The OEM is usually responsible for technical support on the software that you bought.

The retail license (usually purchased from your office or computer store or over the Internet) allows you move it from one machine to another. Of course, retail software usually costs more than OEM software. Another disadvantage of using retail software from Microsoft is that you need to enter a key code to activate the software. Another disadvantage is that if you move the software to another computer or you make semi-significant changes such as adding RAM or a new hard drive, you may need to re-activate the software.

Finally, Microsoft has several volume licensing programs available to organize their licenses and to keep you up to date with the newest software at a discounted price. The Open license is intended for businesses with at least 5 PCs, and Select License and Enterprise Agreement Plans are licensing programs intended for corporations with at least 250 PCs. Each of these programs may have additional benefits such as free take-home licenses and training.

Volume licensing can be further broken down into Multiple Activation Key (MAK) and Key Management Services (KMS). With MAK, each key has to be registered and activated individually, while Key Management Services (KMS) uses a KMS server to automatically connect to Microsoft's license warehouse and activate the key.

Understanding Windows Activation

Microsoft product activation, including *Windows activation*, is an anti-piracy technology designed to verify that software products are legitimately licensed. The goal of product activation is to reduce software piracy through casual copying and hard drive cloning. The Windows Server 2008 R2 family of retail products contains activation technology, which requires you to activate your retail or volume license copy of Windows Server 2008 R2.

If you have not activated Windows Server 2008 R2, you are reminded each time you log in and at common intervals until the end of the activation grace period of 30 days. If you have not activated Windows Server 2008 R2 during the grace period, the system then will be unlicensed. Persistent notifications will alert you of the need to activate. While in the notification condition, you will be able to log on and off, and the system will function normally. However, the desktop background will change to black, and Windows Update will only install critical updates. The notifications will continue until you activate the operating system.

In the Welcome Center, the Activation Status entry specifies whether you have activated the operating system. If Windows Server 2008 R2 has not been activated, you can activate the operating system by clicking More Details to access the System console and then selecting Click Here to Activate Windows Now under Windows Activation. See Figure 1-10.

Figure 1-10

Activation Status

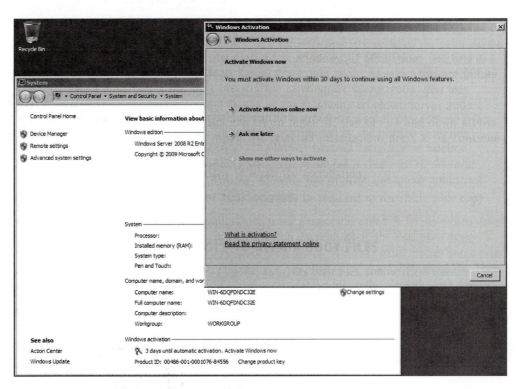

If you choose to activate your product over the Internet, the activation wizard detects your Internet connection and securely connects to a Microsoft server to transfer your installation ID when you submit it. A confirmation ID is passed back to your computer, automatically activating Windows Server 2008 R2. This process typically takes just a few seconds to complete. No personally identifiable information is required to activate Windows Server 2008 R2. If you do not have an Internet connection, you will have to activate Windows Server 2008 R2 over the phone.

Understanding Windows Updates

CERTIFICATION READY
Why is it important to keep Windows updated?
6.3

After installing Windows, check whether Microsoft has any *Windows updates* including fixes, patches, service packs, and device drivers, and apply them to the Windows system. By adding fixes and patches, you will keep Windows stable and secure. If there are many fixes or patches, Microsoft releases them together as a service pack or a cumulative package.

To update Windows Server 2008 R2, Internet Explorer, and other programs that ship with Windows, go to Windows Update in the Control Panel or click the Start button and select All Programs, and then select Windows Update. Then in the left pane, click Check for updates. See Figure 1-11. Windows will scan your system to determine what updates and fixes your system still needs. You then have the opportunity to select, download, and install each update.

Figure 1-11

Running Windows update

Microsoft routinely releases security updates on the second Tuesday of each month on what is known as "Patch Tuesday." Most other updates are released as needed, which are known as "out of band" updates. Since servers are often used as production systems, you should test updates to make sure they do not cause problems for you. While Microsoft does intensive testing, occasionally problems do occur either as a bug or a compatibility issue with a third-party software.

For small environments, you can configure your system to perform Auto Updates to ensure that critical, security and compatibility updates are made available for installation automatically without significantly affecting your regular use of the Internet. Auto Update works in the background when you are connected to the Internet to identify when new updates are available and to download them to your computer. When download is completed, you will be notified and prompted to install the update. You can install it then, get more details about what is included in the update, or let Windows remind you about it later. Some installations may require you to reboot, but some do not.

To change the Windows Update settings, click the Change settings option in the left pane of the Windows Update window. See Figure 1-12. The options allow you to specify whether to download and let you specify which ones to install, specify which updates to install and then download, or just disable Windows Updates all together. You can also specify whether

Figure 1-12

Choose how Windows installs updates

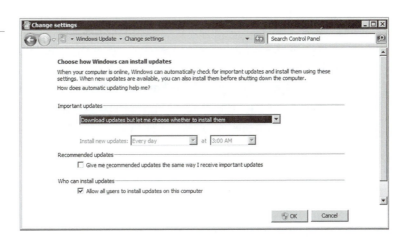

Windows Update will check for Microsoft products other than the operating system and also install software that Microsoft recommends.

If Windows update fails to get updates, you should check your proxy settings in Internet Explorer to determine whether it can get through your proxy server (if any) or firewall. You should also check whether you can access the Internet by attempting to access http://www.microsoft.com.

To see all updates that have been installed, click the View Update History link on the left pane. If you suspect a problem with a specific update, you can then click Installed Updates at the top of the screen to open the Control Panel's Programs. From there, you can view all installed programs and updates. If the option is available, you can then remove the update.

Larger organizations don't typically expect each user to download updates for his or her computer. Instead, a Windows Server Update Service (WSUS) or System Center Configuration Manager (SCCM) is used to automatically install Windows updates. Different from getting updates from the Windows Update Web site, WSUS and SCCM allow the administrators to test the updates and approve which updates will get installed on the client computers.

SKILL SUMMARY

IN THIS LESSON YOU LEARNED:

- A server is a computer that is a meant to be a dedicated service provider, and a client is a computer that requests services.

- Before selecting the hardware and software components of a server, you should identify the server roles and network services that the server will need to provide and how many people will be accessing the server at once to help determine the load the server needs to fulfill.

- The primary subsystems that make up a server are processor, memory, storage, and network.

- The computer, including servers, is built around one or more integrated chips called the processor. It is considered the brain of the computer because all of the instructions it performs are mathematical calculations and logical comparisons.

- A 64-bit processor is a processor with a default word size of 64 bits and a 64-bit external data bus, which allows you to access much more RAM than a 32-bit processor.

- The amount of RAM can be one of the largest factors in your overall computer performance.

- For the processor to communicate with the rest of the system, the processor plugs in or connects to a large circuit board called the motherboard or system board. The motherboard allows the processor to branch out and communicate with all of the other computer components.

- Instructions that control most of the computer's input/output functions, such as communicating with disks, RAM, and the monitor kept in the System ROM chips, are known as the BIOS (basic input/output system).
- The process of updating your system ROM BIOS is called flashing the BIOS.
- While a server needs to have solid performance, the server needs to be reliable.
- Virtual machines technologies enable multiple operating systems to run concurrently on a single machine.
- Windows Server 2008 R2 has organized the most common services into server roles. A server role describes the function of the server.
- Windows Server 2008 R2 Features are software programs that are not directly part of a role, or they can support or augment the functionality of one or more roles, or enhance the functionality of the entire server.
- Server Core installation provides a minimal environment with no Windows Explorer shell for running specific server roles and no Start button.
- Before installing software, you should look at the system requirements as a starting point to make sure your server meets those requirements.
- A clean installation is installing the software from scratch on a new drive or on newly reformatted drive. Many people find that doing a clean install of an operating system is the best way to go because you are starting fresh.
- In some instances, you will want to take a current system and upgrade from an older version of Windows to Windows Server 2008 R2.
- One way to install Windows Server 2008 R2 is to use disk cloning software such as Norton Ghost to create an image file, which is a sector-by-sector copy stored in a large file.
- If you clone a computer, you need to run the System Preparation Tool (Sysprep), which removes the security identifiers and all other user-specific or computer-specific information from the computer before you run the disk cloning software to make the cloned disk image.
- An Answer file, which is used to automatically install Windows, is an XML file that stores the answers for a series of graphical user interface (GUI) dialog boxes.
- Windows Deployment Services (WDS) is a technology from Microsoft for network-based installation of Windows operating systems including Windows XP, Windows Vista, Windows Server 2003, and Windows Server 2008. The deployment of Windows can be fully automated and customized through the use of unattended installation scripting files.
- Microsoft product activation is an anti-piracy technology designed to verify that software products are legitimately licensed.
- After installing Windows, check to see if Microsoft has any fixes, patches, service packs, and device drivers, and apply them to the Windows system.

■ Knowledge Assessment

Fill in the Blank

Complete the following sentences by writing the correct word or words in the blanks provided.

1. A _____ is a primary duty that a server performs.

2. The computer, including servers, is built around one or more integrated chips called the _____.

3. A _____ processor can typically process more data at the same time and can access much more memory than a 32-bit processor.

4. Making sure you have sufficient _____ is one of the biggest factors in performance, even more than disk and processor.

5. For the processor to communicate with the rest of the system, the processor plugs in or connects to a large circuit board called the _____.

6. Firmware is software contained in _____ chips.

7. Instructions that control much of the computer's input/output functions, such as communicating with disks, RAM, and the monitor kept in the System ROM chips, are known as the _____.

8. The process of updating your system ROM BIOS, is called _____ the BIOS.

9. _____ installation provides a minimal environment with no Windows Explorer shell for running specific server roles and no Start button.

10. A(n) _____ is an XML file that stores the answers for a series of graphical user interface (GUI) dialog boxes.

Multiple Choice

Circle the letter that corresponds to the best answer.

1. What technology provided by Microsoft is used to perform a network-based installation of Windows operating systems including Windows XP, Windows Vista, Windows Server 2003, and Windows Server 2008?
   a. IAS
   b. Server Core
   c. SIM
   d. WDS

2. What does the name of the answer file on a USB drive have to be to perform an automatic installation?
   a. autounattend.xml
   b. auto.xml
   c. auto.txt
   d. automatic.xml

3. What is the program you should use to create or validate an answer file used to install Windows?
   a. IAS
   b. Server Core
   c. SIM
   d. WDS

4. What is the maximum amount of memory that Windows Server 2008 R2 Standard Edition requires?
   a. 2 GB
   b. 4 GB
   c. 32 GB
   d. 64 GB

5. How many grace period days do you have in which to activate Windows Server 2008 R2?
   a. 3 days
   b. 10 days
   c. 15 days
   d. 30 days

6. Which of the following is not a primary subsystem found in a server?
   a. Processor
   b. Memory
   c. Sound
   d. Storage

7. What type of installation do you use that starts from scratch?
   a. A clean upgrade
   b. A clean installation
   c. A formatting installation
   d. A backup installation

8. What command would you use to prepare a Windows installation for imaging that will remove the SID and computer name?
   a. Sys
   b. Sysprep
   c. SIDPrep
   d. WDSPrep

9. What does Microsoft use to fight pirated copies of Windows?
   a. WDS
   b. IAS
   c. Sysprep
   d. Activation

10. Which edition of Windows Server 2008 R2 gives you the most access to processors and memory?
    a. Foundation
    b. Standard
    c. Enterprise
    d. Datacenter

True / False

Circle T if the statement is true or F if the statement is false.

T | F   1. If you have a power outage while you are flashing the BIOS, you can just restart the process when the power is restored.

T | F   2. Windows Server 2008 R2 can be only on 64-bit processors.

T | F   3. The lowest edition of Windows Server 2008 R2 is the Standard edition.

T | F   4. When you clone a server with Windows Server 2008 R2, you just need to blank the computer name and administrator password.

T | F   5. The standard protocol to share files on Windows Server 2008 is SMB.

■ Competency Assessment

Scenario 1-1: Server Analysis

You are designing a new network for the Acme Corporation. You expect to have a lot of sales over the Internet. How many servers do you think you will need, what hardware requirements should you use, and what role would you assign to each server? Hint: When you purchase something over the Internet, what type of server do you access? Then what type of server do you think you will need in the background that will keep track of those sales?

Scenario 1-2: Identify Ports

Look at the back of your computer and draw a diagram that shows all of the ports and the purpose of each port.

■ Proficiency Assessment

Scenario 1-3: Installing Windows Server 2008 R2

Go to Microsoft's Web site and find and download the evaluation copy of Windows Server 2008 R2. Burn the image to a DVD. Then boot a computer and install Windows Server 2008 following the steps listed in the Clean Installation section. When configuring your disk, only use half of the disk for your C drive.

Scenario 1-4: Using Windows Updates

Use the Windows Update program to patch Windows.

Workplace Ready

Selecting the Right Server

If you are new to server administration, trying to determine the right server can be quite challenging. So what can you do?

First, you will need to do a lot of reading including looking for the minimum requirements. Always go beyond the minimum. If it says it needs 2 GB of memory, plan for at least 4 GB. If it needs a single processor running at 2 GHz, plan for dual processors running at 2.4 GHz. Always double the specification for the operating system, as a minimum. In addition, don't forget to research load recommendations or load specifications or guidelines.

Next, if you have a similar server, try to compare its current load to the predicted load on your new server. You can also look at processor, memory, disk, and network performance.

You should also ask people who use the server about perceived performance to see if it is adequate or if it should be increased. You should then verify the performance by using the network application in the same way and measure how long it takes for a task to complete.

2 | LESSON

Managing Windows Server 2008 R2

OBJECTIVE DOMAIN MATRIX

SKILLS/CONCEPTS	MTA EXAM OBJECTIVE	MTA EXAM OBJECTIVE NUMBER
Managing Devices and Device Drivers	Understand device drivers.	1.1
Managing Services	Understand services.	1.2
Using the Control Panel	Understand remote access.	2.3

KEY TERMS

Administrative Tools

Computer Management console

Control Panel

device drivers

device manager

domain

Initial Configuration Tasks

Microsoft Management console (MMC)

Plug and Play (PnP)

registry

Remote Assistance

Remote Desktop

Remote Server Administration Tools

Server Management console

secure desktop

services

signed drivers

workgroup

You just installed several computers for the Acme Corporation. Now, you have to get each server connected to the network and add each computer to the domain. You then need to install the network services that each server is going to host.

■ Performing Initial Configuration Tasks

↓ **THE BOTTOM LINE**

Because configuring Windows servers can be time consuming, Windows Server 2008 and Windows Server 2008 R2 include *Initial Configuration Tasks* that automatically launch when you first log on to Windows after an installation. With the Initial Configuration Tasks, you can activate Windows, set the time zone, configure networks, provide computer name and *domain*, update Windows, add roles and features, enable remote desktop, and configure the Windows Firewall.

Although Initial Configuration Tasks can be accessed within the ***Control Panel***, because it launches automatically it acts as a reminder and a quick method to access key options so that you can quickly get your Windows server up and running with minimal effort. See Figure 2-1. The Initial Configuration Tasks will appear every time you log on until you select "Do not show this window at logon" at the bottom of the window.

Figure 2-1

Initial Configuration Tasks

Using the Control Panel

THE BOTTOM LINE   As with previous versions of Windows, the main graphical utility to configure the Windows environment and hardware devices is the Control Panel.

You can also display the Control Panel in any Windows Explorer view by clicking the leftmost option button in the Address bar and selecting Control Panel.

To access the Control Panel, you can click the Start button on the taskbar and select Control Panel. See Figure 2-2. Of the eight categories that are listed, each category includes a top-level link, and under this link are several of the most frequently performed tasks for the category. Clicking a category link provides a list of utilities in that category. Each utility listed within a category includes a link to open the utility, and under this link are several of the most frequently performed tasks for the utility.

Figure 2-2

Windows Server 2008 R2
Control Panel in Category View

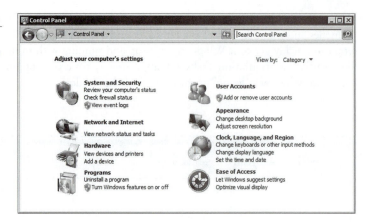

As with current and previous versions of Windows, you can change from the default category view to classic view (large icon view or small icon view). Icon view is an alternative view that provides the look and functionality of Control Panel in Windows 2000 and earlier versions of Windows where all options are displayed as applets or icons (see Figure 2-3).

Figure 2-3

Windows Server 2008 R2
Control Panel in Large Icon
View

Understanding User Account Control

User Account Control (UAC) is a feature that started with Windows Vista and is included with Windows Server 2008 that helps prevent unauthorized changes to your computer. If you are logged in as an administrator, UAC asks you for permission, and if you are logged in as a standard user, UAC asks you for an administrator password before performing actions that can potentially affect your computer's operation or that change settings that affect other users. Because the UAC is designed to make sure that unauthorized changes are not made, especially by malicious software that you may not know you are running, you need to read the warnings carefully, and then make sure the name of the action or program that's about to start is one that you intended to start.

As a standard user, in Windows Server 2008 R2, you can do the following without requiring administrative permissions or rights:

- Install updates from Windows Update.
- Install drivers from Windows Update or those that are included with the operating system.
- View Windows settings.
- Pair Bluetooth devices with the computer.
- Reset the network adapter and perform other network diagnostic and repair tasks.

When an application requests elevation or is run as administrator, UAC will prompt for confirmation and, if consent is given, allow access as an administrator.

UAC cannot be enabled or disabled for any individual user account. Instead, you enable or disable UAC for the entire computer. If you disable UAC for user accounts, you lose the additional security protections UAC offers and put the computer at risk. However, if you perform a lot of administrative tasks on a computer, the UAC prompts can be annoying and can stop you from performing certain actions including saving to the root directory of a drive.

ENABLE OR DISABLE UAC

GET READY. To enable or disable UAC for a particular user account, follow these steps:

1. In Control Panel, click User Accounts.
2. On the User Accounts page, click User Accounts.
3. Click the Change User Account Control settings. See Figure 2-4.
4. Then slide the slider to the appropriate option level as shown in Table 2-1.
5. When prompted to restart the computer, click Restart Now or Restart Later as appropriate for the changes to take effect.

Figure 2-4

UAC Settings

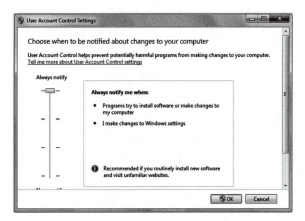

Table 2-1

UAC Settings

SETTING	DESCRIPTION	SECURITY IMPACT
Always notify	You will be notified before programs make changes to your computer or to Windows settings that require the permission of an administrator. When you're notified, your desktop will be dimmed, and you must either approve or deny the request in the UAC dialog box before you can do anything else on your computer. The dimming of your desktop is referred to as the *secure desktop* because other programs can't run while it's dimmed.	This is the most secure setting. When you are notified, you should carefully read the contents of each dialog box before allowing changes to be made to your computer.
Notify me only when programs try to make changes to my computer	You will be notified before programs make changes to your computer that require the permission of an administrator. You will not be notified if you try to make changes to Windows settings that require the permission of an administrator. You will be notified if a program outside of Windows tries to make changes to a Windows setting.	It's usually safe to allow changes to be made to Windows settings without you being notified. However, certain programs that come with Windows can have commands or data passed to them, and malicious software can take advantage of this by using these programs to install files or change settings on your computer. You should always be careful about which programs you allow to run on your computer.
Notify me only when programs try to make changes to my computer (do not dim my desktop)	You will be notified before programs make changes to your computer that require the permission of an administrator. You will not be notified if you try to make changes to Windows settings that require the permission of an administrator. You will be notified if a program outside of Windows tries to make changes to a Windows setting.	This setting is the same as "Notify only when programs try to make changes to my computer," but you are not notified on the secure desktop. Because the UAC dialog box isn't on the secure desktop with this setting, other programs might be able to interfere with the dialog's visual appearance. This is a small security risk if you already have a malicious program running on your computer.
Never notify	You will not be notified before any changes are made to your computer. If you are logged on as an administrator, programs can make changes to your computer without you knowing about it. If you are logged on as a standard user, any changes that require the permission of an administrator will automatically be denied. If you select this setting, you will need to restart the computer to complete the process of turning off UAC. Once UAC is off, people that log on as administrator will always have the permission of an administrator.	This is the least secure setting. When you set UAC to never notify, you open up your computer to potential security risks. If you set UAC to never notify, you should be careful about which programs you run, because they will have the same access to the computer as you do. This includes reading and making changes to protected system areas, your personal data, saved files, and anything else stored on the computer. Programs will also be able to communicate and transfer information to and from anything that your computer connects with, including the Internet.

Introducing System Settings

Some of the most important configuration settings for a server administrator are the system settings within the Control Panel. These include gathering generation information about your system, changing the computer name, adding the computer to a domain, accessing the device manager, configuring remote settings, configuring startup and recovery options, and configuring overall performance settings.

To access the system settings, you can do one of the following:

- If you are in Category view, click System and Security, and click System or click View amount of RAM and processor speed.
- If in classic view, double-click the System applet.
- Right-click Computer and select Properties.

In Windows, there are often several ways to do the same thing.

At the top of the screen you see the Windows edition you have and the system type. Because Windows Server 2008 R2 comes only in 64-bit, it will show 64-bit Operating System in the middle of the screen. Toward the bottom of the screen you will see the computer name and domain (if any) if Windows is activated and the Product ID. See Figure 2-5.

Figure 2-5

Control Panel system settings

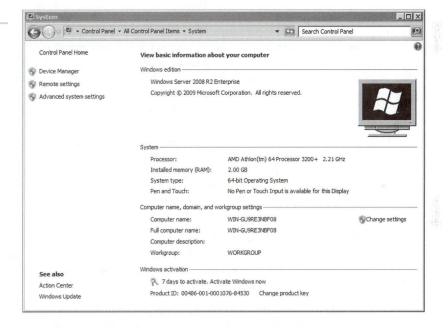

Changing Computer Name and Domain Settings

To help identify computers, you should name a computer with a meaningful name. This can be done within the System settings within the Control Panel. You can also add a computer to a domain or workgroup.

Every computer must have a unique computer name assigned to a network. If two computers have the same name, one or both of the computers will have trouble communicating on the network. To change the computer name, open System from the Control Panel. Then click the Change Settings option in the Computer name, domain, and workgroup settings. When the System

Properties box appears with the Computer Name tab selected, you then click the Change button. See Figure 2-6. Any changes to the computer name or workgroup/domain name will require a reboot.

Figure 2-6

Control Panel System Properties

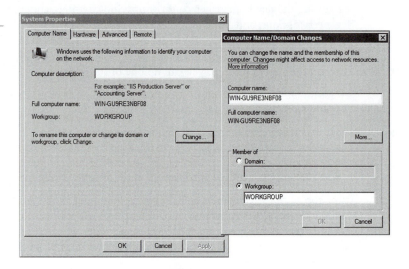

By default, a computer is part of a workgroup. A *workgroup* is usually associated with a peer-to-peer network in which user accounts are decentralized and stored on each individual computer. If several users need to access the computer (while requiring unique usernames and passwords), you will need to create a user account for each user. If you want those users to access another stand-alone computer, you will have to create the same computer accounts and password on that computer as well. As you can imagine, with several computers, this can become a lot of work as you keep creating and managing accounts on each individual computer.

A domain is a logical unit of computers that define a security boundary, and it is usually associated with Microsoft's Active Directory. The security of the domain is generally centralized and controlled by Windows servers acting as domain controllers. As a result, you can manage the security much easier for multiple computers while providing better security.

If a computer is added to a domain, a computer account is created to represent the computer. In addition, information stored on the computer is used to uniquely identify the computer. When these items match, it shows that a computer is who it says is, which contributes to a more secure work environment.

To add the computer to the domain, open System Properties and click the Change button. You will then select the Domain option and type in the name of the domain. Next, click the OK button. It will prompt you to log in with a domain account that has the ability to add computers to the domain. This is typically a domain administrator or account administrator. After you enter the credentials (username and password), a Welcome dialog box appears. Click OK to close the Welcome dialog box. When you close the System Properties dialog box, it will prompt you to reboot the computer.

To remove a computer from a domain, join an existing workgroup, or create a new workgroup, you select the workgroup option and type in the name of the workgroup and click OK. If you are removing yourself from the domain, you will be asked for administrative credentials so that it can delete the account from Active Directory. If you don't specify administrative credentials, it will still remove the computer from the domain, but the computer account will still remain within Active Directory.

CERTIFICATION READY
How do you manage a
server from your desk?
2.3

Configuring Remote Settings

As with most enterprise versions of Windows including Windows Server 2008 and Windows Server 2008 R2, you can remotely connect to a server using *Remote Assistance* and *Remote Desktop*.

With Remote Assistance and Remote Desktop, you can access a computer running Windows with another computer that is connected to the same network or over the Internet just as if you were sitting in front of the server. You will be able to use your mouse and keyboard to access the desktop, taskbar, and Start menu. You will be able to run programs and access all of the configuration tools.

Remote Assistance is designed for support personnel to connect to an active login session to assist or troubleshoot a problem. Unlike Remote Desktop, Remote Assistance allows the user to interact with the current session including seeing the same computer screen. If you decide to share control of your computer with your remote user, you both will be able to control the mouse cursor.

To keep the system secure and to make sure you want the option available, you must first install Remote Assistant as a feature. It must also be enabled in the Remote tab of the System properties dialog box. Next, you will have to invite the person using email or an instant message. You can also reuse an invitation that you sent before. After the person accepts the invitation, a two-way encrypted connection will be created.

To start a Remote Assistance session and to create an invitation, open the Start Menu, click All Programs, Select Maintenance, and click Windows Remote Assistance. See Figure 2-7.

Figure 2-7

Windows Remote Assistance

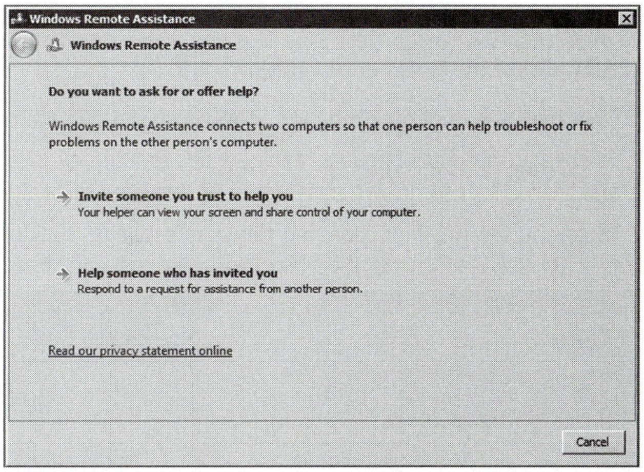

TAKE NOTE*

Before you can use Remote Assistance with Windows Server 2008 R2, you must first install the Remote Assistance feature.

TAKE NOTE*

Before you can use Remote Desktop, you must first enable it using System Properties. In addition, by default, administrators and users are members of the Remote Desktop users group and have access to Remote Desktop.

Remote Desktop allows a user running the Remote Desktop program to access a server remotely. By default, Windows Server 2008 R2 supports two remote desktop connections (three if you also count the console mode, which is the active connection as if you were actually sitting in front of the server keyboard and monitor).

Unlike Remote Assistance, Remote Desktop is installed but must be enabled before you connect to the server. To enable Remote Desktop, open the System Properties and select one of the following settings:

• Allow connections from computer running any version of Remote Desktop (less secure).
• Allow connections running Remote Desktop with Network Level Authentication (more secure).

Network Level Authentication is an authentication method that completes user authentication before you establish a full Remote Desktop connection and the logon screen appears. The Allow connections running Remote Desktop with Network Level Authentication (more secure) option is available to the Remote Desktop program that is included with Windows 7 or you may download a newer version of Remote Desktop from Microsoft. To determine if your version of Remote Desktop supports Network Level Authentication, start a Remote Desktop Connection (under Accessories), click the icon in the upper-left corner of the Remote Desktop Connection dialog box, and then click About. If it supports Network Level Authentication, it will say "Network Level Authentication supported."

By default, administrators and users are members of the Remote Desktop Users. Therefore, for someone to connect to a computer running Remote Desktop, you should add his or her user account to one of these groups.

Changing Date and Time

One of the simplest but most essential tasks is making sure that the server has the correct date and time. This is essential for logging purposes and for security. If a secure packet is sent with the wrong date or time, the packet may be automatically denied because the date and time is used to determine if the packet is legitimate.

To access the date and time settings, do one of the following:

- Click Clock, Language, and Region in the Control Panel while in Category view and click Set the time and date.
- Double-click Date and Time while in Icon view.
- If the date and time show in the Notification area, double-click the date and time.

 SET THE CLOCK

GET READY. To set the clock, do the following:

1. Click the Date and Time tab, and then click Change date and time.
2. To change the hour, minutes, and seconds, double-click the hour, minutes, or seconds, and then click the arrows to increase or decrease the value.
3. When you are finished changing the time settings, click OK. See Figure 2-8.

Figure 2-8

Changing date and time

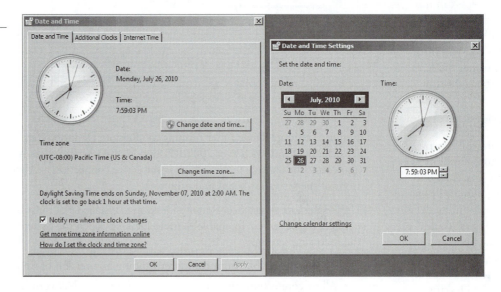

To change the time zone, click Change time zone and click your current time zone in the drop-down list. Then click OK.

If you are part of a domain, the server should be synchronized with the domain controllers. If you have a stand-alone server, you can synchronize with an Internet time server by clicking the Internet Time tab and selecting the check box next to Synchronize with an Internet time server. Then select a time server and click OK.

Configuring IP Address Settings

 THE BOTTOM LINE   For a server to serve other clients, it will need connect to and communicate over the network. Therefore, you need to know how to connect the server and configure the TCP/IP properties.

Although servers may use wireless cards to connect to the network, most servers use wired connections to communicate. The cable connections will be faster, more reliable, and more secure. In either case, you need to configure the following on a computer running Windows Server 2008 R2:

- IP address and its corresponding subnet mask (uniquely identifies the computer using a logical address)
- Default gateway (nearest router that connects to the other networks or the Internet)
- One or more DNS servers provide name resolution (domain/host name to IP address).

The IP address, subnet mask, default gateway, and DNS servers can be configured manually or automatically via a DHCP server. Because servers provide *services* to multiple clients, the network addresses are manually assigned and don't change much.

CONFIGURE THE IP

GET READY. To configure the IP in Windows Server 2008 R2, do the following:

1. Open the Control Panel.
2. To access the network connection properties, do one of the following:
   - While in Category view, click Network and Internet, then click Network and Sharing Center, and finally, click Change adapter settings.
   - If you are in Icon view, double-click Network and Sharing Center, and then click Change adapter settings.
   - Right-click the network icon in the notification area, select Open Network and Sharing Center (Figure 2-9), and then click Change adapter settings.

Figure 2-9

Network and Sharing Center

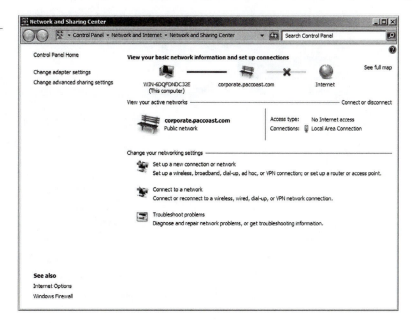

3. Right-click the connection that you want to change, and then click Properties.
4. Under the Networking tab, click either Internet Protocol Version 4 (TCP/IPv4) or Internet Protocol Version 6 (TCP/IPv6), and then click Properties.

To specify IPv4 IP address settings, do one of the following:

- To obtain IP settings automatically from a DHCP server, click Obtain an IP address automatically, and then click OK.
- To specify an IP address, click Use the following IP address, and then, in the IP address, Subnet mask, Default gateway, Preferred DNS server, and Alternate DNS server boxes, type the appropriate IP address settings. See Figure 2-10.

Figure 2-10

Configuring IPv4

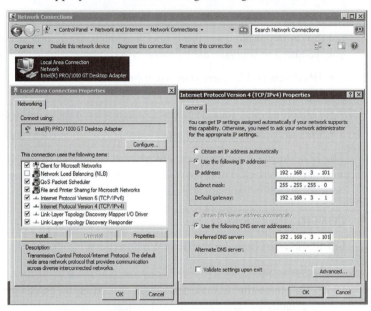

To specify IPv6 IP address settings, do one of the following:

- To obtain IP settings automatically, click Obtain an IPv6 address automatically, and then click OK.
- To specify an IP address, click Use the following IPv6 address, and then, in the IPv6 address, Subnet prefix length, and Default gateway boxes, type the IP address settings. See Figure 2-11.

Figure 2-11

Configuring IPv6

X REF

For more information about IP Configuration, see Appendix B Understanding TCP/IP.

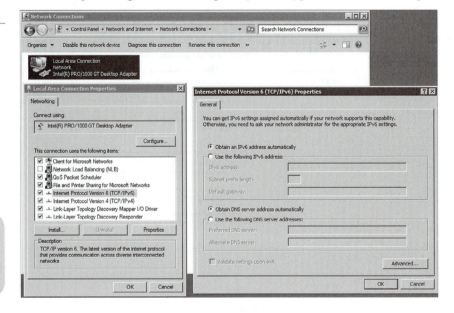

Before moving on to the next section, you should understand how proxy settings affect your access to the network or the Internet. A proxy server is a server that is used to translate between public and private networks using Network Address Translation (NAT). It is usually placed on the edge of a corporate network. With NAT, you can have a single public address and multiple private addresses. A proxy server hides the internal addresses and allows you to have a multitude of private addresses.

When you purchase a wireless router for your house, you connect your cable or DSL modem to the wireless router, which will be assigned a public external address. You can then connect multiple computers or hosts inside your house, which are assigned private addresses. The router will then translate between the public address and the private addresses.

Usually when you go to the Internet within a corporation, you need to specify the address and port of the proxy server. If not, while you may be able to access internal resources, you will not be able to access resources on the Internet.

To change the proxy settings for Internet Explorer (which is also used for other applications), you can do one of the following:

- Start Internet Explorer. Then select the Connections tab and click the LAN settings button.
- While in Category view in the Control Panel, click network and Internet, then click Internet Options. Next select the Connections tab and click the LAN settings button.
- While in Icon view, double-click Internet Options. Then select the Connections tab and click the LAN settings button.

Most corporations should have servers that automatically configure the proxy settings when you have Automatically detect settings enabled. However, if you need to use a different proxy server, you will need to deselect the Automatically detect settings and select the Use a proxy server for your LAN option. You will then specify an address and port number for your proxy server. Common ports are 80, 8080, and 3128. Because you don't want to go through the proxy server for your internal servers, you should select the Bypass proxy server for local address box. See Figure 2-12.

Figure 2-12

Proxy settings in Internet Explorer

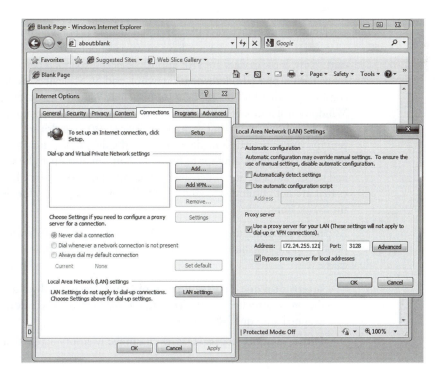

■ Managing Devices and Device Drivers

THE BOTTOM LINE

Because a computer running Windows Server 2008 R2 can have a wide array of devices, it can sometimes be a challenge to make all devices operate correctly, especially because servers often have nonstandard hardware that may require you to manually install or update drivers.

CERTIFICATION READY
How do you manage device drivers in Windows?
1.1

Device drivers are programs that control a device. You can think of them as a translator between the device and the operating system and programs that use the device. Programmers write code that accesses generic commands, such as sending sound, and the device driver will translate those generic commands to specific commands understood by the device, such as a specific sound card. Although Windows Server 2008 R2 includes many drivers (built-in or included on the installation DVD), some drivers come with the device. Because these drivers are software, there may be times when you need to go to the manufacturer's Web site to retrieve newer drivers (although sometimes older drivers work better than newer drivers) or download them through Microsoft's updates.

To prevent you from constantly inserting the Windows Server 2008 R2 installation DVD, Windows Server 2008 R2 includes a driver store with an extensive library of device drivers. Drivers will be located in the C:\Windows\System32\DriverStore. In the DriverStore folder, you will find subfolders with located driver information such as en-US for U.S. English, which will have hundreds of different drivers. When you add a hardware device, Windows can check the Driver Store for the correct driver.

Understanding Plug and Play Devices

For years, Windows has benefited from *Plug and Play* (PnP) where you install or connect a device, and the device is automatically recognized and configured, and the appropriate driver is installed. Today, this technology has been expanded beyond expansion cards to include other technologies.

Intel and Microsoft released Plug and Play in 1983. For a computer technician, PnP made life a lot easier because you did not have to worry about setting DIP switches or jumpers on the card. Now, most devices are PnP, and it has been expanded beyond expansion cards to include USB, IEEE 1394 (also known as Firewire), and SCSI devices. Today, if you use PnP hardware combined with a PnP operating system such as Windows, you can plug in the hardware, and Windows will automatically recognize the device, load the appropriate driver, and configure it to work without interfering with other devices. When a driver cannot be found, Windows will prompt you to provide a media or path to the driver, or it may even ask if you want to connect to the Internet in an attempt to find one. You can also open the Control Panel, click Hardware, and select Add a device under the Devices and Printers section. It will then search for any devices that are not currently recognized by Windows. Eventually, the device driver will be added to the driver store.

As part of the configuration process, Windows assigns the following system resources to the device you are installing so that the device can operate at the same time as other expansion cards:

- **Interrupt request (IRQ) line numbers:** A signal sent by a device to get the attention of the processor when the device is ready to accept or send information. Each device must be assigned a unique IRQ number.
- **Direct memory access (DMA) channels:** Memory access that does not involve the processor.

- **Input/output (I/O) port addresses:** A channel through which data is transferred between a device and the processor. The port appears to the processor as one or more memory addresses that it can use to send or receive data.
- **Memory address ranges:** A portion of computer memory that can be allocated to a device and used by a program or the operating system. Devices are usually allocated a range of memory addresses.

Understanding Signed Drivers

Windows was designed to work with a large array of devices. Unfortunately, in the past, there were times when a device was added and a driver was loaded, the driver caused problems with Windows. As a result, Microsoft started using *signed drivers* to help fight faulty drivers. Although signed drivers will not fix a faulty driver, they make sure the publisher of the driver is identified, the driver has not been altered, and the driver has been thoroughly tested to be reliable so that it will not cause a security problem.

A signed driver is a device driver that includes a digital signature, which is an electronic security mark that can indicate the publisher of the software and information that can show if a driver has been altered. When Microsoft signs it, the driver has been thoroughly tested to make sure that the driver will not cause problems with the system's reliability and not cause a security problem.

Drivers that are included on the Windows installation DVD or downloaded from Microsoft's update Web site are digitally signed. A driver that lacks a valid digital signature, or was altered after it was signed, cannot be installed on 64-bit versions of Windows. If you have problems with a device driver, you should download only drivers that are from Microsoft's update Web site or the manufacturer's Web site.

TAKE NOTE* You cannot install a driver that lacks a valid digital signature or that has been altered after it was signed on Windows Server 2008 R2.

Windows Server 2008 R2 is delivered only in 64-bit versions; all drivers must be signed for Windows Server 2008. If you are using a newer version of Windows that is not a 64-bit version, you can use the File Signature Verification program (Sigverif.exe) to check whether unsigned device drivers are in the system area of a computer.

Using Devices and Printers

Starting with Windows Server 2008 and Windows Vista, Windows includes the Devices and Printers folder to quickly allow users to see all the devices connected to the computer and to configure and troubleshoot these devices. It also allows you to view information about the make, model, and manufacturer and gives you detailed information about the sync capabilities of a mobile phone or other mobile devices.

The Devices and Printers folder gives you a quick view of devices connected to your computer that you can connect or disconnect from your computer through a port or network connection. This includes mobile devices such as music players and digital cameras, USB devices, and network devices. See Figure 2-13. It does not include items installed inside your computer such as internal disk drives, expansion cards, or RAM, and it will not display legacy devices such as keyboards and mice connected through a PS/2 or serial port.

Figure 2-13

Devices and Printers folder

To open the Devices and Printers folder, open the Control and click View devices and printers under Hardware while in Category view or double-click Devices and Printers in Icon view. You can also open the Devices and Printers folder by clicking the Start button and clicking Devices and Printers.

When you right-click a device icon in the Devices and Printers folder, you can select from a list of tasks that vary depending on the capabilities of the device. For example, you might be able to see what's printing on a network printer, view files stored on a USB flash drive, or open a program from the device manufacturer. For mobile devices that support the new Device Stage feature in Windows, you can also open advanced, device-specific features in Windows from the right-click menu, such as the abilities to sync with a mobile phone or change ringtones.

Using Device Manager

Device Manager provides you with a graphical view of the hardware (internal and external) that is installed on your computer and gives you a way to manage and configure your devices. With Device Manager, you can determine whether Windows recognizes a device and if the device is working properly. You can also enable, disable, or uninstall the device; roll back the previous version of the driver; and identify the device driver including its version and change hardware configuration settings.

To open the Device Manager, you can do one of the following:

- Open the Control Panel in Category view, click Hardware, and click Device Manager.
- Open the Control Panel in Icon view and double-click Device Manager.
- Open the System Properties and click Device Manager.
- Open the Computer Management console and click Device Manager.
- Open the Server Manager and click Device Manager under Diagnostics.
- Start Search box or Run box and execute the following command from a command prompt: mmc devmgmt.msc.

If you are logged on as the built-in Administrator account, Device Manager opens. If you are logged on as the user that is a member of the Administrator group and you have User Account Control enabled, you will have to click Continue to open Device Manager. See Figure 2-14.

Figure 2-14

Device Manager

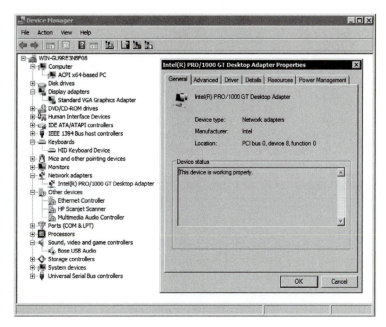

If you locate and double-click a device or right-click a device and select properties, you can view the details of the driver in the General tab including the status of the device. The Details tab will give you detailed settings of various properties assigned to the hardware device. As a server administrator, most of the items you will need are located at the Driver tab:

1. **Driver Details:** Shows the driver file(s) and their location, the provider of the driver, the version of the file, and the digital signer of the file.
2. **Update Driver:** Allows you to update the driver software for a device.
3. **Roll Back Driver:** Used to roll back a driver if problems exist when you update a device driver. If there's no previous version of the driver installed for the selected device, the Roll Back Driver button will be unavailable.
4. **Disable/Enable:** Instead of uninstalling the driver, you can use the Device Manager to disable the device.
5. **Uninstall:** Used to remove the driver software from the computer.

Additional tabs such as Advanced, Resources (Memory Range, I/O Range, IRQ, and DMA), and Power Management may be shown depending on the type of device. See Figure 2-15. If there is conflict for your resources, you can try to use Device Manager to change the memory range, I/O range, IRQ, or DMA of the device). In addition, if you right-click a device in Device Manager, you can update driver software, disable the device, uninstall the device, or scan for hardware changes.

Figure 2-15

Device Properties

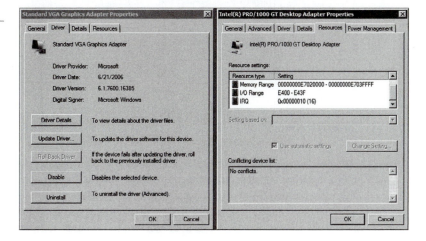

When you use the Device Manager that comes with Windows Vista, Windows 7, and Windows Server 2008, you should note the following:

- A down black arrow indicates a disabled device. A disabled device is a device that is physically present in the computer and is consuming resources, but does not have a driver loaded.
- A black exclamation point (!) on a yellow field indicates the device is in a problem state.
- You also need to check whether any devices are listed under Other devices or have a generic name such as Ethernet Controller or PCI Simple Communications Controller, which indicates that the proper driver is not loaded.

■ Using Microsoft Management Console and Administrative Tools

THE BOTTOM LINE

The *Microsoft Management Console* (MMC) is one of the primary administrative tools used to manage Windows and many of the network services provided by Windows. It provides a standard method to create, save, and open the various administrative tools provided by Windows. When you open Administrative Tools, most of these programs are an MMC.

To start an empty MMC, go to the command prompt, Start Search box or Run box, type mmc or mmc.exe. Every MMC has a console tree that displays the hierarchical organization of snap-ins or pluggable modules) and extensions (a snap-in that requires a parent snap-in). By adding and deleting snap-ins and extensions, users can customize the console or access tools that are not located in Administrative Tools. You can add snap-ins to a MMC by opening the File menu and selecting Add/Remove Snap-ins. See Figure 2-16.

Figure 2-16

Adding snap-ins to a blank MMC

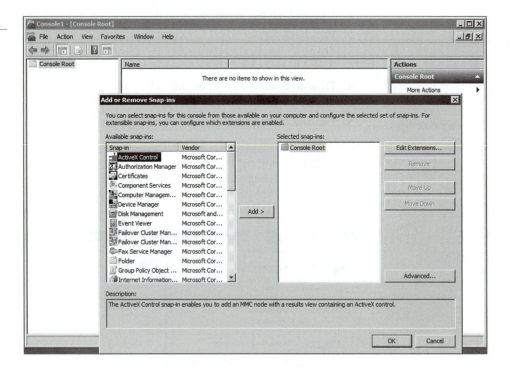

Administrative Tools is a folder in the Control Panel that contains tools for system administrators and advanced users. To access the Administrative Tools folder, open the Control Panel, open Administrative Tools by clicking Start, Control Panel, System, and Security while in Category View or double-click the Administrative Tools applet while in Icon view. There is also a quick link on Windows Servers that can be accessed by clicking the Start button.

Some common administrative tools in this folder include the following:

- **Component Services:** Configure and administer Component Object Model (COM) components. Component Services is designed for use by developers and administrators.
- **Computer Management:** Manage local or remote computers by using a single, consolidated desktop tool. Using Computer Management, you can perform many tasks, such as monitoring system events, configuring hard disks, and managing system performance.
- **Data Sources (ODBC):** Use Open Database Connectivity (ODBC) to move data from one type of database (a data source) to another.
- **Event Viewer:** View information about significant events, such as a program starting or stopping, or security errors, that are recorded in event logs.
- **iSCSI Initiator:** Configure advanced connections between storage devices on a network.
- **Local Security Policy:** View and edit Group Policy security settings.
- **Performance Monitor:** View advanced system information about the processor, memory, hard disk, and network performance.
- **Print Management:** Manage printers and print servers on a network and perform other administrative tasks.
- **Security Configuration Wizard:** A wizard that walks you through how to create a security policy that you can apply to any server on the network.
- **Server Management:** A console that allows you to manage and secure multiple server roles including managing the server's identity, system information; displaying server status; identifying problems with the server role configuration; and managing all roles installed on the server.
- **Services:** Manage the different services that run in the background on your computer.
- **Share and Storage Management:** A centralized location for you to manage folders and volumes that are shared on the network and volumes in disks and storage subsystems.
- **Storage Explorer:** View and manage Fibre Channel and iSCSI fabrics that are available in your storage area network (SAN).
- **System Configuration:** Identify problems that might be preventing Windows from running correctly.
- **Task Scheduler:** Schedule programs or other tasks to run automatically.
- **Windows Firewall with Advanced Security:** Configure advanced firewall settings on both this computer and remote computers on your network.
- **Windows Memory Diagnostics:** Check your computer's memory to see whether it is functioning properly.
- **Windows PowerShell Modules:** A task-based command-line shell and scripting language designed especially for system administration.
- **Windows Server Backup:** Back up and restore the server.

When you use these tools, you might assume that they are used only to manage the local computer. However, many of them can be used to manage remote computers as well. For example, you can use the Computer Management and Server Management console to connect to and manage other computers, assuming you have administrative rights to the computer.

Using Computer Management Console and Server Management Console

The *Computer Management console* and *Server Management console* are two of the primary tools to manage a Windows server, and they include the most commonly used MMC snap-ins.

The Computer Management console is available in Windows Server 2003, Windows Server 2008, Windows XP, Windows Vista, and Windows 7. It includes multiple snap-ins including Task Scheduler, Event Viewer, Shared Folders, Local Users and Groups, Performance, Device Management, Routing and Remote Access, Services, and WMI Control. See Figure 2-17. If you are using Windows Server 2003, Windows XP, Windows Vista, or Windows 7, you can access the Computer Management console through the Administrative Tools or by right-clicking Computer/My Computer and clicking Manage. If you are running Windows Server 2008 or Windows Server 2008 R2, you can access only it from the Administrative Tools folder.

Figure 2-17

Computer Management console

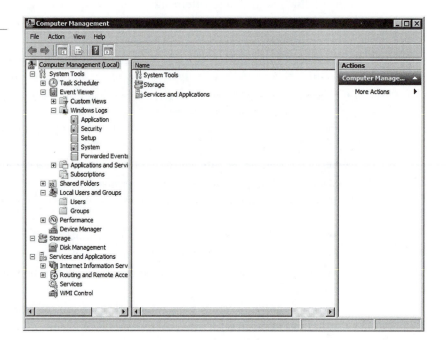

If you right-click Computer on a computer running Windows Server 2008 or Windows Server 2008 R2, you will open the Server Management console instead. Also when you log in to a computer running Windows Server 2008 or Windows Server 2008 R2 as an administrator, Server Manager will automatically open by default. The Server Manager allows you to install Windows server Roles and Features; view the Event Viewer logs; access performance monitoring tools, Device Manager, Task Scheduler, Windows Firewall with Advanced Security, Services, Local Users and Groups, Windows Server Backup and Disk management. See Figure 2-18.

Figure 2-18

Server Manager console

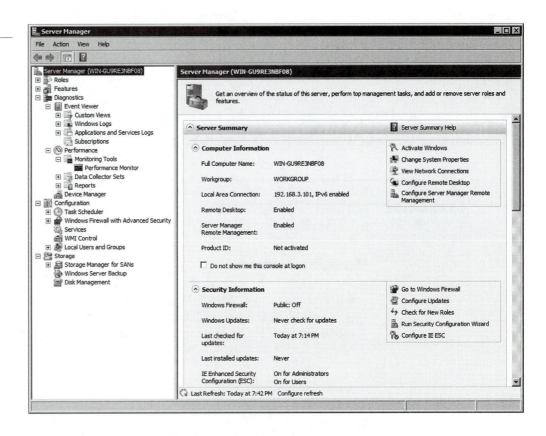

The ***Remote Server Administration Tools*** pack is a feature available with Windows Server 2008 R2 that enables remote management of Windows Server 2008 R2, Windows Server 2008, and Windows Server 2003 from a computer running Windows Server 2008 R2, by allowing you to open and run management tools and snap-ins to manage roles, role services, or features on a remote computer.

The Remote Server Administration Tools pack includes tools for the following roles:

- Active Directory Certificate Services Tools
- Active Directory Domain Services (AD DS) and Active Directory Lightweight Directory Services (AD LDS) Tools
- Active Directory Rights Management Services (AD RMS) Tools
- DHCP Server Tools
- DNS Server Tools
- Fax Server Tools
- File Services Tools
- Hyper-V Tools
- Network Policy and Access Services Tools
- Print and Document Services Tools
- Remote Desktop Services Tools
- Web Server (IIS) Tools
- Windows Deployment Services Tools

The Remote Server Administration Tools pack includes tools for the following features:

- BitLocker Drive Encryption Administration Utilities
- BITS Server Extensions Tools

- Failover Clustering Tools
- Network Load Balancing Tools
- SMTP Server Tools
- WINS Server Tools

■ Installing Programs, Roles, and Features

THE BOTTOM LINE

By default, most of the roles and features that are available for Windows Server 2008 must be installed or enabled before you can use them. This is to reduce the surface attack that hackers or malicious software can utilize. When managing servers, if you don't need a service or program running, you should not install or enable it.

Managing Programs

Windows Server 2008 R2 includes many roles and features to provide a wide range of network services. However, you will often have to install programs. Some of these programs such as SQL Server or Exchange come from Microsoft, while many others do not. Therefore, you will need to know how to install and uninstall these applications.

If you need to install a program in Windows such as an antivirus software package, Microsoft Exchange, Microsoft SQL Server, or any other program that does not come with Windows Server, you usually insert the disk, usually a CD or DVD, into the drive and the installation program will automatically start. With other programs, you may need to run a command, download and install using your browser, or double-click on an executable file with an.exe or msi extension.

Most Windows programs allow you to uninstall a program from your computer if you no longer use it or if you want to free up space on your hard disk. For Windows Server 2008, you can use Programs and Features to uninstall programs or to change a program's configuration by adding or removing certain options. Before Windows Server 2008, you would use Add/Remove Programs from the Control Panel.

 UNINSTALL OR CHANGE A PROGRAM

GET READY. To uninstall a program or change a program in Windows Server 2008 R2, perform the following:

1. Open the Control Panel.
2. If you are in Category View, click Programs and click Programs and Features. If you are in Icon view, double-click Programs and Features.
3. Select a program, and then click Uninstall. See Figure 2-19.

Figure 2-19

Programs and Features

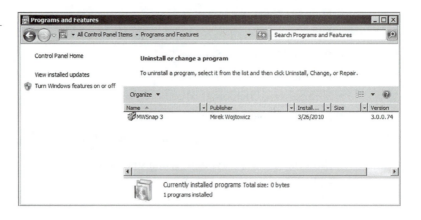

If the program you want to uninstall isn't listed, it might not have been written for Windows. You should check the documentation for the software.

Some programs include the option to repair the program in addition to uninstalling it, but many simply offer the option to uninstall. To change the program, click Change or Repair. If you are prompted for an administrator password or confirmation, type the password or provide confirmation.

Managing Roles and Features

As mentioned in Lesson 1, a server is designed to provide network services and resources. Windows Server 2008 R2 has organized the most common services into server roles. Typically, you would install those roles using Server Manager. In addition, Windows Server 2008 R2 includes many features that are not directly part of a role or that are used to support or augment the functionality of one or more roles or enhance the functionality of the entire server.

A server role is a set of software programs that, when installed and properly configured, enables a computer to perform a specific function for multiple users or computers within a network. Many of these roles were listed in Lesson 1.

Role services are software programs that provide the functionality of a role or service. When you install a role, you can choose which services the role provides for other users and computers in your enterprise. Some roles, such as DNS Server, have only a single function and do not have available role services. Other roles, such as Remote Desktop Services, have several role services that can be installed, depending on the remote computing needs of your organization.

To add roles, open Server Manager, click Roles in the left pane, and click Add Roles. See Figure 2-20. Roles can also be added using the Initial Configuration Tasks window. To remove a role, click the Remove Roles. To manage a specific role that has already been installed, you can scroll down to the service or click on the link in the Roles Summary. If there are any problems with the roles, you will see Red circles with an X or Red circles with exclamation points.

Figure 2-20

Managing Roles

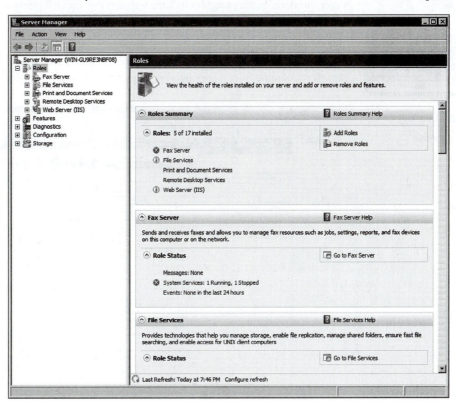

Also mentioned in Lesson 1, features are software programs that are not directly part of a role. Instead, they can support or augment the server. Similar to installing and removing roles, you would install and remove features with Server Manager console or by using the Initial Configuration Tasks window. See Figure 2-21.

Figure 2-21

Managing Features

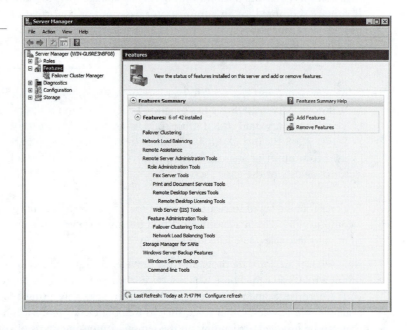

■ Managing Services

THE BOTTOM LINE

A *service* is a program, routine, or process that performs a specific system function to support other programs or to provide a network service. A service runs in the system background without a user interface. Some examples include web serving, event logging, and file serving.

CERTIFICATION READY
How does a service run in Windows?
1.2

To manage services, use the Services console located under Administrative Tools. The Services snap-in is also included in the Computer Management and Server Manager consoles. You can also execute mmc services.mmc from a command prompt, Start Search box, or Run box. See Figure 2-22.

Figure 2-22

The Services console

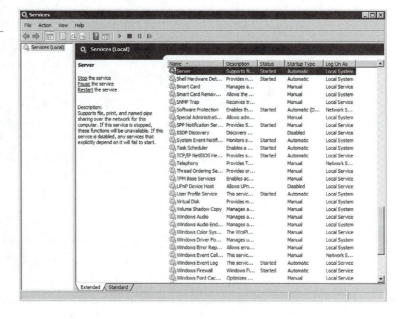

To start, stop, pause, resume, or restart services, right-click on the service and click on the desired option. To the left of the service name is a description. To configure a service, right-click the service and click on the Properties option or double-click the service. See Figure 2-23. On the General tab, under the start-up type pull-down option, set the following:

Figure 2-23

Managing an individual service

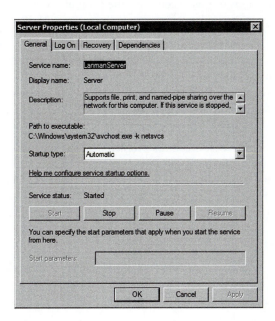

- **Automatic:** Specifies that the service should start automatically when the system starts.
- **Automatic (Delayed Start):** Specifies that the service should start automatically after the services marked as automatic have started (which is approximately 2 minutes).
- **Manual:** Specifies that a user or a dependent service can start the service. Services with manual start-up do not start automatically when the system starts.
- **Disable:** Prevents the service from being started by the system, a user, or any dependent service.

If you like doing things at the command prompt or you have a need use a script to start or stop a service, you would use the *sc* command to communicate with the Service Control Manager and Services. The *scconfig* command is used to modify a service entry in the ***registry*** and Service Database. You can also use the *net start* and *net stop* commands to start and stop services.

When you configure a service, you need to configure what account the service runs under. You can use the built-in accounts included with Windows or you can use a service account that you create locally or on the domain. The built-in accounts include:

- **Local System:** Highly privileged account that can access most resources on the local computer.
- **NT Authority\LocalService:** Has the same privileges of the local Users group on the computer. When it accesses Network resources, it uses no credentials and a null session.
- **NT Authority\NetworkService:** Has the same level of access as the Users group on the local computer. When it accesses network resources, it does so under the context of the local computer account.

You should always take care when changing the Startup parameters for a service including the Startup Type and Log On As settings because these changes might prevent key services from running correctly. In addition, Microsoft recommends that you do not change the Allow service to interact with desktop settings because this will allow the service to access any information displayed on the interactive user's desktop. A malicious user can then take control of the service or attack it from the interactive desktop. If you specify an account that does not have permission to log on as a service, the Services snap-in automatically grants the appropriate permissions to that account on the computer that you are managing. If you use a local or domain account, make sure that you use a strong password and that the account uses a password that does not expire.

As a general rule, you should use the account with minimum rights and permissions for the service to operate. In addition, you should use different service accounts for different services. So if you install Exchange and SQL on a server, you should have a service account for Exchange and a different service account for SQL. SQL and Exchange should be on the same server only for small businesses that have a handful of employees.

If you enable or disable a service and a problem occurs, you can try to start the service manually to see what happens. You can also check the Event Viewer for more information on some of the errors. If the system does not boot because of the enabled or disabled service, you should try to start the computer in Safe mode, which starts only the core services needed to operate, load only the necessary drivers to operate, and load in 640x480 screen resolution with the minimum number of colors. By using Safe mode, you should have an opportunity to fix the problem.

If you are new to Windows, particularly in administering and configuring Windows, you should take some time, click on each service, and read the description. You will learn that many service names are very descriptive. For now, let's cover two specific services:

- **Server:** Supports file, print, and named-piped sharing over the network. If the Services service is not started, you will not be able to access shared folders including administrative shares such as C$ and IPC$.
- **Workstation:** Creates and maintains client network connections to remove servers using the SMB protocol. Without this service, you will not be able to access shared folders on other computers.

■ Understanding the Registry

THE BOTTOM LINE

The *registry* is a central, secure database in which Windows stores all hardware configuration information, software configuration information, and system security policies. Components that use the registry include the Windows kernel, device drivers, setup programs, hardware profiles, and user profiles.

Most of the time, you will not need to access the registry because programs and applications typically make all the necessary changes automatically. For example, when you change your desktop background or change the default color for Windows, you access the Display settings within the Control Panel, and it saves the changes to the registry.

If you do need to access the registry to make changes, you should follow the instructions from a reputable source closely because an incorrect change to your computer's registry can render your computer inoperable. However, there may be a time when you need to make a change in the registry because there is no interface or program to make the change. To view and manually change the registry, you use the Registry Editor (Regedit.exe), which can be executed from the command prompt, Start Search box, or Run box. See Figure 2-24.

Figure 2-24

The Registry Editor

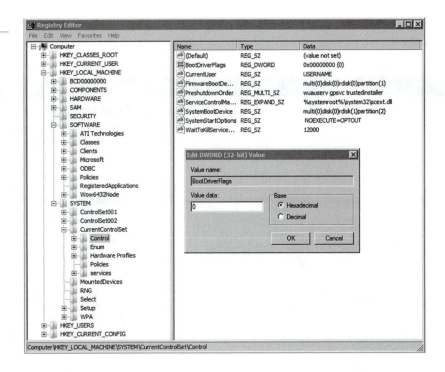

The Registry is split into several logical sections, often referred to as hives, which are generally named by their Windows API definitions. The hives begin with HKEY and are often abbreviated to a three- or four-letter short name starting with "HK." For example, HKCU is HKEY_CURRENT_USER and HKLM is HKEY_LOCAL_MACHINE. Windows Server 2008 R2 has five Root Keys/HKEYs:

- **HKEY_CLASSES_ROOT:** Stores information about registered applications, such as the file association that tells which default program opens a file with a certain extension.
- **HKEY_CURRENT_USER:** Stores settings that are specific to the currently logged-in user. When a user logs off, the HKEY_CURRENT_USER is saved to HKEY_USERS.
- **HKEY_LOCAL_MACHINE:** Stores settings that are specific to the local computer.
- **HKEY_USERS:** Contains subkeys corresponding to the HKEY_CURRENT_USER keys for each user profile actively loaded on the machine.
- **HKEY_CURRENT_CONFIG:** Contains information gathered at run time. Information stored in this key is not permanently stored on disk, but rather regenerated at the boot time.

Registry keys are similar to folders, which can contain values or subkeys. The keys within the registry follow a syntax similar to a Windows folder or file path using backslashes to separate each level. For example:

HKEY_LOCAL_MACHINE\Software\Microsoft\Windows

refers to the subkey "Windows" of the subkey "Microsoft" of the subkey "Software" of the HKEY_LOCAL_MACHINE key.

Registry values include a name and a value. There are multiple types of values. Some of the common key types are shown in Table 2-2.

Table 2-2

Common Registry key types

NAME	DATATYPE	DESCRIPTION
Binary value	REG_BINARY	Raw binary data. Most hardware component information is stored as binary data and is displayed in Registry Editor in hexadecimal format.
DWORD value	REG_DWORD	Data represented by a number that is 4 bytes long (a 32-bit integer). Many parameters for device drivers and services are this type and are displayed in Registry Editor in binary, hexadecimal, or decimal format.
Expandable string value	REG_EXPAND_SZ	A variable-length data string. This datatype includes variables that are resolved when a program or service uses the data.
Multi-string value	REG_MULTI_SZ	A multiple string. Values that contain lists or multiple values in a form that people can read are generally this type. Entries are separated by spaces, commas, or other marks.
String value	REG_SZ	A fixed-length text string.
QWORD value	REG_QWORD	Data represented by a number that is a 64-bit integer. This data is displayed in Registry Editor as a binary value, and it was introduced in Windows 2000.

Reg files (also known as Registration entries) are text files used for storing portions of the registry. They have a.reg filename extension. If you double-click a reg file, it will add the registry entries into the registry. You can export any registry subkey by right-clicking the subkey and choosing Export. You can back up the entire registry to a reg file by right-clicking Computer at the top of Regedit and selecting export, or you can back up the system state with Windows Backup.

■ Managing Server Core

THE BOTTOM LINE

As mentioned in Lesson 1, the Server Core installation provides a minimal environment with no Windows Explorer shell for running specific server roles and no Start button. It should be noted that while you would usually use commands to manage server core, these commands will also work with a full Windows installation.

To discover the available server roles, open a command prompt and type the following:

oclist

To shut down or restart Windows Server 2008 Server Core, you need to use the shutdown.exe file. To shut down the computer, you use the following command:

shutdown /s

To restart the computer, you use the following command:

shutdown /r /t 0 or shutdown /r

The /r specifies reboot while the /t 0 (short for 0 seconds) indicates a reboot immediately.

To log off, use:

> shutdown /l

To open the Date and Time applet, type the following command at the command prompt:

> controltimedate.cpl

To change the International settings including changing your keyboard for different layouts, type the following at the command prompt:

> controlintl.cpl

To change the computer name, you must first know the current computer name. To find the current name, you can use the hostname or ipconfig command. Then use the following command to change the computer name:

> netdomrenamecomputer<ComputerName>
> /NewName:<NewComputerName>

Then restart the computer.

To join a domain, use the following command:

> netdom join <ComputerName> /domain:<DomainName>
> /userd:<Admin_UserName> /passwordd:*

You are prompted for the admin password. Next, restart the computer.

If you need to add a domain user account to the local Administrators group, type the following command:

> netlocalgroup administrators /add <DomainName>\<UserName>

Setting up IP configuration is a little bit more complicated because it is done at the command prompt. To view the IP configuration, you can execute the following command:

> ipconfig /all

To view your interfaces, execute the following command:

> netsh interface ipv4 show interfaces

When you view the output of the netsh command, you need to note of the number shown in the Idx column for your network adapter.

To set a static IP address and default gateway, you would use the following command:

> netsh interface ipv4 set address name="<ID>" source=static
> address=<StaticIP> mask=<SubnetMask> gateway=<DefaultGateway>

To set the static DNS address, use the following command:

> netsh interface ipv4 add dnsserver name=<name of primary DNS
> server> address=<IP address of the primary DNS server> index=1

For each DNS server that you want to set, increment the index = number each time. Therefore, the first DNS server, index number would be 1. For the second DNS server, index number would be 2.

To change a server to the DHCP-provided IP address from a static IP address, use the following command:

> netsh interface ipv4 set address name="<ID>" source=dhcp

where ID is the number of the network adapter.

Besides running these commands, there are a few simple but essential programs that are still available including:

- Notepad (notepad.exe)
- Task Manager (taskmgr.exe) command or pressing the Ctrl+Alt+Del keys.
- Registry Editor (regedit.exe)
- System Information (msinfo32.exe)

You can use cscript.exe to run scripts. For example, to verify the current automatic settings, execute the following command:

> cscript scregedit.wsf /AU /v

To enable automatic updates, execute the following command:

> cscript scregedit.wsf /AU /4

To disable automatic updates, execute the following command:

> cscript scregedit.wsf /AU /1

After the server is communicating on the network, you can connect to the server remotely using administrative tools based on the Microsoft Management Console including Computer Management and Server Manager consoles.

 MANAGE A SERVER CORE SERVER USING AN MMC SNAP-IN

GET READY. To manage a server core server using an MMC snap-in, do the following:

1. Log on to a remote computer.
2. Start an MMC snap-in, such as Computer Management or Server Manager console.
3. In the left pane, right-click the top of the tree and click Connect to another computer. For example, in the Computer Management, you would right-click Computer Management (Local).
4. On another computer, type the computer name or IP address of the server running a Server Core installation and click OK. See Figure 2-25.

Figure 2-25

Accessing a remote computer using Computer Management console

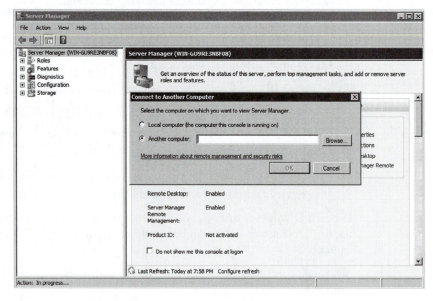

To use the Disk Management MMC snap-in remotely on a Server Core computer, you must start the Virtual Disk Service on the Server Core computer by typing the net start VDS command at the command prompt.

SKILL SUMMARY

- The Initial Configuration Tasks acts as a reminder and a method to access key options so that you can quickly get your Windows server up and running with minimal effort.

- Every computer on a network must have a unique computer name assigned to it.

- A workgroup is usually associated with a peer-to-peer network on which user accounts are decentralized and stored on each individual computer.

- A domain is a logical unit of computers that defines a security boundary and is usually associated with Microsoft's Active Directory.

- The security of the domain is generally centralized and controlled by Windows servers acting as domain controllers.

- With Remote Assistance and Remote Desktop, you can access a computer running Windows with another computer that is connected to the same network or over the Internet just as if you were sitting in front of the server.

- Make sure that the server has the correct date and time. It is essential for logging purposes and security.

- Device drivers are programs that control a device. You can think of them as a translator between the device and the operating system and programs that use that device.

- Plug and Play (PnP) allows you to install or connect a device; the device is automatically recognized, automatically configured and the appropriate driver is installed.

- An interrupt is a signal sent by a device to get the attention of the processor when the device is ready to accept or send information. Each device must be assigned a unique IRQ number.

- A signed driver is a device driver that includes a digital signature, which is an electronic security mark that can indicate the publisher of the software and show if a driver has been altered.

- A driver that lacks a valid digital signature, or was altered after it was signed, cannot be installed on 64-bit versions of Windows.

- The Devices and Printers folder gives you a quick view of devices connected to your computer, which you can connect or disconnect from your computer through a port or network connection.

- Device Manager provides you with a graphical view of the hardware (internal and external) that is installed on your computer and gives you a way to manage and configure your devices.

- A black down arrow in Device Manager indicates a disabled device.

- A black exclamation point (!) on a yellow field in Device Manager indicates the device is in a problem state.

- Administrative Tools, including Computer Management console and Server Manager console, is a folder in the Control Panel that contains tools for system administrators and advanced users.

- To install Roles and Features in Windows Server 2008, you would use the Server Manager console or the Initial Configuration Task window.

- A service is a program, routine, or process that performs a specific system function to support other programs or to provide a network service. It runs in the system background without a user interface.

- The registry is a central, secure database in which Windows stores all hardware configuration information, software configuration information, and system security policies.

■ Knowledge Assessment

Fill in the Blank

Complete the following sentences by writing the correct word or words in the blanks provided.

1. The primary tool used to configure the Windows environment and hardware is the _____.

2. _____ is a feature that helps prevent a program making a change without you knowing about it.

3. Every computer in a network should have a _____ computer name assigned to it.

4. A _____ is a logical unit of computers that share the same security database and is usually associated with Microsoft's Active Directory.

5. _____ allows you to connect to a server remotely to run programs just as if you were sitting in front of the computer.

6. For many security mechanisms to work, your computer needs to have the correct _____.

7. _____ are programs that control a device and act as a translator between the device and the operating system and programs that use the device.

8. _____ allows you to install or connect a device, and the operating system will automatically recognize, configure, and install the appropriate drivers for the device.

9. A _____ is a device driver that includes a digital signature proving who published the device driver and whether the device driver has been altered.

10. _____ provides you with a graphical view of the hardware that is installed your computer and gives you a way to manage and configure your devices.

Multiple Choice

Circle the letter that corresponds to the best answer.

1. Which tool allows support personnel to interact with your session to help troubleshoot problems?
   a. Remote Desktop
   b. Remote Assistance
   c. Credential Manager
   d. Control Panel

2. If you connected to your internal network, what should you check if you cannot connect to web servers on the Internet?
   a. UAC
   b. Administrative rights
   c. Proxy settings
   d. NTFS permissions

3. What technology automatically configures IRQs, DMA channels, I/O port addresses, and memory address ranges for an expansion card?
   a. Credential Manager
   b. Signed drivers
   c. Services Manager
   d. Plug and Play

4. Which built-in account gives full access to the computer system?
   a. Local System
   b. Local Service
   c. Network Service
   d. Local User

5. What is a central secure database that stores all hardware configuration information, software configuration information, and system security configuration policies?
   a. Credential Manager
   b. The Registry
   c. Server Manager
   d. Computer Management

6. When installing drivers on a 64-bit version of Windows Server 2008 R2, you must _____.
   a. Install only signed drivers
   b. Install the driver with Device Manager
   c. First disable UAC
   d. Enable the Windows Installer service

7. To install a network role, you would use the _____.
   a. Computer Management console
   b. Server Manager console
   c. Device Manager
   d. Services console

8. What program would you use to assign IRQ for a device?
   a. Credential Manager
   b. Device Manager
   c. Registry Editor
   d. UAC

9. Which of the following is not a start-up type for a service?
   a. Automatic
   b. Manual
   c. Disable
   d. Self-configuring

10. Which registry key holds the specific settings of a local computer?
    a. HKEY_CLASSES_ROOT
    b. HKEY_CURRENT_USER
    c. HKEY_LOCAL_MACHINE
    d. HKEY_USERS

True / False

Circle T if the statement is true or F if the statement is false.

T | F   1. By default, UAC is disabled.

T | F   2. When you right-click Computer in Windows Server 2008, the Computer Management console will open.

T | F   3. You can install signed 32-bit drivers on Windows Server 2008 R2.

T | F   4. A black exclamation point in the Device Manager means the device is disabled.

T | F   5. To connect to a remote computer running a Server Core, you can use only a command prompt escalated as an administrator.

■ Competency Assessment

Scenario 2-1: Managing Server Core

You just installed Windows Server 2008 R2 Server Core to act as a web server. You now need to configure the server. What are all of the different tools you can use?

Scenario 2-2: Configuring Services

You are installing a new network program that will install a network service. You need to choose which account you want the service to run under. What are the guidelines in choosing the account?

■ Proficiency Assessment

Scenario 2-3: Using Device Manager

Open Device Manager. Verify that all devices are enabled and that all devices have the proper device driver. If necessary, find and install the correct drivers for any unknown devices.

Scenario 2-4: Configuring Network Adapter

1. Configure the following IP parameters (unless otherwise assigned by your instructor):

   IP address: 172.24.1.XX where XX is your student number. If you do not have a student number, use .31.

   Subnet Mask: 255.255.255.0
   Default Gateway: 172.24.1.20
   DNS Server: 172.24.24.1.30

2. Save your settings.
3. If necessary, change your settings back DHCP and save your settings.

✳ Workplace Ready

Configuring and Managing the Servers

Installing the server is usually a straightforward task. The real work comes when you have to patch Windows, install roles and features, install applications, and configure Windows and the applications. It also takes time to add users and grant permissions to the computers, folders, and applications. Backups allow you to recover any irreplaceable data and data that may take hours to re-create. It also allows you to restore a server that took many hours to install and configure if you have to replace or rebuild the server.

Managing Storage

OBJECTIVE DOMAIN MATRIX

SKILLS/CONCEPTS	MTA EXAM OBJECTIVE	MTA EXAM OBJECTIVE NUMBER
Identifying Storage Technologies	Identify storage technologies.	4.1
Introducing Redundant Arrays of Independent Disks	Understand RAID.	4.2
Understanding Disk Structure	Understand disk types.	4.3

KEY TERMS

FAT32

Fibre Channel

File Allocation Table (FAT)

host bus adapter (HBA)

hot spare

integrated drive electronics (IDE)

internet small computing system interface (iSCSI)

logical unit number (LUN)

network attached storage (NAS)

New Technology File System (NTFS)

partition

partitioning style

redundant array of independent disks (RAID)

serial ATA standard (SATA)

small computer system interface (SCSI)

storage area network (SAN)

volume cloning

You just installed several new servers running Windows Server 2008 for the Acme Corporation, and they have been connected to your network. Now you need to expand several of these servers by adding drives to the servers and configuring RAID so that the drives are fault tolerant. In addition, you need to connect to a SAN so that several servers connect to a centralized storage device.

■ Identifying Storage Technologies

THE BOTTOM LINE

While you need sufficient processing power and a sufficient amount of RAM, you will also most likely need a large amount of storage. Although simple servers usually require that you install Windows Server on a local IDE (parallel and serial) or SCSI hard drive, more complex systems may use a form of RAID or attached remote computer storage devices such as a storage area network (SAN) or network attached storage (NAS).

Comparing IDE and SCSI Drives

Today's hard drives are either integrated drive electronics (IDE) or small computer system interface (SCSI), pronounced "skuzzy," drives. Even if you use RAID, a NAS, or a SAN, they most likely still use IDE or SCSI drives.

IDE drives are designed as fast, low-cost drives. Traditional IDE drives were based on the parallel AT attachment (ATA) standard that used a parallel 40-pin/80-conductor connector. Today's IDE drives follow the *serial ATA standard (SATA)*, which uses a connector that is attached with only four wires and a smaller power connector. Although the serial ATA uses fewer wires and connectors, it provides faster throughput than parallel ATA IDE drives.

When configuring parallel IDE drives, you can connect two drives on the same ribbon cable. You then need to configure one drive as the master and the other drive as the slave using jumpers on the drive. You can also select a cable that will automatically configure the drives. Today, if a system has parallel IDE drives, the motherboard will have two IDE connectors, allowing you to connect four IDE drives. Because you can connect only one serial ATA drive to a cable, you do not need to configure serial ATA drives.

Servers and high-performance workstations usually use SCSI drives. *SCSI* drives typically offer faster performance and throughput than IDE drives, and SCSI drives can support a larger number of drives that can be attached using the same interface. Legacy SCSI devices used a 50-pin connector. Newer drives use a 68-pin connector if you are using copper cabling, although some SCSI drives support Fibre Channel for even faster throughput.

When connecting SCSI drives, each SCSI device must have a unique SCSI ID number on the chain. In addition, both ends of the chain must be terminated with resistors. Today, most devices are auto-terminating so you don't have to do much configuring.

Introducing Redundant Arrays of Independent Disks

Because most drives are half-electronic and half-mechanical devices, you can connect multiple drives to special controllers to provide data production, system reliability, and better performance. A *redundant array of independent disks (RAID)* uses two or more drives in combination to create a fault-tolerant system that protects against physical hard drive failure and increases hard drive performance. A RAID can be accomplished with either hardware or software and is usually used with network servers.

There are several levels of RAID available for use, based on your particular needs. RAID 0 stripes data across all drives. With striping, all available hard drives are combined into a single large virtual file system, with the file system's blocks arrayed so that they are spread evenly across all the drives. For example, if you have three 500 GB hard drives, RAID 0 provides for a 1.5 TB virtual hard drive. When you store files, they are written across all three of these drives. For instance, when a large file is written, one part of it may be written to the first drive, the next chunk to the second drive, more to the third drive, and perhaps more is wrapped back to the first drive to start the sequence again. Unfortunately, with RAID 0, there is no parity control or fault tolerance; therefore, it is not a true form of RAID. Here, if one drive fails, you lose all data on the array. However, RAID 0 does have several advantages because it offers increased performance through load balancing.

RAID 1 is another common RAID that is used in networked PCs and servers. RAID 1 is sometimes known as disk mirroring. Disk mirroring copies a disk or partition onto a second hard drive. Specifically, as information is written, it is written to both hard drives simultaneously. This means that if one of the hard drives fails, the PC will still function because it can access the other hard drive. Then, should you later replace the failed drive, data will be copied from the remaining good drive to the new drive.

Yet another common RAID is RAID 5, which is similar to striping, except the space equivalent to one of the hard drives is used for parity (error correction) to provide fault tolerance. To increase performance, the error correction function is spread across all hard drives in the array to avoid having one drive doing all the work in calculating the parity bits. Therefore if one drive fails, you can still continue working because parity calculations with the remaining drives will fill in any missing data. Later, when the failed drive is replaced, the missing information will be rebuilt. However, if two drives fail, you will lose all data on the array. Generally speaking, RAID 5 offers better performance than RAID 1. RAID 5 requires at least three drives, with more than three drives preferable. For instance, if you have just 3×500 GB drives, you will have only 2×500 GB or 1,000 GB of disk space because one of the three drives must be used for parity. Similarly, if you have 6×500 GB drives, you will have 5×500 GB or 2,500 GB of disk space available.

There are two other forms of RAID worth mentioning, both of which are considered hybrid or nested RAIDs:

- RAID 1+0 is a mirrored dataset (RAID 1), which is then striped (RAID 0). A RAID 1+0 array requires a minimum of four drives: two mirrored drives to hold half the striped data, plus another two mirrored drives for the other half of the data. The array continues to operate if one or more drives fail in the same mirror set, but if drives fail on both sides of the mirror, all the data on the RAID system will be lost.

- RAID 0+1 is a striped dataset (RAID 0), which is then mirrored (RAID 1). Similar to RAID 1+0, RAID 0+1 requires a minimum of four drives: two to hold the striped data, plus another two to mirror the first pair. The array continues to operate if one or more drives fail within the striped set. If you have drives that fail on both striped set, all the data on the RAID system will be lost.

RAID can be implemented with hardware using a special controller that is built into the motherboard or an expansion card. More expensive servers typically use hardware RAID because software RAID requires some processing by the computer, whereas the controller handles hardware RAID. One disadvantage of hardware RAID is that it usually requires a longer boot time.

RAID can also be implemented with software, specifically operating systems. Windows clients such as Windows XP, Windows Vista, and Windows 7 can support RAID 0 and RAID 1, whereas Windows Servers including Windows Server 2003 and Windows Server 2008 support RAID 0, RAID 1, and RAID 5.

A third form, which is sometimes difficult to distinguish, is firmware/driver-based RAID (sometimes referred to as FakeRAID or HostRAID). With firmware/driver-based RAID, the RAID is initially implemented by the firmware and is then taken over by the operating system when the appropriate driver is loaded. Therefore, the firmware/driver can protect the boot process, which isn't always true with operating system-based RAID. In addition, firmware/driver-based RAID is usually much less expensive than hardware RAID.

Introducing Hot Spares

A ***hot spare*** is much like it sounds. When drives need to be fault tolerant, you can combine a hot spare drive with a RAID. Then, if a drive fails, the system will automatically grab the hot spare drive to replace the failed drive and rebuild or restore the missing data.

Remember that most hard drives are half-electronic/half-mechanical devices. Mechanical devices are considered high-failure items because they fail more often than nonmechanical electronic devices. This is one reason why servers use some form of RAID that provides fault tolerance.

To take the idea of fault tolerance a step further, a hot spare drive is an extra drive installed within a RAID set that is inactive until an active drive fails. When this happens, the system automatically replaces the failed drive with the hot spare drive and rebuilds the array with the spare. (Of course, any time you have to rebuild an array, it can take several hours, especially on busy systems.) A hot spare can be shared by multiple RAID sets.

■ Looking at Network Attached Storage and Storage Area Networks

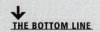
THE BOTTOM LINE

For larger corporations, servers may connect to centralized devices that contain large amounts of storage. These devices offer better performance and better fault tolerance and offer quick recovery.

Network attached storage (NAS) is a file-level data storage device that is connected to a computer network to provide shared drives or folders, usually using SMB/CIFS. NAS devices usually contain multiple drives in a form of RAID for fault tolerance and are managed usually using a web interface.

A ***storage area network (SAN)*** is an architecture used for disk arrays, tape libraries, and optical jukeboxes to appear as locally attached drives on a server. A SAN always uses some form of RAID and other technology to make the system redundant against drive failure and to offer high performance. SANs also usually contain spare drives. To provide a high level of data throughput, SANs use the SCSI protocol and either iSCSI or Fibre Channel interface.

Although SANs offer performance and redundancy, there are also other benefits to consider. For instance, because you designate storage areas within the SAN and assign them to servers, if you have problems with a particular server, you can quickly and easily move the storage areas to another server.

Some SANs also offer snapshotting. When you need to install or upgrade a component within a server, you can first take a snapshot, which is a temporary image at the time of the snapshot. You can then make changes or upgrades to the server. Later, if you have a problem, you can roll back to the snapshot and continue on with things the way they were before you made the changes. A roll back can take minutes.

In addition, certain SANs offer volume cloning. ***Volume cloning*** allows you to copy a storage area to another storage area within a SAN or to another SAN. This allows you to quickly create a test environment or duplicate an existing environment. You can also establish storage replication between SAN units even if the units are in different locations.

A host adapter, sometimes referred to as ***host bus adapter*** (***HBA***), connects a host system such as a computer to a network or storage device. It is primarily used to refer to connecting SCSI, Fibre Channel, and eSATA devices; however, devices for connecting to IDE, Ethernet,

FireWire, USB, and other systems may also be called host adapters. Today, the term host bus adapter (HBA) is most often used to refer to a Fibre Channel interface card.

Logical unit numbers (usually referred to as LUNs) allow a SAN to break its storage down into manageable pieces, which are then assigned to one or more servers in the SAN. It is a logical reference that can comprise a disk, a section of a disk, a whole disk array, or a section of a disk array. LUNs serve as logical identifiers through which you can assign access and control privileges. If a LUN is not mapped to a given server, that server cannot see or access the LUN. You only need to identify the server or cluster that will access the LUN and then select which HBA ports, identified on the SAN by the World Wide Name on that server or cluster, will be used for LUN traffic.

Introducing Fibre Channel

Optic fiber cabling offers higher bandwidths and can be used over longer distances than copper cabling because signals travel with less loss and are immune to electromagnetic interference. For these reasons, storage systems often use fiber cabling.

Fibre Channel or FC is a gigabit-speed technology primarily used for storage networking. It uses a Fibre Channel Protocol (FCP) as its transport protocol, which allows SCSI commands to be issued over Fibre Channel.

The network topology or layout used in Fibre Channel is known as a fabric, in which devices are connected to each other through one or more data paths. To provide redundancy and faster performance, Fibre Channel uses one or more Fibre Channel switches that allow servers and storage devices to connect to each other through virtual point-to-point connections. When a host or device communicates with another host or device, the fabric routes data from the source to the target.

A port, much like in a network switch, communicates over the network usually implemented in a device such as disk storage, an HBA on a server, or a Fibre Channel switch. There are three major Fibre Channel topologies that describe how multiple ports are connected together:

- **Point-to-point (FC-P2P):** This is the simplest topology, in which two devices are connected back to back.
- **Arbitrated loop (FC-AL):** Here, all devices are connected in a loop or ring, similar to token-ring networking. Unfortunately, adding or removing a device from the loop causes interruption of communication on the loop, as well as failure of one of the devices, which causes a break in the ring. Some hubs can bypass failed devices.
- **Switched fabric (FC-SW):** In this topology, all devices or loops of devices are connected to Fibre Channel switches, similar to what you find on today's Ethernet network. The switches manage the state of the fabric to provide optimized connections. In an FC-SW, the media is not shared. Therefore, any device that communicates with another device communicates at full bus speed regardless of whether other devices and hosts are also communicating. One advantage of FC-SW is that the failure of a particular port is isolated and should not affect the operation of other ports.

The Fibre Channel and iSCSI fabrics include one or more Internet Storage Name Service (iSNS) servers to provide discoverability and partitioning of resources. When a host or device is powered on, it logs on to the fabric and is assigned a unique fabric address. Also, when a host or device communicates with another device, it establishes a connection to that device before transmitting data. The switch then routes the packets in the fabric.

Each device including the host bus adapter is called a node. Much like a MAC address used in network interface cards, each node has a fixed 64-bit World Wide Name (WWN) assigned by the manufacturer and registered with the IEEE to ensure it is globally unique. Also similar to a server, each node can have multiple ports, each with a unique 64-bit port name and 24-bit port ID.

To make storage more manageable, Fibre Channel uses zoning and LUNs. Zoning is a method of restricting which ports or WWNs can communicate with each other.

Introducing iSCSI

Internet Small Computing System Interface or *iSCSI* is an Internet Protocol (IP)-based storage networking standard for linking data storage facilities. iSCSI allows clients to send SCSI commands over a TCP/IP network using TCP port 3260. Similar to Fibre Channel, iSCSI can communicate using Gigabit Ethernet or Fibre, and it can connect a SAN to multiple servers over a distance.

Although iSCSI uses normal network technology to communicate, the network adaptor must be dedicated to iSCSI. This means that servers will typically need at least two sets of networks cards, one for iSCSI and one for the network connection. However, like network connections, each iSCSI initiator can have one or more network adapters through which communication is established to provide increased bandwidth and redundancy. The iSCSI software could be built into the iSCSI host adapter or host bus adapter, allowing increased performance for the server.

After the SAN grants access, an iSCSI session emulates a SCSI hard disk so that the server treats the LUN just like any other hard drive. Similar to Fibre Channel, you can define which servers communicate with each LUN and what type of communication is permitted.

iSCSI initiators find storage devices by using the Internet Storage Name Service (iSNS) protocol to provide both naming and resource discovery services for storage devices on the IP network. In particular, iSCSI uses the following information to connect to the SAN:

- Host name or IP address
- Port number (default port is 3260)
- iSCSI name (For example, "iqn.2003-01.com.ibm:00.fcd0ab21.shark128")
- Optional CHAP secret password

The iSCSI name will follow one of the following formats:

- **iSCSI Qualified Name (IQN):** IQN follows the iqn.yyyy-mm.{reversed domain name} format. (For example, iqn.2001-04.com.acme:storage.tape.sys1.xyz.) IQN addresses are the most common format.
- **Extended Unique Identifier (EUI):** EUI follows the eui.{EUI-64 bit address} format. (For example, eui.02004567A425678D.) The IEEE Registration Authority provides the EUI in accordance with EUI-64 standard.
- **T11 Network Address Authority (NAA):** NAA follows the naa.{NAA 64 or 128-bit} identifier. (For example, naa.52004567BA64678D.) NAA is part OUI, which is provided by the IEEE Registration Authority. NAA name formats were added to iSCSI in RFC 3980 to provide compatibility with naming conventions used in Fibre Channel and SAS storage technologies.

iSCSI INITIATOR SOFTWARE

Microsoft Windows Server 2008 includes two iSCSI Initiator software interfaces to connect an iSCSI storage array or volume of a storage array to a server and mount the array or volume as a local volume. These interfaces are:

- iSCSI Initiator (located in the Administrative Tools and Control Panel)
- iSCSICLI command interface

When you open the iSCSI Initiator program, you will see the following six tabs:

- **Targets:** Specifies which storage devices the server has access to and allows you to log on to those devices.
- **Discovery:** Specifies the location of the SAN and Internet Storage Name Service (iSNS) servers.
- **Favorite Targets:** Specifies which targets reconnect each time you start your computer.
- **Volumes and Devices:** Shows volumes and devices that are connected to the server and allows you to bind or connect an iSCSI device to a volume.
- **RADIUS:** Specifies a RADIUS server to connect to for authentication.
- **Configuration:** Allows you to globally configure settings that will affect any future connections made with the initiator.

See Figure 3-1.

Figure 3-1

iSCSI Initiator included with Windows Server 2008 R2

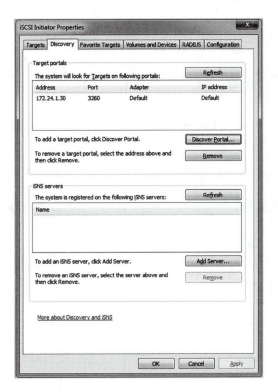

CONNECT TO AN iSCSI ARRAY

GET READY. To connect to an iSCSI target device using Quick Connect:

1. Click Start, type iSCSI in Start Search, and then under Programs, click iSCSI Initiator.
2. If the UAC page appears, click Continue.
3. If this is the first time you have launched Microsoft iSCSI Initiator, you will receive a prompt that says the Microsoft iSCSI service is not running. You must start the service for Microsoft iSCSI Initiator to run correctly. Click Yes to start the service. The Microsoft iSCSI Initiator Properties dialog box will open, and the Targets tab will be displayed.
4. On the Targets tab, type the name or IP address of the target device in the Quick Connect text box, and then click Quick Connect. The Quick Connect dialog box is displayed.

5. If multiple targets are available at the target portal that is specified, a list will be displayed. Click the desired target, then click Connect.

6. Click Done.

iSCSICLI

iSCSICLI is a command-line tool suitable for scripting the Microsoft iSCSI initiator service. Although some of the commands may become lengthy and complex, they allow you to access all features of iSCSI. Some of the functions include:

- **iSCSICLI AddTarget:** Creates a connection to a volume or device.
- **iSCSICLI AddPersistentDevices:** Makes an iSCSI device persistent.
- **iSCSICLI RemovePersistentDevices:** Prevents the reconnection to a specified volume.
- **iSCSICLI ClearPersistentDevices:** Removes all volumes and devices from the list of persistent devices.

Using Storage Explorer and Storage Manager

Windows Server 2008 includes Storage Explorer and Storage Manager for SANs to manage Fibre Channel, iSCSI fabrics, and LUNs.

Storage Explorer allows you to view and manage the Fibre Channel and iSCSI fabrics that are available in your SAN. Storage Explorer can display detailed information about servers connected to the SAN, as well as components in the fabrics such as host bus adapters (HBAs), Fibre Channel switches, and iSCSI initiators and targets. See Figure 3-2.

Figure 3-2

Storage Explorer

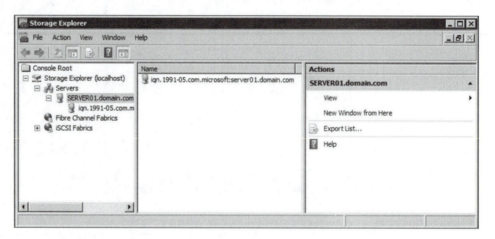

The Storage Manager for SANs is a Windows Server 2008 feature that allows you to create and manage LUNs on both Fibre Channel and iSCSI disk storage subsystems that support Virtual Disk Service (VDS) using the Provision Storage Wizard. You can also use Storage Manager for SANs to assign a LUN to a server or cluster using the Assign LUN wizard. To start the Assign LUN wizard, click LUN Management in Storage Manager, then select the LUN you want to assign in the Results pane. Finally, click Assign LUN in the Actions pane.

■ Understanding Disk Structure

THE BOTTOM LINE Before you use a disk, you must prepare the disk for usage by creating *partitions* or volumes and formatting the disk.

When you want to use a disk in Windows, you have several choices to make:

- Disk partitioning style
- Disk type
- Type of volume
- File system

Partitioning is defining and dividing a physical or virtual disk into logical volumes called *partitions*. Each partition functions as if it were a separate disk drive, which can be assigned a drive letter. To keep track of how a disk is divided, the disk uses a partition table. Formatting a disk prepares the volume's file system by creating a file allocation table to keep track of the files and folders on the volume.

Introducing Disk Partitioning Styles

Partitioning style refers to the method that Windows uses to organize partitions on a disk.

Windows Server 2008 supports two types of disk partitioning styles:

- **Master Boot Record (MBR):** This is the traditional partitioning style that has been around since DOS, as well as for all versions of Windows. MBR supports partitions up to 2 terabytes (TB) and allows up to 4 primary partitions per disk. Each partition can contain a bootable operating system. Although not used as much as in the past, you can also create three primary partitions and one extended partition. The extended partition can hold an unlimited number of logical drives.
- **GUID Partition Table (GPT):** This is a newer partitioning style that supports up to 18 exabtyes (EB) or 18 billion gigabytes and can store up to 128 partitions on each disk. In addition, this style is more fault tolerant because it stores a duplicate set of partition tables.

Comparing Types of Disks

Most versions of Windows servers—including Windows Server 2008—support two types of hard disk storage: basic and dynamic. Basic disks are the traditional disk type, whereas dynamic disks offer software-based RAID and the ability to resize volumes without rebooting.

CERTIFICATION READY
What are the differences between basic and dynamic disks?
4.3

In Windows Server 2008, a basic disk is the same type of disk as found in earlier versions of Windows. When using MBR, basic disks gave you either four primary partitions or three primary partitions and one extended partition. The partition table and master boot record are located on the first sector of each hard disk.

Dynamic disks were created for increased flexibility. Instead of the basic partition table found in a basic disk, a dynamic disk uses the Logical Disk Manager (LDR) database to store information about the basic disk. Because it uses the LRD, the disk can be divided into 2,000 separate volumes. However, you should limit the number of volumes to 32 to allow the system to reboot in a reasonable amount of time.

Dynamic disks are meant to be dynamic, which means you can extend or shrink a dynamic disk without having to reboot. In addition, dynamic disks support five types of volumes:

- **Simple volume:** A single volume consists of disk space on a single physical disk. This can be a single area or multiple linked areas on the same disk.

- **Spanned volume:** A spanned volume consists of disk space from more than one physical disk. You can add more space to a spanned volume by extending it at any time. You can create spanned volumes on dynamic disks only, and you need at least two dynamic disks to create a spanned volume. You can extend a spanned volume onto a maximum of 32 dynamic disks. Spanned volumes cannot be mirrored or striped, and they are not fault tolerant.

- **Striped volume:** A striped volume (RAID 0) stores data in stripes on two or more physical disks. Data in a striped volume is allocated alternately and evenly (in stripes) to the disks contained within the striped volume. Striped volumes can substantially improve the speed of data access. However, striped volumes are not fault tolerant. You need at least two physical dynamic disks to create a striped volume, and you can extend a striped volume onto a maximum of 32 disks. If you need to make a striped volume larger by adding another disk, you must first delete the volume and then re-create it.

- **Mirrored volume:** A mirrored volume uses volumes stored on two separate physical disks to "mirror" (write) the data onto both disks simultaneously and redundantly. This configuration is also referred to as RAID 1. If one of the disks in the mirrored configuration fails, Windows Server 2008 writes an event into the system log of the Event Viewer. The system will then continue to function normally until the failed disk is replaced.

- **RAID-5 volume:** A RAID-5 volume is a form of RAID (striping with parity) that uses a minimum of three disks (and a maximum of 32 disks) to create a fault-tolerant drive among the drives. Here, if one drive fails, the system will continue to work until you replace the drive.

You can create mirrored and RAID-5 volumes only on dynamic disks running on Windows Server 2008, Windows Server 2003, or Windows Server 2000 computers. Both mirrored and RAID-5 volumes are considered fault tolerant because these configurations can handle a single disk failure and still function normally. Mirrored and RAID-5 volumes both require that an equal amount of disk space be available on each disk that is a part of these volumes. As previously mentioned, a mirrored volume must use two physical disks, and a RAID-5 volume must use at least three but no more than 32 physical hard disks.

Many network administrators and consultants agree that hardware-based fault-tolerant solutions are more robust and reliable than software-based fault-tolerant configurations. By installing one or more RAID controller adapter cards into a server, you can set up several different types of hardware fault tolerance, such as mirroring, RAID 5, RAID 1+0 (mirrored volumes that are part of a striped array set), and RAID 0+1 (striped volumes that are part of a mirrored set). When you use hardware RAID, you can retain basic disks or you can convert disks to dynamic; hardware RAID is hidden from Windows Server 2008. Of course, it's less expensive to implement a software solution, such as setting up mirrored or RAID-5 volumes using the Disk Management console in Windows Server 2008, but often the performance, reliability, and flexibility of hardware-based RAID far outweighs its extra cost.

Introducing File Systems

A file system is a method of storing and organizing computer files and the data they contain to make it easy to find and access this information. A file system also maintains the physical location of the files so that you can find and access the files in the future. Windows Server 2008 supports FAT16, FAT32, and NTFS file systems on hard drives.

After you partition a disk, you next need to format the disk. In particular, you can format the disk as FAT16, FAT32, or NTFS. Of these three options, NTFS is the preferred file system for use in today's Windows operating systems.

FAT16, sometimes referred to generically as *File Allocation Table (FAT)*, is a simple file system that uses minimum memory and was even used with DOS. Originally, FAT16 supported the

8.3 naming scheme, which allowed up to an 8-character filename and a 3-character filename extension. Later, it was revised to support longer file names. Unfortunately, FAT can only support volumes up to 2 GB.

FAT32 was released with the second major release of Windows 95. Although this file system can support larger drives, today's Windows versions support volumes only up to 32 GB. FAT32 also supports long file names.

As mentioned earlier, **New Technology File System (NTFS)** is the preferred file system, largely because it supports both a much larger hard disk (up to 16 exabytes) and long file names. In addition, NTFS is more fault tolerant than previous file systems used in Windows because it uses journaling to make sure that disk transactions are written properly before they can be recognized. Last, NTFS offers better security through permissions and encryption.

■ Using Disk Management Tools

THE BOTTOM LINE

The main disk management tool in Windows Server 2008 is the MMC snap-in called Disk Management, which is also part of the Computer and Management consoles. In addition, you can use a diskpart.exe and the Format command to partition and format a drive, as well as Windows Explorer to format a drive.

Disk Management is a system utility for managing hard disks and the volumes or partitions they contain. With Disk Management, you can initialize disks, create volumes, and format volumes with the FAT16, FAT32, or NTFS file systems. See Figure 3-3.

Figure 3-3

The Disk Management snap-in

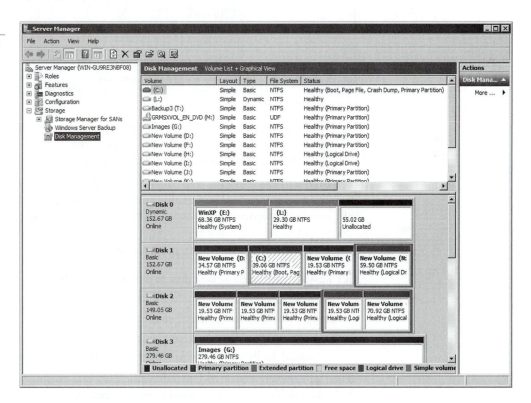

Whenever you add a new disk (either a local hard drive or a virtual drive, such as from a SAN) to a Windows Server 2008 system, you need to open Disk Management and initialize the disk.

INITIALIZE A NEW DISK

GET READY. To initialize new disks:

1. Right-click the disk you want to initialize, and then click Initialize Disk.
2. In the Initialize Disk dialog box, select the disk(s) to initialize. You can select whether to use the Master Boot Record (MBR) or GUID Partition Table (GPT) partition style. See Figure 3-4. Click the OK button.

Figure 3-4

Initializing a disk

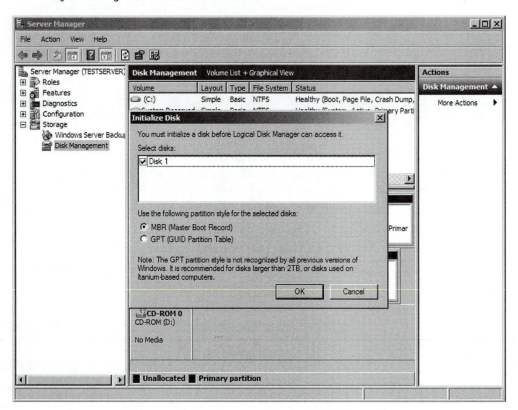

If the disk that you want to initialize does not appear, you may need to right-click Disk Management and click Refresh or Rescan Disks. If the disk still does not appear, you need to make sure that it is connected properly and running.

New disks will automatically start as basic disks. To convert a basic disk to a dynamic disk, there must be at least 1 MB of unallocated space on the disk. Disk Management automatically reserves this space when creating partitions or volumes on a disk.

 CONVERT A BASIC DISK TO A DYNAMIC DISK

GET READY. To convert a basic disk to a dynamic disk from the Disk Management console, perform the following steps:

1. Open the Disk Management snap-in.
2. Right-click the basic disk you want to convert to a dynamic disk, and then click Convert to Dynamic Disk. Click the OK button. See Figure 3-5.

When you convert a basic disk to a dynamic disk, any existing partitions or logical drives on the basic disk become simple volumes on the dynamic disk.

After you convert a basic disk to a dynamic disk, you cannot change the dynamic volumes back to a basic disk. Instead, you must delete all dynamic volumes on the disk and then use the Convert To Basic Disk command. If you want to keep your data, you must back it up or move it to another volume.

Figure 3-5

Convert a basic disk to
dynamic disk

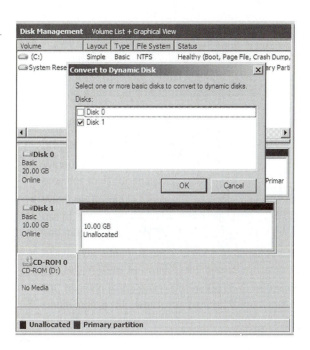

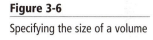 **CREATE OR DELETE A PARTITION OR LOGICAL DRIVE**

GET READY. To create or delete a partition or logical drive, perform the following steps:

1. Open the Disk Management console.
2. Perform one of the following options:
   - Right-click an unallocated region of a basic disk and click New Partition.
   - Right-click an area of free space within an extended partition and click New Logical Drive.
   - Right-click a partition or logical drive and select Delete Partition to remove that partition or logical drive. Click Yes to confirm the deletion.
3. When you choose to create a new partition or logical drive, the New Partition Wizard appears. Click Next to continue.
4. Specify the size of the volume and click the Next button. See Figure 3-6.

Figure 3-6

Specifying the size of a volume

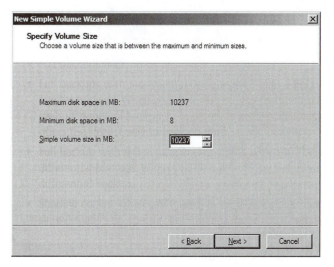

5. Assign a drive letter or mount the volume to an empty NTFS folder and click the Next button. See Figure 3-7.

Figure 3-7

Assigning a drive letter to a new volume

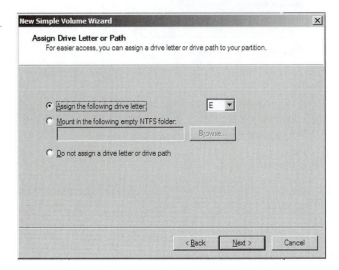

6. Specify the file system, allocation unit size, and volume label. You can also perform a quick format and enable file and folder compression if desired. Click the Next button. See Figure 3-8.

Figure 3-8

Formatting the volume

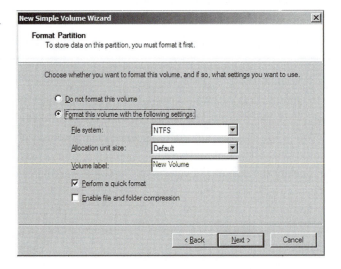

7. When the wizard is complete, click the Finish button.

For basic disks, you must first create an extended partition before you can create a new logical drive, if no extended partition exists already.

If you choose to delete a partition, all data on the deleted partition or logical drive will be lost unless you previously backed it up. In addition, you cannot delete the system partition, boot partition, or any partition that contains an active paging file. Windows Server 2008 requires that you delete all logical drives and any other partitions that have not been assigned a drive letter within an extended partition before you delete the extended partition itself.

EXTEND A SIMPLE OR SPANNED VOLUME

GET READY. To extend a simple or a spanned volume, perform the following steps:

1. Open Disk Management.
2. Right-click the simple or spanned volume you want to extend, and then click Extend Volume.
3. Specify the available disk and the size you wish to extend to. Click the Next button. See Figure 3-9.

Figure 3-9

Extending a volume

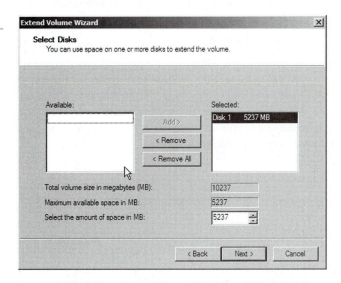

4. When the wizard is complete, click the Finish button.

 CREATE A NEW EMPTY MIRRORED VOLUME

GET READY. To create a new empty mirrored volume from unallocated space, perform the following steps:

1. Open Disk Management.
2. Right-click an area of unallocated space on a dynamic disk and select New Volume.
3. Click Next for the New Volume Wizard welcome window.
4. Click Mirrored as the volume type option and click Next.
5. Select one of the available dynamic disks and click Add.
6. Enter the amount of storage space to be used (in MB) for this mirrored volume, up to the maximum available space on the first disk you selected, and then click Next.
7. Assign the new volume a drive letter, mount the volume in an empty NTFS folder, or choose not to assign the volume a drive letter or path; then click Next.
8. Choose whether to format the new mirrored volume. If you choose to format the new volume, you must do the following:

   • Specify the file system. (NTFS is the only option for dynamic volumes under the Disk Management console.)
   • Specify the allocation unit size.
   • Specify the volume label.
   • Mark the check box for Perform a Quick Format (if desired).
   • Mark the check box for Enable File and Folder Compression (if desired).

9. Click Next to continue.

10. Click Finish to complete the New Volume Wizard.

 CREATE A MIRRORED VOLUME FROM A BOOT OR SYSTEM VOLUME

GET READY. To create a mirrored volume from a boot or system volume, or to create a mirrored volume from an existing volume that already contains data, perform the following steps:

1. Open Disk Management.

2. Right-click an existing dynamic volume and select Add Mirror.

3. Select one of the available dynamic disks on which to create the redundant volume and click Add Mirror.

You can stop mirroring a volume by either breaking or removing the mirror. When you break a mirrored volume, each volume that makes up the mirror becomes an independent simple volume, and they are no longer fault tolerant. When you remove a mirrored volume, the removed volume becomes unallocated space on its disk, whereas the remaining mirrored volume becomes a simple volume that is no longer fault tolerant. All data that was stored on the removed mirrored volume is erased.

 BREAK A MIRRORED VOLUME

GET READY. To break a mirrored volume, perform the following steps:

1. Open Disk Management.

2. Right-click one of the mirrored volumes that you want to break and select Break Mirrored Volume.

3. Click Yes in the Break Mirrored Volume message box.

If you want to completely destroy one of the mirrored volumes and leave just one of the volumes intact, you need to perform a removal procedure instead of simply breaking the mirrored volume.

 REMOVE A MIRRORED VOLUME

GET READY. To remove a mirrored volume, perform the following steps:

1. Open Disk Management.

2. Right-click a mirrored volume and then select Remove Mirror.

3. In the Remove Mirror dialog box, select the disk from which you want to completely erase the mirrored volume and turn it into unallocated space. The remaining volume will stay, with all of its data intact as a simple volume.

4. Click the Remove Mirror button.

5. Click Yes to confirm the removal action in the Disk Management message box that appears.

CREATE A STRIPED VOLUME

GET READY. To create a striped volume from unallocated space, perform the following steps:

1. Right-click an area of unallocated space and select New Striped Volume.

2. When the Welcome screen appears, click the Next button.

3. Select the remaining disk and click the Add button. Then, click the Next button.

4. Assign the F drive and click the Next button.

5. When asked whether to format the volume, click the Next button.

6. When the wizard is complete, click the Finish button.

→ CREATE A RAID-5 VOLUME

GET READY. To create a RAID-5 volume using Disk Management, perform the following steps:

1. Open Disk Management. Be sure the computer has three or more dynamic disks, each with unallocated space.

2. Right-click an area of unallocated space on one of the dynamic disks that you want to use for the RAID-5 volume, then select New Volume.

3. Click Next for the Welcome to the New Volume Wizard window.

4. Select the RAID-5 option button and click Next.

5. Select each available disk that you want to use as part of the RAID-5 volume from within the Available list box and click Add for each of them. You must select at least three disks and no more than 32.

6. Select any disks that you do not want to use as part of the RAID-5 volume within the Selected list box and click Remove.

7. Enter your desired storage capacity for the RAID-5 volume in the Select the Amount of Space in MB box, then click Next to continue.

8. Choose to assign the volume a drive letter, to mount the volume in an empty NTFS folder, or to not assign a drive letter or path to the new RAID-5 volume and click Next.

9. Choose whether to format the new RAID-5 volume. If you choose to format the volume, you must do the following:

   • Specify the file system. (NTFS is the only option for dynamic volumes under the Disk Management console.)

   • Specify the allocation unit size.

   • Specify the volume label.

   • Mark the check box for Perform a Quick Format (if desired).

   • Mark the check box for Enable File and Folder Compression (if desired).

10. Click Next to continue.

11. Click Finish to complete the New Volume Wizard.

If one disk within a RAID-5 volume is intermittently failing, you can attempt to reactivate it by right-clicking the disk and selecting Reactivate Disk. In addition, if one disk within a RAID-5 volume appears to have permanently failed, you can replace the failed disk with another dynamic disk attached to the computer, or you can install a new disk. To regenerate the RAID-5 volume, right-click the RAID-5 volume on the failed disk and select Repair Volume. The replacement disk must contain at least as much unallocated space as that used by the failed disk for the RAID-5 volume.

To format a disk, you can right-click the volume in Disk Management and select Format. You can also right-click the drive in Windows Explorer and select Format. You can then specify the volume label, the file system, and the allocation unit size (the smallest space allocated to a file). You can also perform a quick format, which only empties the FAT table, and you can enable file and folder compression.

When you prepare a volume in Windows, you can assign a drive letter to the new volume, or you can create a mount point for the new volume as an empty NTFS folder. The available drive letters range from drive C through drive Z (i.e., there are 24 different drive letters). Drives A and B are reserved for floppy disk drives. To assign or change a drive letter for a volume, right-click the volume in the Disk Management console and select Change drive letters and path. Then click either the Add or Change button.

By using volume mount points, you can graft or mount a target partition into a folder on another drive. The mounting is handled transparently to the user and applications. With the NTFS volume mount points feature, you can surpass the 26-drive-letter limitation.

→ **ASSIGN A MOUNT-POINT FOLDER PATH**

GET READY. To assign a mount-point folder path to a drive using the Windows interface, perform the following steps:

1. In Disk Management, right-click the partition or volume where you want to assign the mount-point folder path, then click Change Drive Letter and Paths.

2. To assign a mount-point folder path, click Add. Click Mount in the following empty NTFS folder, type the path to an empty folder on an NTFS volume, or click Browse to locate the folder.

SKILL SUMMARY

IN THIS LESSON YOU LEARNED:

- Today's drives are either IDE drives (mostly found on consumer computers) or SCSI drives (mostly found in servers).

- A redundant array of independent disks (RAID) uses two or more drives in combination to create a fault-tolerant system that protects against physical hard drive failure and increase hard drive performance.

- With striping (RAID 0), all available hard drives are combined into a single large virtual file system, with the file system's blocks arrayed so that they are spread evenly across all the drives. Unfortunately, striping offers no fault tolerance.

- Disk mirroring (RAID 1) copies a disk or partition onto a second hard drive. Then, as information is written, it is written to both hard drives simultaneously.

- RAID 5 is similar to striping except that one of the hard drives is used for parity (error correction) to provide fault tolerance.

- RAID 1+0 is a mirrored dataset (RAID 1), which is then striped (RAID 0).

- When a drive fails, some systems use hot spares so that the system will automatically replace the failed drive and rebuild or restore the missing data.

- Network attached storage (NAS) is a file-level data storage device that is connected to a computer network to provide shared drives or folders, usually using SMB.

- A storage area network (SAN) is an architecture used for disk arrays, tape libraries, and optical jukeboxes to appear as locally attached drives on a server.

- A host adapter, sometimes referred to as host bus adapter (HBA), connects a host system such as a computer to a network or storage devices.

- Logical unit numbers (usually referred to as LUNs) allow a SAN to break its storage into manageable pieces, which are then assigned to one or more servers in the SAN.

- Fibre Channel and iSCSI are gigabit-speed technologies primarily used for storage networking.

- Microsoft Windows Server 2008 includes two iSCSI Initiator software interfaces (iSCSI Initiator and iSCSICLI command interface) to connect an iSCSI storage array or volume of a storage array to a server and mount the array or volume as a local volume.

- Windows Server 2008 includes Storage Explorer and Storage Manager for SANs to manage Fibre Channel, iSCSI fabrics, and LUNs.

- Partitioning is defining and dividing a physical or virtual disk into logical volumes called partitions. Each partition functions as if it were a separate disk drive that can be assigned a drive letter.

- Formatting a disk prepares the disk's file system.

- Windows Server 2008 supports two types of disk partitioning styles: Master Boot Record (MBR) and GUID Partition Table (GPT).

- In Windows Server 2008, a basic disk is the same type of disk found in earlier versions of Windows.

- When using MBR, basic disks gave you either four primary partitions or three primary partitions and one extended partition.
- Dynamic disks offer increased flexibility, including up to 2,000 volumes and the ability to extend or shrink a disk without requiring a reboot.
- Dynamic disks support five types of volumes: simple volumes, spanned volumes, striped volumes, mirrored volumes, and RAID-5 volumes.
- A file system is a method of storing and organizing computer files and the data they contain to make it easy to find and access this information. A file system also maintains the physical location of the files so you can find and access the files in the future.
- Currently, NTFS is the preferred file system, in part because it supports much larger hard disks (up to 16 exabytes) and long filenames.
- NTFS is a journaling file system that makes sure a disk transaction is written properly before it is recognized.
- NTFS offers better security through permissions and encryption.
- The main tool used to manage disks in Windows Server 2008 is the MMC snap-in called Disk Management, which is also part of the Computer and Management consoles.
- When you prepare a volume in Windows, you can assign a drive letter to the new volume, or you can create a mount point to the new volume as an empty NTFS folder.

■ Knowledge Assessment

Fill in the Blank

Complete the following sentences by writing the correct word or words in the blanks provided.

1. _____ uses two or more drives used in combination to create a fault-tolerant system.
2. _____ is a commonly used RAID technology that does not provide fault tolerance.
3. A(n) _____ is an extra drive that can be automatically swapped when a drive fails.
4. A(n) _____ is an architecture used for disk arrays, tape libraries, and optical jukeboxes based on networking technology.
5. The _____ sends SCSI commands to a SAN over a TCP/IP network.
6. The _____ is a Windows Server 2008 feature that allows you to create and manage logical unit numbers (LUNs) on both Fibre Channel and iSCSI disk storage subsystems that support VDS.
7. A(n) _____ is a method of storing and organizing computer files so that you can easily find them and access them.
8. NTFS can support up to _____ of storage space for each volume.
9. The _____ program is the command interface to partition drives.
10. A(n) _____ uses volumes stored on two separate physical disks to write data onto both disks simultaneously and redundantly.

Multiple Choice

Circle the letter that corresponds to the best answer.

1. Which type of drives offer faster performance and are usually found on servers?
   a. SCSI
   b. IDE

    c. RLL

    d. MFM

2. Which common form of RAID uses three or more disks to provide fault tolerance?

    a. RAID 0

    b. RAID 1

    c. RAID 3

    d. RAID 5

3. How much disk space would you have if you use four 2TB drives in a RAID 5 configuration?

    a. 2 TB

    b. 4 TB

    c. 6 TB

    d. 8 TB

4. Which type of RAID uses a striped dataset that is mirrored with RAID 1?

    a. RAID 4

    b. RAID 5

    c. RAID 1+0

    d. RAID 0+1

5. Which device is a file-level data storage drive that provides access to shared files and folders?

    a. SAN

    b. NAS

    c. RAID

    d. Hot spare

6. What is the default port used by iSCSI?

    a. 3000

    b. 8080

    c. 3260

    d. 443

7. Windows Server 2008 uses an _____ to communicate to a SAN based on iSCSI.

    a. iSCSI connector

    b. iSCSI initiator

    c. iSCSI plug-in

    d. iSCSI snap-in

8. Which Fibre Channel topology provides optimized connection when isolating failed ports?

    a. FC-P2P

    b. FC-AL

    c. FC-SW

    d. FC-SNP

9. What units used in a SAN can be assigned to a server?

    a. HBAs

    b. snapshots

    c. LUNs

    d. ANSIs

10. Which type of volume do dynamic disks not support?

    a. Simple volume

    b. Striped volume

    c. Stripped mirror volume

    d. RAID-5 volume

True / False

Circle T if the statement is true or F if the statement is false.

T | F **1.** When configuring IDE drives, you must configure a SCSI ID and terminate both ends of the chain.

T | F **2.** Two volume types used by Windows Server 2008 are MBR and GPT.

T | F **3.** NTFS is the preferred file system used by Windows Server 2008.

T | F **4.** Basic disks can be resized without rebooting.

T | F **5.** GUID partition types can support up to 18 EB drives.

■ Competency Assessment

Scenario 3-1: Planning Your Disks

You are configuring a computer that is running Windows Server 2008 R2 and will run Microsoft Exchange 2010. So far, you have a single 80 GB drive with Windows running on it. What drives and drive configuration should you add to the server to support Microsoft Exchange if it requires 100 GB of mailboxes?

Scenario 3-2: Researching Disks

Every day, disks become faster and gain more capacity. In addition, disks are starting to transition from mechanical magnetic disks to solid-state disks. Do a search on the Internet, find the fastest disk currently available, and research its features. List the drive, its highlights, and where you found the information.

■ Proficiency Assessment

Scenario 3-3: Connecting a Second Hard Drive

Connect a second hard drive to your system. Next, create a volume on the second drive that takes up half the available space. Format the disk as an NTFS file system. Then expand the drive to take up the rest of the available space. When you can access the volume successfully, delete the volumes on the second hard drive.

Scenario 3-4: Creating a Striped Volume

Using the free disk space on the first drive and the space on the second disk, create a striped volume.

✳ Workplace Ready

Disk Management Software

You can do a lot with the Disk Management snap-in and with the diskpart command. However, these tools cannot do everything. For example, in some situations, you cannot extend certain disks because something is in the way or because the disks are working as system disks. Tools such as Partition Magic can come in handy. Also, even though the Check Disk utility can help you fix some basic errors, you may need to use a third-party tool to recover disks or rebuild a disk.

LESSON 4

Monitoring and Troubleshooting Servers

OBJECTIVE DOMAIN MATRIX

SKILLS/CONCEPTS	MTA EXAM OBJECTIVE	MTA EXAM OBJECTIVE NUMBER
Understanding Performance	Understand performance monitoring.	5.2
Using the Event Viewer	Understand logs and alerts.	5.3
Booting the System	Identify steps in the startup process.	6.1
Introducing Business Continuity	Understand business continuity.	6.2
Introducing Troubleshooting Methodology	Understand troubleshooting methodology.	6.4

KEY TERMS

active-passive cluster

Advanced Boot Options

backup

Boot Configuration Data (BCD)

boot.ini file

cluster

differential backup

Event Viewer

failover cluster

full backup

grandfather-father-son (GFS)

incremental backup

Information Technology Infrastructure Library (ITIL)

Knowledge Base

last known good configuration

master boot record (MBR)

Microsoft TechNet

network load balancing (NLB)

paging file

Performance Monitor

Power-On Self Test (POST)

Recovery console

Resource Monitor

safe mode

shadow copies

System Information

Task Manager

teaming

uninterruptible power supply (UPS)

virtual memory

volume boot record (VBR)

Windows Preinstallation Environment (Windows PE)

You have been with the Acme Corporation for several months. Since then, you have upgraded several servers, installed several servers, and inventoried the servers and services you manage. When your boss asks you, "If we had a disaster, how would you deal with it?" you did not give your boss a very thorough answer. A couple of weeks later, one of your servers crashes and will no longer start.

■ Managing Information Technology

THE BOTTOM LINE

For most companies, an Information Technology (IT) department can be very complex. With all of the network services and applications that are available, larger companies usually need a team of people because of the workload and specialization needed. To help manage all of this, several standards have been created to give an organization some guidelines to follow.

TAKE NOTE*

Remember that the IT department is there to service the rest of the organization, not the other way around.

When you are managing complicated systems that your company depends on, you need to have processes in place to plan, design, implement, monitor, and retire servers, services, and applications to ensure that your time and money is well managed and that the needs of your organization are met.

The *Information Technology Infrastructure Library (ITIL)* is a set of concepts and practices for managing Information Technology (IT) systems, IT Service Management (ITSM), IT development, and IT operations. ITIL gives detailed descriptions of a number of important IT practices and provides comprehensive checklists, tasks, and procedures that any IT organization can tailor to its needs. ITIL is published in a series of books, each of which covers an IT management topic.

The ITIL version 3 core books include:

+ **MORE INFORMATION**

For more information about the ITIL, visit the following two Web sites:
http://www.itil-officialsite.com
http://en.wikipedia.org/wiki/Information_Technology_Infrastructure_Library

- **Service Strategy:** A view of ITIL that aligns business and IT together. It focuses on customer outcomes. Subsequent titles in the core set will link deliverables to meeting the business goals, requirements, and service management principles described in this publication.
- **Service Design:** Provides guidance on the production and maintenance of IT policies, architectures, and documents for the design of appropriate and innovative IT infrastructure service solutions and processes.
- **Service Transition:** Provides guidance and process activities for the transition of services in the operational business environment. It covers the broader, long-term change management role; release; and deployment practices so that risks, benefits, delivery mechanisms, and the support of ongoing operational services are considered.
- **Service Operation:** Introduces, explains, and details delivery and control activities to achieve operational excellence on a day-to-day basis.
- **Continual Service Improvement:** Focusing on the process elements involved in identifying and introducing service management improvements, this publication also deals with issues surrounding service retirement.

In either case, the ITIL publications will only give you a starting place in developing your organization's processes to help manage your IT department. You will also need to discuss the needs of the organization with various managers including managers of your core business and managers of other support departments such as human resources, accounting, and legal departments to gather what services your organization should provide and what other requirements you must follow.

For example, if you work with medical records, you have certain standards that you have to follow to keep the data secure such as the Health Insurance Portability and Accountability Act (HIPAA). In a publicly traded company, you have to follow certain financial requirements including archiving data. Finally, your organization may have its own standards in place.

When you want to start using a server, service, or application, you should follow certain steps to implement it properly. Those steps include:

- Collecting requirements
- Designing and planning
- Implementing
- Managing and monitoring

By collecting requirements, you define what the server, service, or application is supposed to do, including its workload. Without properly collecting requirements, you may not select the correct hardware or software that will support your objectives. You must then plan and design the server, service, or application to make sure that it does what it is supposed to do without interfering with other servers, services, or applications. Next, you implement the server, service, or application, which includes installing and configuring it. Finally, you need to manage and monitor your server, service, or application to make sure it does what it is intended to do and that the proper users and services can access it. If a problem occurs, you will need to fix and troubleshoot the problem. As you monitor the system, you should look at the performance of the system so that you know when your server, service, or application should be replaced. You may also need to identify potential problems to correct them before they affect your server, service, or application to the point that it cannot be used or that it is significantly degraded.

Most of the information available from Microsoft to design, plan, implement, manage, and monitor Microsoft products can be found at Microsoft's Web site, particularly at **Microsoft TechNet** (http://technet.microsoft.com). It includes Microsoft Knowledge Base, service packs, security updates, resource kits, technical training, operations and deployment guides, white papers, and case studies.

Within these documents and Web sites, you should always pay attention to the Best Practices sections. By following these guidelines, your system or application will run more efficiently and reliably, be more secure and more scalable. Some of the more complex software components including Microsoft Exchange and Microsoft SQL Server include Best Practices Analyzer software, which will automatically analyze the server and give recommendations.

When managing your servers, you can take one of two approaches: proactive or reactive. Being proactive means that you are planning ahead and anticipating problems before they disable or degrade your server, service, or application. Being reactive means that you are waiting for problems to occur before addressing them. In the long run, the best approach is to be proactive so that you can avoid system downtime. Of course, you must allocate some time and effort and possible additional hardware and software to help you efficiently monitor your servers, services, and applications. Finally, remember that while you make an effort to be proactive, you will eventually have to deal with unforeseen or unexpected problems.

■ Introducing Troubleshooting Methodology

THE BOTTOM LINE

As a computer technician, a server administrator, or a network administrator, you will eventually have to deal with problems. Some problems will have obvious solutions and be easy to fix. Many problems will need to be figured out by following a troubleshooting methodology to efficiently resolve a problem.

There are two methods when troubleshooting and fixing a problem: specific approach and systematic approach. The specific approach is usually used when you have seen the exact problem before and you already know what to do. There is not much that needs to be done in investigating the scope of the problem and little research needs to be done. Of course, if you see the same problem frequently, you should investigate further to permanently fix the problem.

The systematic approach is a more formal approach. The whole reason for using an effective troubleshooting methodology is to reduce the amount of guesswork needed to troubleshoot and fix the problem in a timely manner.

CERTIFICATION READY
What steps would you use to troubleshoot a problem?
6.4

Microsoft Product Support Service engineers use the "detect method," which consists of the following six steps:

1. **Discover the problem:** Identify and document problem symptoms, and search technical information resources including searching Microsoft Knowledge Base (KB) articles to determine whether the problem is a known condition.

2. **Evaluate system configuration:** Ask the client or customer and check the system's documentation to determine if any hardware, software, or network changes have been made including any new additions. Also check any available logs including looking in the Event Viewer.

3. **List or track possible solutions and try to isolate the problem by removing or disabling hardware or software components:** You may also consider turning on additional logging or running diagnostic programs to gather more information and test certain components.

4. **Execute a plan:** Test potential solutions and have a contingency plan if these solutions do not work or have a negative impact on the computer. Of course, you don't want to make the problem worse, so if possible, back up any critical system or application files.

5. **Check results:** If the problem is not fixed, go back to track possible solutions.

6. **Take a proactive approach:** Document changes that you made along the way while troubleshooting the problem. Also notify the customer or client and document internal symptoms of the problem in case it happens in the future or in case those changes that fixed the problem affect other areas.

When troubleshooting problems, you do have several tools that can help isolate and fix the problems. The Device Manager was already discussed in Lesson 2. Other tools include:

- System Information
- Event Viewer
- Task Manager
- Resource Monitor
- Performance Monitor
- System Configuration
- Memory Diagnostics tool
- Troubleshooting Wizard
- Boot Menu including Safe mode
- Windows Repair

When troubleshooting issues within Windows and related programs, you will eventually deal with problems that you do not know how to fix. Therefore, you may have to ask coworkers and do some research on the Internet. Good search engines such as Google and Bing are invaluable. You will also need to check the vendor Web sites, including Microsoft's (www.microsoft.com).

Microsoft also includes a Knowledge Base and several online forums (http://social.microsoft.com/forums and http://social.technet.microsoft.com/Forums), which you can use to find help for a wide range of problems and that allow you to leave messages for others to answer. The Microsoft *Knowledge Base* is a repository of thousands of articles made available to the public by Microsoft Corporation that contains information on problems encountered by users of Microsoft products. Each article bears an ID number, and articles are often referred to by their Knowledge Base (KB) ID. The Knowledge Base can be accessed by entering keywords or the ID at http://support.microsoft.com/search/.

System Information

When you first start troubleshooting a server, you need to know what the server contains, such as the type and number of processors and the amount of RAM. You will also need to know what programs and services are running on the server. System properties can give you information about the system processor and amount of RAM. By looking at the Device Manager you can see what hardware is recognized and what drivers are loaded. However, if you want a more detailed look at what your system consists of and what is running on your system, you can use the System Information program.

System Information (also known as msinfo32.exe) shows details about your computer's hardware configuration, components, and software, including drivers. It was originally included with Windows to assist Microsoft support people in determining what a particular machine contains, especially when talking to end users.

System Information lists categories in the left pane and details about each category in the right pane. See Figure 4-1. The categories include:

- **System Summary:** Displays general information about your computer and the operating system, such as the computer name and manufacturer, the type of basic input/output system (BIOS) your computer uses, and the amount of memory that's installed.

- **Hardware Resources:** Displays advanced details about your computer's hardware and is intended for IT professionals.

- **Components:** Displays information about disk drives, sound devices, modems, and other components installed on your computer.

- **Software Environment:** Displays information about drivers, network connections, and other program-related details.

Figure 4-1

System Information

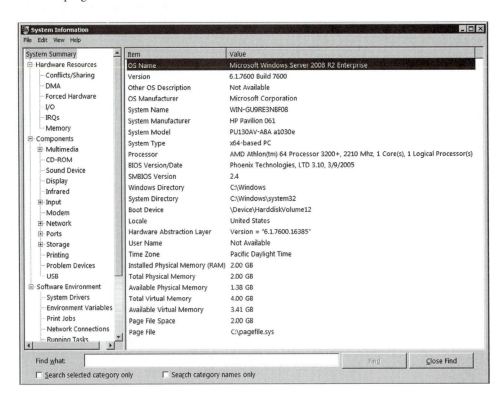

To find a specific detail in System Information, type the information you're looking for in the Find what box at the bottom of the window. For example, to find your computer's Internet protocol (IP) address, type "ip address" in the Find what box, and then click Find.

Using the Event Viewer

CERTIFICATION READY
How you would see the errors and warnings in the Windows logs?
5.3

One of the most useful troubleshooting tools is the Event Viewer MMC snap-in, which is essentially a log viewer. Whenever you have problems, you should look in the Event Viewer to see any errors or warnings that may reveal what a problem is.

The *Event Viewer* is a Microsoft Management Console (MMC) snap-in that enables you to browse and manage event logs. It is included in the Computer Management and Server Manager MMC and is included in Administrative Tools as a stand-alone console. You can also execute the eventvwr.msc command.

Event Viewer enables you to perform the following tasks:

- View events from multiple event logs. (See Figure 4-2.)
- Save useful event filters as custom views that can be reused.
- Schedule a task to run in response to an event.
- Create and manage event subscriptions.

Figure 4-2

Windows Event Viewer

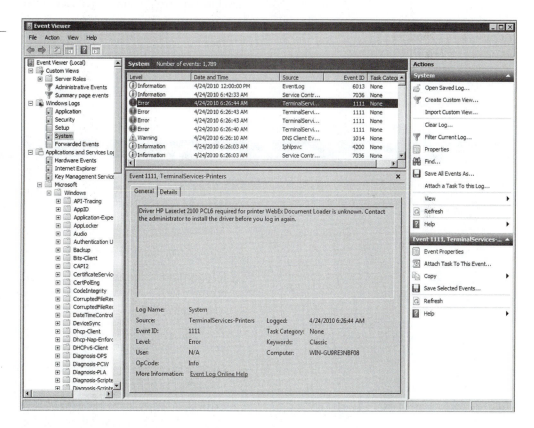

The Windows Logs category includes default logs that were available in previous versions of Windows. They include:

- **Application log:** Contains events logged by applications or programs.
- **Security log:** Contains events such as valid and invalid log on attempts and access to designated objects such as files and folders, printers, and Active Directory objects. By default, the Security log is empty until you enable auditing.

- **Setup log:** Contains events related to application setup.
- **System log:** Contains events logged by Windows system components including errors displayed by Windows during boot and errors with services.
- **Forwarded Events log:** Used to store events collected from remote computers allowing you to centralize Windows logs. To collect events from remote computers, you must create an event subscription. It should be noted that Forwarded Events will not appear in operating systems found before Windows 7 and Windows Server 2008 operating systems.

Based on the roles and programs installed on a server, Windows may have additional logs such as DHCP, DNS, or Active Directory.

Applications and Services logs were first introduced with Windows Vista. These logs store events from a single application or component rather than events that might have a system-wide impact, such as:

- **Admin:** Primarily targeted at end users, administrators, and support personnel. The events that are found in the Admin channels indicate a problem and a well-defined solution that an administrator can act on.
- **Operational:** Used for analyzing and diagnosing a problem or occurrence. They can be used to trigger tools or tasks based on the problem or occurrence.
- **Analytic:** Published in high volume. They describe program operation and indicate problems that cannot be handled by user intervention.
- **Debug:** Used by developers in troubleshooting issues with their programs.

Table 4-1 shows the common fields displayed in the Event Viewer logs.

Table 4-1

Common fields displayed in the Event Viewer logs

Property Name	Description
Source	The software that logged the event, which can be either a program name, such as "SQL Server," or a component of the system or of a large program, such as a driver name.
Event ID	A number identifying the particular event type.
Level	A classification of the event severity: **Information:** Indicates that a change in an application or component has occurred, such as an operation has successfully completed, a resource has been created, or a service started. **Warning:** Indicates that an issue has occurred that can impact service or result in a more serious problem if action is not taken. **Error:** Indicates that a problem has occurred, which might impact functionality that is external to the application or component that triggered the event. **Critical:** Indicates that a failure has occurred from which the application or component that triggered the event cannot automatically recover. **Success Audit:** Shown in security logs to indicate that the exercise of a user right was successful. **Failure Audit:** Shown in security logs to indicate that the exercise of a user right has failed.

When you open any of these logs, particularly the Application, Security, and System, they may have thousands of entries. Unfortunately, this means that it may take some time to find what you are looking for if you look entry by entry. To cut down on the time it takes to find what you want, you can use a filter to cut the number of entries down. To filter a log, open the Action menu and click Filter Current Log.

Event Viewer allows you to view events on a single remote computer. However, troubleshooting an issue might require you to examine a set of events stored in multiple logs on multiple computers.

Today's Event Viewer can be used to collect copies of events from multiple remote computers and store them locally. To specify which events to collect, you create an event subscription. Among other details, the subscription specifies exactly which events will be collected and in which log they will be stored locally. Once a subscription is active and events are being collected, you can view and manipulate these forwarded events as you would any other locally stored events.

Third party applications, non-Microsoft servers, and many network devices will not use the Event Viewer. Instead, logs are saved to text files. Many of these servers and devices can be configured to save the logs to a centralized syslog server. Syslog is a standard for logging program messages.

■ Booting the System

 THE BOTTOM LINE

One of the most frustrating problems to troubleshoot is when Windows does not boot and you cannot log in to Windows. To overcome these problems, you need to understand how the computer boots and be familiar with the tools available during boot up.

CERTIFICATION READY
If your server fails to start properly, do you know how to isolate the point at which it fails?
6.1

Every time you turn on a computer, it goes through the *Power-On Self Test (POST)*, which initializes hardware and finds an operating system to load. The POST includes the following steps:

1. The computer does a quick power check to make sure it has enough power to supply the system.
2. When the processor receives a power good signal, the processor initializes and tests essential PC components as specified in the System ROM BIOS.
3. If a problem is found, the computer identifies the problem with a series of beeps based on the system ROM BIOS.
4. The processor then initializes the video card and starts sending information to the monitor. Next, the system initializes additional components. If a problem is discovered, it displays a message to indicate the problem.
5. The system will search for a boot device (such as a hard drive, optical disk, or USB flash drive) from which to boot.
6. The system will read the master boot record on a boot device to determine operating system boot files.

If the system is running Windows XP or Windows Server 2003, the system will go through the following steps:

1. NT loader (NTLDR) is loaded, which reads the boot.ini file to display the boot menu or to boot from a partition or volume.
2. NTDetect.com gathers information about the computer hardware as reported by the BIOS.
3. NTOSKRNL.EXE is the main part of Windows, which is responsible for various system services and process and memory management.
4. HAL.DLL implements a number of functions different ways by various hardware platforms based on processor and chipset.

If the system is running Windows Vista, Windows 7, or Windows Server 2008, the system will go through the following steps:

1. BOOTMGR is loaded, which accesses the Boot Configuration Data Store to display the boot menu or to boot from a partition or volume.
2. WINLoad is the operating system boot loader, which loads the rest of the operating system.
3. NTOSKRNL.EXE is the main part of Windows, which is responsible for various system services and process and memory management.
4. Boot-class device drivers implement a number of functions in different ways by various hardware platforms based on processor and chipset.

A *master boot record (MBR)* is the first 512-byte boot sector of a partitioned data storage device such as a hard disk. It is used to hold the disk's primary partition table, contains the code to bootstrap an operating system, which usually passes control to the volume boot record and uniquely identifies the disk media. By default, the master boot record contains the primary partition entries in its partition table.

A *volume boot record (VBR)*, also known as a volume boot sector or a partition boot sector, is a type of boot sector, stored in a disk volume on a hard disk, floppy disk, or similar data storage device that contains code for booting an operating system such as NTLDR and BOOTMGR.

The active partition is the partition or volume that is marked as the partition from which to boot. The active partition or volume that contains the boot file (NTLDR or BOOTMGR) is known as the system partition/volume. The partition or volume that contains the Windows operating system files (usually the Windows or WINNT folder) is called the boot partition. It is common for the systems to have one drive and one partition/volume that makes up the partition, system partition, and boot partition.

The %SystemRoot% variable is a special system-wide environment variable found on Microsoft Windows systems. Its value is the location of the system folder, including the drive and path. By default, on a clean installation of Windows, the %SystemRoot% is C:\Windows.

Understanding Boot.ini

The Windows XP and Windows Server 2003 NTLDR will read the *boot.ini file* to determine which operating system to load even if your system only has one operating system. If your system has multiple operating systems, the boot.ini file can display a boot menu so that you can choose which operating system to load and automatically select a default operating system if one is not selected during boot up.

The menu options are stored in boot.ini, which itself is located in the root of the same disk as NTLDR. It is a read-only, hidden, system file.

The boot.ini file is divided into two sections, [boot loader] and [operating system]. The [boot loader] section configures the number of seconds the Boot Loader Operating System Selection menu appears on the screen and the default operating system loaded. For example, the following section:

    [boot loader]

    Timeout = 30

    Default = multi(0)disk(0)ridsk(0)partition(1)\Windows

will display the Boot Loader Operating System Selection menu for 30 seconds. If no operating system is selected Windows will load in the Windows folder.

The [operating system] section contains the list of available operating systems. The location of the operating system is written as an Advanced RISC Computing (ARC) path. An example of the [operating system] section is:

> [operating systems]
>
> multi(0)disk(0)rdisk(0)partition(1)\WINNT="Microsoft Windows Server 2003"/ fastdetect

The ARC path is used to specify the location of the operating system. It follows the format:

> multi(x)disk(y)rdisk(z)partition(a)

or

> scsi(x)disk(y)rdisk(x)partition(a)

SCSI is used for a SCSI disk with its BIOS disabled. Multi is used for disks other than SCSI or a SCSI with its BIOS enabled. The number after Multi is the ordinal number of the hardware adapter starting with 0. The number after Disk is the SCSI bus number and will always be 0 for a non-SSCI disk or for a SCSI disk with its BIOS enabled. The number after Rdisk is the ordinal number of the disk starting from 0. The number after partition is the ordinal number of the partition starting with 1. After the partition, you then specify the folder that contains the Windows folder. This will usually be \Windows or \Winnt.

There are several options that can be used in the [operating system] section. Some of the popular settings include:

/FASTDETECT[:comx[,comy]]: Turns off serial and bus mouse detection for the specified port(s), or for all ports if none are specified. Use this switch when there is a component other than a mouse attached to a serial port during the startup process. Ports may be separated with commas to turn off more than one port.

/BASEVIDEO: Forces the system into standard 640 × 480 16-color VGA mode by using a video device driver that is compatible with any video adapter. If the operating system fails to load due to a faulty or incorrectly configured video driver, this switch allows the system to load, so that the user may then remove, update, or roll back the problem video driver.

/3GB: Forces ×86-based systems to increase the virtual address space allocated for user programs to 3 GB, and to decrease to 1 GB allocated to the kernel and to executive components. Some configurations of Windows Server 2003 that run virtual memory intensive applications such as database servers or Microsoft Exchange Server 2003 may require this switch for better performance.

/PAE: Enables Physical Address Extension support, which allows the system to see more than 4 GB of memory. Note: In safe mode, the computer starts by using normal kernels, even if the /PAE switch is specified.

/NOEXECUTE: Data Execution Prevention (DEP) uses a processor feature to prevent malicious code from exploiting buffer overflow bugs with unexpected program input in order to execute arbitrary code. The /NOEXECUTE option is only available with 32-bit versions of Windows running on processors that support DEP. The NoExecute option is always enabled on 64-bit versions of Windows. To disable DEP, you would include /NOEXECUTE=ALWAYSOFF.

When using Windows XP or Windows Server 2003, you can modify the default operating system and the amount of time the list of operating systems appear by right-clicking My Computer, selecting Properties, selecting the Advanced tab, and clicking the Settings button in the Startup and Recovery section. You can also edit the boot.ini file by clicking the Edit button and specifying what type of dump occurs during a system failure. See Figure 4-3.

Figure 4-3

Windows startup and recovery options

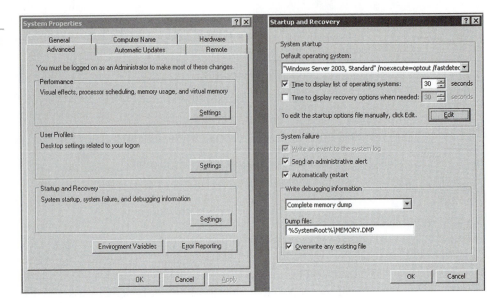

Understanding BCDEdit

> **Boot Configuration Data (BCD)** is a firmware-independent database for boot-time configuration data used by Microsoft's Windows Boot Manager found with Windows Vista, Windows 7, and Windows Server 2008. To edit the Boot Configuration, you typically use Bcdedit.exe.

Unlike previous versions of Windows that used the boot.ini file to designate the boot configuration, newer versions of Windows store the configuration in a \Boot\bcd on the system volume on machines that use IBM PC compatible firmware. To edit the Windows Boot Menu Options, the Boot Configuration Data Editor (Bcdedit) is used.

The Bcdedit.exe command-line tool can be used to add, delete, and edit entries in the BCD store, which contains objects. Each object is identified by a GUID (Globally Unique Identifier). Every drive or partition on the system will have its own GUID and could be:

- **{legacy}:** Describes a drive or partition on a pre-Windows Vista operating system,
- **{default}:** Describes the drive or partition containing the current default operating system, or
- **{current}:** Describes the current drive or partition to which you are booted.

For example {c34b751a-ff09-11d9-9e6e-0030482375e7} describes another drive or partition on which an operating system has been installed.

Some of the options available for the BCDEdit command are:

- **/createstore:** Creates a new empty BCD store.
- **/export:** Exports the contents of the system BCD store to a specified file.
- **/import:** Restores the state of the system BCD store from a specified file.
- **/copy:** Makes copies of boot entries.
- **/create:** Creates new boot entries.
- **/delete:** Deletes boot entries.
- **/deletevalue:** Deletes elements from a boot entry.
- **/set:** Creates or modifies a boot entry's elements.
- **/enum:** Lists the boot entries in a store.

- **/bootsequence:** Specifies a one-time boot sequence.
- **/default:** Specifies the default boot entry.
- **/displayorder:** Specifies the order in which Boot Manager displays its menu.
- **/timeout:** Specifies the Boot Manager Timeout value.
- **/toolsdisplayorder:** Specifies the order in which Boot Manager displays the tools menu.
- **/bootems:** Enables or disables Emergency Management Services (EMS) for a specified boot application.
- **/ems:** Enables or disables EMS for an operating system boot entry.
- **/emssettings:** Specifies global EMS parameters.
- **/store:** Specifies the BCD store upon which a command acts.
- **bcdedit /?:** Specifies the available options.

To change the title of the boot menu entry, such as its type, you would use the following command, which changes the title to Windows XP from "Earlier Windows Version":

> bcdedit /set {ntldr} description "Windows XP"

To change the timeout showing on the boot menu:

> bcdedit /timeout 5

To change the default OS to boot first:

> bcdedit /default {ntldr}

When using Windows Vista, Windows 7, and Windows Server 2008, you can modify the default operating system and the amount of time the list of operating systems appear by right-clicking Computer, selecting Properties, clicking Advanced system settings, selecting the Advanced tab, and clicking the Settings button in the Startup and Recovery section. You can also specify what type of dump occurs during a system failure.

+ MORE INFORMATION

For more information about Bcdedit, visit the following Web sites:

http://technet.microsoft.com/en-us/library/cc709667(WS.10).aspx

http://www.windows7home.net/how-to-use-bcdedit-in-windows-7

Understanding Advanced Boot Menu

When problems occur during boot up, you may need to take some extra steps to get the computer into a usable state so that you can fix the problem. Since the release of Windows XP, you can access the *Advanced Boot Options* to get to advanced troubleshooting modes.

To access the Advanced Boot Options screen, you turn your computer on and press F8 before the Windows logo appears. See Figure 4-4. If you have Windows Server 2008 R2, you can then select one of the following options:

- **Repair Your Computer:** Shows a list of system recovery tools you can use to repair startup problems, run diagnostics, or restore your system. This option is available only if the tools are installed on your computer's hard disk.
- **Safe Mode:** Starts Windows with a minimal set of drivers and services. If you make a change to the system and Windows no longer boots, you can try safe mode.
- **Safe Mode with Networking:** Starts Windows in safe mode and includes the network drivers and services needed to access the Internet or other computers on your network.
- **Safe Mode with Command Prompt:** Starts Windows in safe mode with a command prompt window instead of the usual Windows interface.
- **Enable Boot Logging:** Creates a file, ntbtlog.txt, that lists all the drivers that are installed during startup and that might be useful for advanced troubleshooting.

Figure 4-4

Advanced boot options

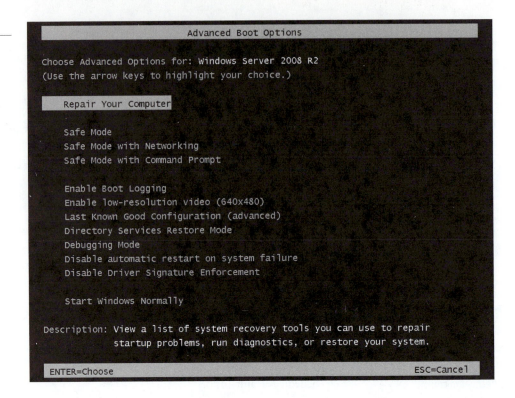

- **Enable low-resolution video (640 × 480):** Starts Windows using your current video driver and low resolution and refresh rate settings. You can use this mode to reset your display settings.
- *Last known good configuration* **(advanced):** Starts Windows with the last registry and driver configuration that worked successfully, usually marked as the last successful login.
- **Directory Services Restore Mode:** Starts Windows domain controller running Active Directory so that the directory service can be restored.
- **Debugging Mode:** Starts Windows in an advanced troubleshooting mode intended for IT professionals and system administrators.
- **Disable automatic restart on system failure:** Prevents Windows from automatically restarting if an error causes Windows to fail. Choose this option only if Windows is stuck in a loop where Windows fails, attempts to restart, and fails again repeatedly.
- **Disable Driver Signature Enforcement:** Allows drivers containing improper signatures to be loaded.
- **Start Windows Normally:** Starts Windows in its normal mode.

Safe mode and its derivatives, enable boot logging, enable low-resolution, last known good configuration, and directory services restore mode, have been around for years.

Safe mode is useful for troubleshooting problems with programs and drivers that might not start correctly or that might prevent Windows from starting correctly. If a problem doesn't reappear when you start in safe mode, you can eliminate the default settings and basic device drivers as possible causes. If a recently installed program, device, or driver prevents Windows from running correctly, you can start your computer in safe mode and then remove the program that's causing the problem.

While in safe mode, you open Control Panel to access the Device Manager, Event Viewer, System Information, command prompt, and Registry Editor.

Devices and drivers that start in safe mode include:

- Floppy disk drives (internal and USB)
- Internal CD-ROM drives (ATA, SCSI)
- External CD-ROM drives (USB)
- Internal DVD-ROM drives (ATA, SCSI)
- External DVD-ROM drives (USB)
- Internal hard disk drives (ATA, SATA, SCSI)
- External hard disk drives (USB)
- Keyboards (USB, PS/2, serial)
- Mice (USB, PS/2, serial)
- VGA video cards (PCI, AGP)

Windows services that start in safe mode include:

- Windows event log
- Plug and Play
- Remote procedure call (RPC)
- Cryptographic Services
- Windows Management Instrumentation (WMI)

Devices and services that start in safe mode with networking include:

- Network adapters (wired Ethernet and wireless 802.11x)
- Dynamic Host Configuration Protocol (DHCP)
- DNS
- Network connections
- TCP/IP-NetBIOS Helper
- Windows Firewall

Using the System Configuration Tool

While safe mode allows you to boot Windows when it will not boot because of a bad driver, service, or application that loads when Windows boots, the System Configuration tool allows you to select or deselect the services or applications that automatically start when you start Windows.

System Configuration (msconfig.exe) is a tool that can help you identify problems that might prevent Windows from starting correctly. When a problem occurs, assuming you can successfully start and log in to Windows, you can open System Configuration and disable certain startup programs or services. If the problem goes away when you restart Windows, you know that the problem is caused by the program or service that you disabled.

The following tabs and options are available in System Configuration:

- **General tab:** Shows the startup selections (Figure 4-5):
  - **Normal startup:** Starts Windows in the usual manner.
  - **Diagnostic startup:** Starts Windows with basic services and drivers only.
  - **Selective startup:** Starts Windows with basic services, drivers, and the other services and startup programs that you select.

Figure 4-5

System Configuration tool
showing the General tab

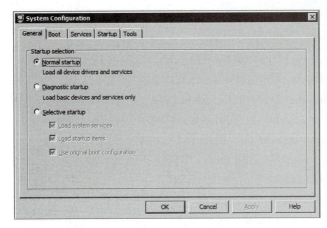

- **Boot tab:** Shows configuration options for the operating system and advanced debugging settings (Figure 4-6) including:
  - **Safe boot:Minimal:** On startup, opens the Windows graphical user interface (Windows Explorer) in safe mode running only critical system services. Networking is disabled.
  - **Safe boot:Alternate shell:** On startup, opens the Windows command prompt in safe mode running only critical system services. Networking and the graphical user interface are disabled.
  - **Safe boot:Active Directory repair:** On startup, opens the Windows graphical user interface in safe mode running critical system services and Active Directory.
  - **Safe boot:Network:** On startup, opens the Windows graphical user interface in safe mode running only critical system services. Networking is enabled.
  - **No GUI boot:** Does not display the Windows Welcome screen when starting.
  - **Boot log:** Stores all information from the startup process in the file %SystemRoot%Ntbtlog.txt.
  - **Base video:** On startup, opens the Windows graphical user interface in minimal VGA mode. This loads standard VGA drivers instead of display drivers specific to the video hardware on the computer.
  - **OS boot information:** Shows driver names as they are being loaded during the startup process.
  - **Make all boot settings permanent:** Doesn't track changes made in System Configuration. Options can be changed later using System Configuration, but they must be changed manually. When this option is selected, you can't roll back your changes by selecting Normal startup on the General tab.

Figure 4-6

System Configuration tool
showing the Boot tab

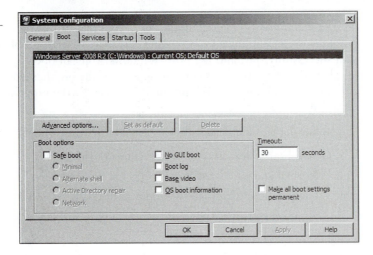

- ○ **Advanced boot options:** Allows you to configure Windows to load quicker or slower based on your needs.
- ○ **Number of processors:** Limits the number of processors used on a multiprocessor system. If the check box is selected, the system boots using only the number of processors in the drop-down list. One processor is selected by default.
- ○ **Maximum memory:** Specifies the maximum amount of physical memory used by the operating system to simulate a low-memory configuration. The value in the text box is megabytes (MB).
- ○ **PCI Lock:** Prevents Windows from reallocating I/O and IRQ resources on the PCI bus. The I/O and memory resources set by the BIOS are preserved.
- ○ **Debug:** Enables kernel-mode debugging for device driver development.
- **Services tab:** Lists all of the services that start when the computer starts, along with their current status (running or stopped). Use this tab to enable or disable individual services at startup to troubleshoot the ones that might be contributing to startup problems. You can also select the Hide all Microsoft services option to show only third-party applications in the services list.
- **Startup tab:** Lists applications that run when the computer starts up, along with the name of their publisher, the path to the executable file, and the location of the registry key or shortcut that causes the application to run (Figure 4-7).

Figure 4-7

System Configuration tool showing the Startup tab

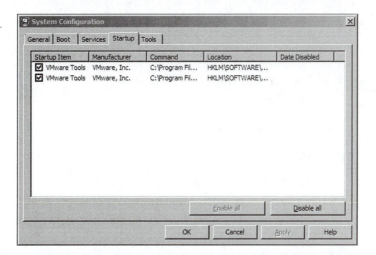

■ Understanding Performance

THE BOTTOM LINE

Performance is the overall effectiveness of how data moves through the system. Of course, it is important to select the proper hardware (processor, memory, disk system, and network) to satisfy the expected performance goals. Without the proper hardware, hardware bottlenecks can limit the effectiveness of software.

CERTIFICATION READY
When your system is slow, what would you use to see why it is slow?
5.2

When a component limits performance, that component is known as a bottleneck. What you do to relieve one bottleneck may cause other bottlenecks. For example, one of the most common bottlenecks is the amount of memory a system has. By increasing the memory, you can often increase the overall performance of a system (up to a point). However, when you add more RAM, the RAM needs to be fed more data from the disk, and now the disk becomes the bottleneck or the processor cannot keep up with the additional data. Overall, the system may become faster, but if your performance is still not where you want it to be, you need to then look for the possibility of another bottleneck.

You cannot identify performance problems by just taking a quick look at performance. Instead, you need a baseline, which can be created by analyzing the performance when the system is running normally and within design specifications. Then when a problem occurs, you compare the current performance to your baseline to see what is different. Since performance can also change gradually over time, it is highly recommended that you baseline your server regularly so that you can chart your performance measures and identify trends. Then, you will know when the server needs to be upgraded or replaced or the workload of the server reduced.

There are several tools available with Windows that enable you to analyze performance. They include:

- Task Manager
- Performance Monitor
- Resource Monitor

Understanding Virtual Memory and Paging File

If your computer lacks the RAM needed to run a program or perform an operation, Windows uses *virtual memory* to compensate. Virtual memory combines your computer's RAM with temporary space on your hard disk. When RAM runs low, virtual memory moves data from RAM to a space called a *paging file*. Moving data to and from the paging file frees up RAM so your computer can complete its work. Unfortunately, when something needs to be accessed from the virtual memory on disk, it is much slower than accessing it directly from RAM. When you have an ample amount of RAM, you do not need as much virtual memory.

 MANAGE YOUR PAGING FILE

GET READY. To manage your paging file in Windows, you will do the following:

1. Right-click Computer and select Properties.
2. In the left pane, click Advanced system settings. If you are prompted for an administrator password or confirmation, type the password or provide confirmation.
3. On the Advanced tab, under performance, click Settings.
4. Click the Advanced tab, and then, under virtual memory, click Change. See Figure 4-8.

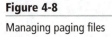

Figure 4-8

Managing paging files

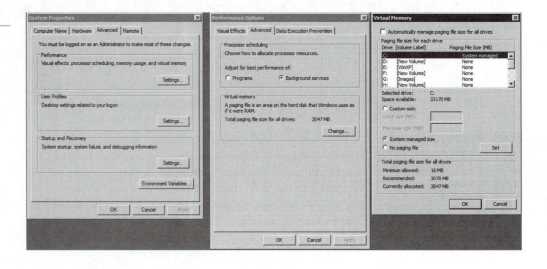

5. Clear the Automatically manage paging file size for all drives check box.
6. Under Drive {Volume Label}, click the drive that contains the paging file you want to change.
7. Click the Custom size radio button, type a new size in megabytes in the Initial size (MB) or Maximum size (MB) box, click Set, and then click OK.

Increases in size usually don't require a restart for the changes to take effect, but if you decrease the size, you will need to restart your computer. It is recommended that you don't disable or delete the paging file.

The default paging file size is equal to 1.5 times the total RAM. However, this default configuration may not be optimal in all cases in particular with servers that contain large databases. Therefore, unless you have an application that uses a larger paging file (usually if your system is utilizing more than 1.5 times your RAM), you should considering adding more RAM to your system. In addition, if you have multiple physical drives, you can move the paging file from the boot volume to another volume.

Using Task Manager

Task Manager gives you a quick glance at performance and provides information about programs and processes running on your computer.

Task Manager is one of the handiest programs you can use to take a quick glance at performance to see which programs are using the most system resources on your computer. You can see the status of running programs and programs that have stopped responding, and you can stop a program running in memory.

To start Task Manager, you can right-click the empty space on the taskbar and select Task Manager or you can open the security menu by pressing the Ctrl+Alt+Del keys and selecting Start Task Manager. When you first start the performance monitor on a computer running Windows Server 2008 R2, you will see six tabs on Task Manager:

- **Applications:** Shows the status of active running programs and programs that have stopped responding. You can end, switch to, or start a program including Windows Explorer (explorer.exe) if it stops unexpectedly.
- **Processes:** Shows all processes running in memory and how much processing and memory each process uses. To see processes owned by other users, you need to select the show processes from all users. To stop a process, right-click the process and select End Process.
- **Services:** Shows all running services.
- **Performance:** Shows the amount of physical memory, CPU usage, and paging file usage.
- **Networking:** Shows how the network interfaces are being used.
- **Users:** Shows the users that are currently logged in and gives you the ability to log off other users.

The Performance tab includes four graphs. The top two graphs show how much the CPU is being used both at the moment and for the past few minutes. (If the CPU Usage History graph appears split, your computer either has multiple CPUs, a single dual-core CPU, or both.) A high percentage means that programs or processes are requiring a lot of CPU resources, which can slow your computer. If the percentage appears frozen at or near 100%, then a program might not be responding. See Figure 4-9.

Figure 4-9

Task Manager Performance tab

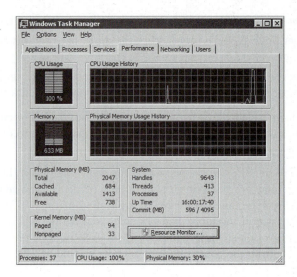

The bottom two graphs display how much RAM, or physical memory, is being used in megabytes (MB) both at the current moment and for the past few minutes. If you have Windows 7 or Windows Server 2008, you can also start the Resource Monitor by clicking the Resource Monitor button. The percentage of memory being used is listed at the bottom of the Task Manager window. If memory use seems consistently high or your computer performance is noticeably slow, try reducing the number of programs you have open at one time or install more RAM.

To view memory use for individual processes on your computer, click the Processes tab. See Figure 4-10. To view all of the processes currently running on the computer, click Show processes from all users. To end a process, click a process, and then click End Process.

Figure 4-10

Task Manager Processes tab

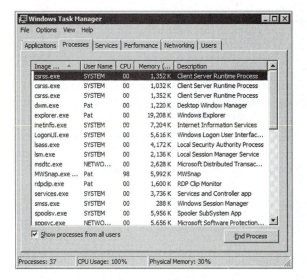

If you are an advanced user, you might want to view other advanced memory values on the Processes tab. To do so, click View, click Select Columns, and then select a memory value:

- **Memory—Working Set:** Amount of memory in the private working set plus the amount of memory the process is using that can be shared by other processes.
- **Memory—Peak Working Set:** Maximum amount of working set memory used by the process.
- **Memory—Working Set Delta:** Amount of change in working set memory used by the process.

- **Memory—Commit Size:** Amount of virtual memory that is reserved for use by a process.
- **Memory—Paged Pool:** Amount of committed virtual memory for a process that can be written to another storage medium, such as the hard disk.
- **Memory—Non-paged Pool:** Amount of committed virtual memory for a process that can't be written to another storage medium.

Using Performance Monitor

Windows *Performance Monitor* is a Microsoft Management Console (MMC) snap-in that provides tools for analyzing system performance. It is included in the Computer Management and Server Manager consoles and it can be executed using perfmon. From a single console, you can monitor application and hardware performance in real time, specify which data you want to collect in logs, define thresholds for alerts and automatic actions, generate reports, and view past performance data in a variety of ways.

Performance Monitor provides a visual display of built-in Windows performance counters, either in real time or as a way to review historical data. See Figure 4-11.

Figure 4-11

Performance Monitor

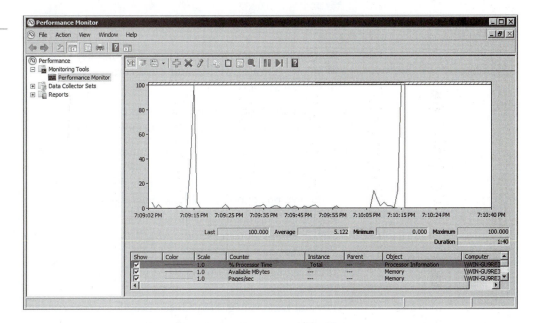

You can add performance counters to Performance Monitor by right-clicking the main pane and selecting Add Counters, or by creating custom Data Collector Sets (Figure 4-12). It features multiple graph views that enable you to visually review performance log data. You can create custom views in Performance Monitor that can be exported as Data Collector Sets for use with performance and logging features.

Windows Performance Monitor uses performance counters, event trace data, and configuration information, which can be combined into Data Collector Sets:

- *Performance counters* are measurements of system state or activity. They can be included in the operating system or can be part of individual applications. Windows Performance Monitor requests the current value of performance counters at specified time intervals.
- *Event trace data* is collected from trace providers, which are components of the operating system or of individual applications that report actions or events. Output from multiple trace providers can be combined into a trace session.

Figure 4-12

Performance Monitor counters

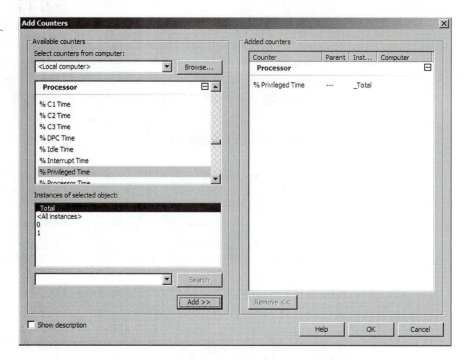

- *Configuration information* is collected from key values in the Windows registry. Windows Performance Monitor can record the value of a registry key at a specified time or interval as part of a file.

There are hundreds of counters that can be added. Often you can look at the Task Manager. Others can only be found in the Performance Monitor. They include:

- Processor: %Processor Time measures how busy the processor is. Although the processor may jump to 100% processor usage, the processor should not be above 80% most of the time. If it isn't, you should upgrade the processor (using a faster processor or add additional processors) or move some of the services to other systems.
- A page fault occurs when a process attempts to access a virtual memory page that is not available in its working set in RAM. If the pages/sec is 20 or higher, you should increase the memory.
- If the paging file is 1.5 times RAM (or higher for specialized applications) you should increase the memory.
- Physical Disk: %Avg. Disk Queue Length is the average number of read requests or write requests queued for the disk in question. A sustained average higher than 2 indicates that the disk is being over utilized.

Using Resource Monitor

Windows Resource Monitor is a system tool that allows you to view information about the use of hardware (CPU, memory, disk, and network) and software resources (file handlers and modules) in real time. You can filter the results according to specific processes or services that you want to monitor. In addition, you can use Resource Monitor to start, stop, suspend, and resume processes and services, and to troubleshoot when an application does not respond as expected.

Windows *Resource Monitor* is a powerful tool for understanding how your system resources are used by processes and services. In addition to monitoring resource usage in real time, Resource Monitor can help you analyze unresponsive processes, identify which applications are using files, and control processes and services. To start Resource Monitor, execute the resmon.exe command. See Figure 4-13.

Figure 4-13

Resource Monitor

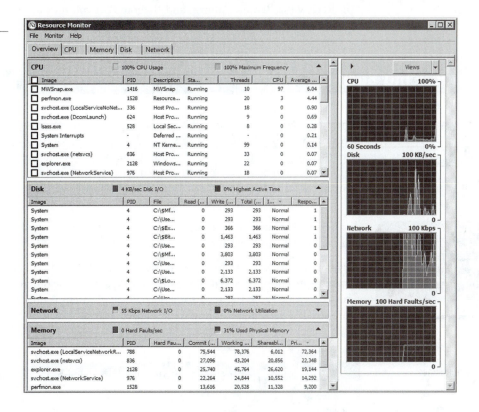

Resource Monitor includes five tabs: Overview, CPU, Memory, Disk, and Network. The Overview tab displays basic system resource usage information; the other tabs display information about each specific resource. Each tab in Resource Monitor includes multiple tables that provide detailed information about the resource featured on that tab.

To identify the process with the highest current CPU usage:

1. Click the CPU tab.
2. In Processes, click CPU to sort processes by current CPU resource consumption.

To view service CPU usage by process:

1. Click the CPU tab.
2. In Processes, in the Image column, select the check box next to the name of the service for which you want to see usage details. You can select multiple services. Selected services are moved to the top of the column.
3. Click the title bar of Services to expand the table. Review the data in Services to see the list of processes hosted by the selected services, and to view their CPU usage.

To identify the process that is using a file:

1. Click the CPU tab, and then click the title bar of Associated Handlers to expand the table.
2. Click in the Search Handlers box, type the name of the file you want to search for, and then click the search button.

To identify the network address that a process is connected to:

1. Click the Network tab, and then click the title bar of TCP Connections to expand the table.

2. Locate the process whose network connection you want to identify. If there are a large number of entries in the table, you can click Image to sort by executable filename.

3. Review the Remote Address and Remote Port columns to see which network address and port the process is connected to.

■ Introducing Business Continuity

THE BOTTOM LINE

When a server goes down, it will most likely cause your company to lose money. If your network contains an external Web site or database that controls your sales, ordering, inventory, or production, server downtime can be detrimental to these business needs. If it is an internal server, it may not allow your users to perform their jobs. In either case, your company is losing money either through revenue or through productivity.

CERTIFICATION READY
If a server failed, do you know how you could have prevented the server from failing?
6.2

As a server administrator, you need to minimize downtime by identifying potential failures and taking steps to avoid those failures and to reduce their effects.

High availability is a system design protocol and associated implementation that ensures a certain degree of operational continuity during a given measurement period. Generally, the term downtime is used to refer to periods when a system is unavailable. Availability is usually expressed as a percentage of uptime in a given year as shown in Table 4-2.

Table 4-2

Availability guidelines

AVAILABILITY %	DOWNTIME PER YEAR	DOWNTIME PER MONTH
99%	3.65 days	7.20 hours
99.9% ("three nines")	8.76 hours	43.2 minutes
99.99% ("four nines")	52.6 minutes	4.32 minutes
99.999% ("five nines")	5.26 minutes	25.9 seconds
99.9999% ("six nines")	31.5 seconds	2.59 seconds

When designing servers and the services they provide, they are often assigned service level agreements (SLA), which state the level of availability those servers or services must maintain. Of course, to have a server design that can support five or six nines is going to be much more expensive than supporting an availability of 99%.

Introducing Fault-Tolerant Components

To make a server more fault tolerant, you should first look at what components are the most likely to fail and implement technology to make a system less likely to fail.

Some of the components that are made redundant within a system are usually:

- **Disks:** Use some form or RAID and hot spares.
- **Power supplies:** Use redundant power supplies.
- **Network cards:** Use redundant network cards.

RAID and hot spare disks have already been discussed in Lesson 3.

It has already been mentioned in this book that mechanical devices fail more often than electrical devices. A Power supply is a mechanical device that converts AC power into clean

DC power and includes fans for cooling. Systems that cannot afford to be down should have redundant power supplies.

While you cannot install fault-tolerant processors and redundant memory, high-end servers have additional features to make the server more resistant to hardware failure and have additional monitoring of key components including processors, RAM, motherboards, and storage. For example, high-end servers use a more expensive Error Correcting Code (ECC) memory that includes special circuitry for testing the accuracy of data as it passes in and out of memory. In addition, ECC memory corrects a single failed bit in a 64-bit block. Some of these servers when combined with Windows Server 2008 Enterprise and Datacenter version allow you to hot add or hot replace processors and memory without taking the server down.

TEAMING OF NETWORK CARDS

NIC *teaming* is the process of grouping together two or more physical NICs into one single logical NIC, which can be used for network fault tolerance and increased bandwidth through load balancing. To make a system truly fault tolerant, you should also have redundant switches where one network card of a team is connected to one switch and the other network card of the team is connected to another switch. This way, if the switch fails, you can still communicate over the network.

To support NIC teaming, the network card, network card driver, and switch must support the same teaming technology, such as 802.3ad link aggregation. You will then most likely have to install and configure specialized software to activate the team.

Understanding Clustering

A computer *cluster* is a group of linked computers that work together as one computer. Based on the technology used, clusters can provide fault tolerance (often referred to as availability), load balancing, or both. If the system fails, including the processor, memory, or motherboard, a cluster that provides fault tolerance can still service requests.

The two most popular forms of clusters are failover clusters and load-balancing clusters. A common use of clusters would include:

- A failover cluster for back end servers such as a database (such as SQL Server) or mail server (such as Exchange Server).
- A load-balancing cluster for the front end that provides the web interface to the back end servers.

INTRODUCING FAILOVER CLUSTERS

A *failover cluster* is a set of independent computers that work together to increase the availability of services and applications. The clustered servers (called nodes) are connected by physical cables and by software. If one of the nodes fails, another node begins to provide services (a process known as failover). Failover clusters can be used for a wide range of network services including database applications such as Exchange Server or SQL Server, file servers, print services, or network services such as DHCP services.

The most common failover cluster is the *active-passive cluster*. In an active-passive cluster, both servers are configured to work as one, but only one at a time. The active node provides the network services while the passive node waits for something to happen to the active node where it cannot provide network services. If the active node goes down, the passive node becomes the active node and resumes providing the network services.

Another type of failover cluster is the active-active node that is designed to provide fault tolerance and load balancing. Network services are split into two groups. One cluster node runs one set of network services while the other cluster node runs the other set of network services. Both nodes are active. If one of the nodes fails, the remaining node will take over providing all of the network services.

To create a failover using Windows Server 2008, you will need two servers that are compatible with Windows Server 2008 and that have identical hardware components. In addition, the servers must run the same Windows Server 2008 Enterprise or Windows Server 2008 Datacenter including the same hardware version, such as 32-bit or 64-bit, and the servers should have the same software updates and service packs. In addition, the servers must be part of the same domain.

Cluster nodes are kept aware of the status of the other nodes and services through the user using heartbeats that are sent through a dedicated network card. Therefore, you need to have at least two network adapters, one for the heartbeat, and one to link normal network traffic. Since the servers provide access to the same files or databases, they will often use the same central storage such as a SAN.

To create a cluster in Windows Server 2008, you would first install the Failover Cluster feature. You then validate your hardware configuration, and then create a cluster using the Failover Cluster Manager.

INTRODUCING LOAD-BALANCING CLUSTERS

Load balancing/**network load balancing (NLB)** is when multiple computers are configured as one virtual server to share the workload among multiple computers. As far as users are concerned, they are accessing the virtual machine and the requests are distributed among the nodes within the cluster. NLB enhances the availability and scalability of Internet server applications such as those used on web, FTP, firewall, proxy, virtual private network (VPN), and other mission-critical servers.

Each node in the NLB cluster is assigned a unique set of cluster IP addresses so that users can access the cluster and the requests are distributed among the various nodes. In addition, each node will have its own dedicated IP addresses for each host. For load-balanced applications, when a host fails or goes offline, the load is automatically redistributed among the computers that are still operating.

For each node to keep track of the status of each other, the NLB cluster exchanges heartbeat messages. By default, when a host fails to send heartbeat messages within five seconds, it has failed. When a host has failed, the remaining hosts in the cluster converge to determine which hosts are still active members, elect the host with the highest priority as the new default host, and to ensure that all new client requests are handled by the surviving hosts. Convergence generally takes only a few seconds, so interruption in client service by the cluster is minimal. During convergence, hosts that are still active continue handling client requests without affecting existing connections. Convergence ends when all hosts report a consistent view of the cluster membership and distribution map for several heartbeat periods.

Understanding Power

Without electricity, the server will not run. Even if you have redundant power supplies, they cannot protect against a power outage or other forms of power fluctuations. In these situations, your company should look at uninterruptible power supplies and power generators to provide power when no power is available from the power company.

An **uninterruptible power supply (UPS)** is an electrical device consisting of one or more batteries to provide backup power when a power outage occurs. UPS units range in size from those designed to protect a single computer without a video monitor (around 200 VA rating) to large units powering entire data centers or buildings. For server rooms that contain many servers, you will most likely install one or more racks full of batteries or UPS devices. For smaller deployments, you may have a single UPS connected to an individual server or essential computer. You also need the UPS to protect other key systems and devices such as primary routers, switches, and telecommunication devices.

What most people new to IT do not realize is that UPSs are not usually designed to provide power for lengthy periods of time. Instead, they are usually designed to provide power for momentary power outages and to allow adequate time to perform a proper shutdown on a server or to switch over to a power generator.

A power generator or a standby power generator is a backup electrical system that operates automatically within seconds of a power outage. Automatic standby generator systems may also be required by building codes for critical safety systems such as elevators in high-rise buildings, fire protection systems, standby lighting, or medical and life-support equipment.

Because power is such a critical component for your server and network, you will need to do periodical tests to make sure that the UPS can supply sufficient power for the necessary time and that the power generator can turn on as needed.

■ Understanding Backups

THE BOTTOM LINE

Data stored on a computer or stored on the network is vital to the users and the organization. It represents hours of work and its data is sometimes irreplaceable. One of the most essential components of any server design is the backup process. No matter how much effort, hardware, and software you put into a system, you will eventually have a failure. Sometimes when the downtime occurs, you may have data loss.

TAKE NOTE*

The best method for data recovery is back up, back up, back up!

A *backup* or the process of backing up refers to making copies of data so that these additional copies may be used to restore the original after a data-loss event. They can be used to restore entire systems following a disaster or to restore small sets of files that were accidentally deleted or corrupted.

When planning your backups, you also need to plan where backup files are going to be stored. It is very difficult to back up all files if you have files stored throughout your corporation, including allowing users to keep files on their local machines. You most likely will need to use some form of technology that keeps your files within a limited number of locations. For example, you can use file redirection for Desktop and My Documents to be stored on a file server by configuring the user profiles.

There are multiple technologies available to help centralize your data. Microsoft offers Distributed File System (DFS), which can be used to replicate shared folders to other servers. In addition, both Microsoft SQL Server and Microsoft Exchange Server have technology to replicate databases to other servers including servers in other locations.

Introducing Backup Media

With early networks and servers, a backup was done with floppy disks. Unfortunately, floppy disks were very limited in size, speed, and life span. Eventually, magnetic tapes were developed and became the standard mechanism used by corporations to perform backup and storage. More recently, hard disk storage and optical disks have become more common for backups.

Traditionally, magnetic tapes have been the most commonly used medium for bulk data storage, backup, and archiving. Tape is a sequential access medium, so even though access times may be poor, the rate of continuously writing or reading data can actually be very fast. For larger organizations, you may use multiple tape drives connected together with a tape library that can automatically swap and manage tapes.

Recently because of increased capacity at lower cost, hard drives have become a viable option for backups. Hard disks can be included in the SAN, NAS, internal hard drives, and external hard drives. Some disk-based backup systems, such as virtual tape libraries, support data de-duplication, which can dramatically reduce the amount of disk storage capacity consumed by daily and weekly backup data.

Usually hard disks are used to provide backup of recent data, and the data will be copied to tape and taken off site for longer term storage and archiving. If a failure occurs, you can quickly restore from the disks. If you need to recover or read data from the past, you will then have to retrieve the tapes from off site and read the tapes.

Another media that is becoming more popular for backups is to use recordable optical disks such as CDs, DVDs, and even Blu-ray. Unfortunately, the newer formats tend to cost more, which may prohibit their use for backups. There is also some concern about the lifetime of a selected optical disk since some optical disks degrade and lose data within a couple of years.

Introducing Backup Items

When a novice thinks of backups, he or she will most likely think of backing up data files such as Microsoft Word or Excel documents. However, there is more to backups than just data files. You also have the program files that make the computer do what it needs to do. Additionally, you have mailboxes, email databases, SQL databases, and other datatypes that may need special software to read and back up. In addition, when determining what and how often to back up, you should also look at the time it would take to reinstall, reconfigure, or recover the item. For example, Microsoft Exchange may take days to install and configure but only a relatively short time to reinstall from backup.

When planning backups, you should isolate your program files and your data files. Program files usually do not change, so they do not have to be backed up often. Data files change often so they should be backed up more often. If you isolate them in different areas, you can create different backup policies for each area.

Databases usually consist of one or more database files and one or more log files. The primary data file is the starting point of the database and points to the other files in the database. Every database has one or more primary data file. The recommended filename extension for primary data files is .mdf.

Log files hold all the log information that is used to recover the database. For example, you can restore the entire database as is or only up to a specific time if you have the complete log files. The recommended filename extension for log files is .ldf.

Another item that must be covered is the system state. The Windows system state is a collection of system components that are not contained in a simple file but can be backed up easily. It includes:

- Boot files (boot.ini, NTLDR, NTDetect.com)
- DLLScache folder
- Registry (including COM settings)
- SYSVOL (Group Policy and log on scripts)
- Active Directory NTDS.DIT (domain controllers)

- Certificate Store (if the service is installed)
- User profiles
- COM+ and WMI information
- IIS metabase

Windows backup and most commercial backup software packages will back up the Windows system state. If you want to perform a complete restore of a system running Windows, you will need to back up all files on the drive and the system state.

Understanding Backup Methods

When planning and implementing backups, you will need to determine when and how often you are going to back up, what hardware and software you are going to use, where you are going to store the backups, and how long you are going to store them.

MEDIA MANAGEMENT METHODS

When you plan a backup, your plan needs to balance between accessibility, security, and cost. Larger organizations will often combine one of the following management methods:

- **On-line:** The most accessible type of data storage usually using hard disks or disk arrays. Restore can begin in milliseconds, but it can be relatively expensive. In addition, on-line storage can be easily deleted or overwritten by accident or intentional action.
- **Near-line:** Typically less accessible and less expensive than on-line storage, usually consisting of a tape library with the restore time beginning with seconds or minutes.
- **Off-line:** Requires some direct human action to physically load tapes into a tape library or drive. Access time can vary from minutes to hours or even days if you have to order tapes from an off-site storage area.
- **Backup site or DR site:** In the event of a disaster, you can switch to the backup site/DR site while you fix or repair the primary site. Unfortunately, this method is the most expensive solution and the most difficult to implement properly.

LOOKING AT BACKUP TYPES

When planning and performing a backup, specialized backup software will usually include different types of backups, each varying in the amount of time it takes to do a backup and restore. Traditional backups include:

- Full backup
- Full backup with incremental backups
- Full backup with differential backup

Full backups back up all designated files and data. For files, it can shut off an archive attribute to indicate that the file has been backed up. For example, with a full backup, you would do a backup once a day, once a week, or once a month depending on the importance of the data and how often it changes. To perform a restore from a full backup, you just need to use the last full backup. A full backup offers the fastest restore.

Full backups with *incremental backups* start with a full backup followed by several incremental backups. For example, once a week, you would perform a full backup on Friday night, which shuts off the archive attribute indicating that the files were backed up. Then any new files or changed files would have the archive attribute turned on. You would then perform an incremental backup Monday, Tuesday, Wednesday, and Thursday night, which only backs up new and changed files and shuts off the archive attribute.

When you do a restore, you restore the last full backup and then restore each incremental backup from oldest to newest. Full backups with incremental backups offer the fastest backup.

Full backup with *differential backup* starts with a full backup followed by several differential backups. For example, once a week, you would perform a full backup on Friday night, which shuts off the archive attribute indicating that the files were backed up. Then any new files or changed files would have the archive attribute turned on. You would then perform a differential backup Monday, Tuesday, Wednesday, and Thursday night, which only backs up new and changed files since the last full backup but will not turn off the archive attribute. When you do a restore, you restore the last full backup and the last differential backup.

Another backup type that is available from backup software packages including Microsoft's backup software is the copy backup. A copy backup backs up the designated files but does not shut off the archive attribute. This is used for impromptu backups such as before you make a system or application change. Since it does not modify the archive attribute, it will not interfere with your normal backup schedules.

LOOKING AT BACKUP ROTATION SCHEMES

One of the questions you should ask yourself is "How often should I do a backup?" The answer will vary based on your needs. You must first look at how important your data is and how much effort would be required to re-create it. You should also consider what it would do to your company if the data were lost. Important or critical data should be backed up nightly. Data that does not change much can be backed up weekly, and data that does not change at all can be backed up monthly.

The next question should be "How often should I keep my backups?" That question is not easy to answer because it is really based on the needs of your organization including the legal requirements that your organization must follow.

Another consideration you should keep in mind is that backups do fail from time to time. Therefore, you should periodically test your backups by doing a restore to make sure that a backup is working and that you are backing up the necessary files. Second, you should have some type of rotation.

One common backup rotation scheme is the **grandfather-father-son (GFS)**. The son backup is done once a day, and those backups are rotated on a daily backup. At the end of the week, the daily backup is promoted to a weekly backup. The weekly or father backups are rotated on a weekly basis with one graduating to grandfather status each month. The monthly backups would traditionally be placed off site; of course, this is based on your needs of what needs to be sent off site.

Introducing Microsoft Windows Backup

Windows includes Microsoft Windows Backup, which will allow you to back up a system. However, third-party backup software packages usually offer more features and options.

To access the backup and recovery tools for Windows Server 2008, you must install the Windows Server Backup Command-line Tools, and Windows PowerShell items that are available in the Add Features Wizard in Server Manager. To run the Windows Server Backup, you must be a member of the Backup Operators or Administrators group.

You can create a backup using the Backup Schedule Wizard or by using the Backup Once option. You can back up to any local drive or to a shared folder on another server.

CREATE A BACKUP SCHEDULE

GET READY. To create a backup schedule using the Windows Server Backup user interface:

1. Click Start, click Administrative Tools, and then click Windows Server Backup.

2. In the Actions pane of the snap-in default page, under Windows Server Backup, click Backup Schedule. This opens the Backup Schedule Wizard.

3. On the Getting started page, click Next.

4. On the Select Backup Configuration page, click Full Server or Custom and click Next (Full Server backs up all volumes on the server, and Custom backs up just certain volumes.). On the Select backup items page, select the check boxes for the volumes that you want to back up and clear the check boxes for the volumes that you want to exclude. See Figure 4-14.

Figure 4-14

Select Backup Configuration

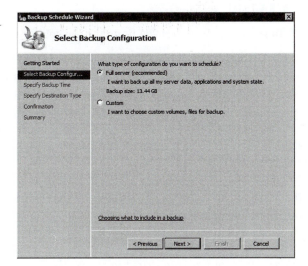

5. On the Specify Backup Time page (Figure 4-15), click Once a day or Click More than once a day. Then Enter the time or times to start the backups. When completed, click Next.

Figure 4-15

Specify Backup Time

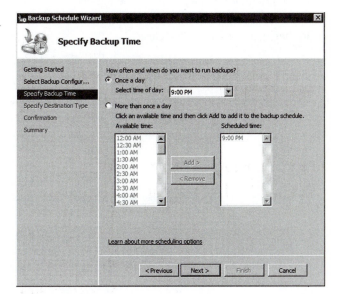

6. On the Select destination disk page, select the check box for the disk that you attached for this purpose, and then click Next.

7. On the Label destination disk page, the disk that you selected is listed. A label that includes your computer name, the current date, the current time, and disk name is assigned to the disk. Click Next.

8. On the Confirmation page, review the details, and then click Finish. The wizard formats the disk, which may take several minutes depending on the size of the disk.

9. On the Summary page, click Close.

Windows Server Backup stores the details about your backups in a file called a backup catalog. The catalog is stored in the same place that you store your backups. Since the catalog specifies what is within a backup, you need the backup catalog to use a Windows backup file.

 RECOVER A BACKUP CATALOG

GET READY. To recover a backup catalog using the Catalog Recovery Wizard:

1. Click Start, click Administrative Tools, and then click Windows Server Backup.

2. In the Actions pane of the snap-in default page, under Windows Server Backup, click Recover Catalog. This opens the Catalog Recovery Wizard.

3. On the Specify storage type page, if you do not have a backup that you can use to recover the catalog, and you just want to delete the catalog, click I don't have any usable backups, click Next, and then click Finish. If you do have a backup that you can use, specify whether the backup is on a local drive or remote shared folder, and then click Next.

4. If the backup is on a local drive (including DVDs), on the Select backup location page, select the drive that contains the backup that you want to use from the drop-down list. If you are using DVDs, make sure the last DVD of the series is in the drive. Click Next.

5. If the backup is on a remote shared folder, on the Specify remote folder page, type the path to the folder that contains the backup that you want to use, and then click Next.

6. You will receive a message that you will not be able to access backups taken after the backup that you are using for the recovery. Click Yes.

7. On the Confirmation page, review the details, and then click Finish to recover the catalog.

8. On the Summary page, click Close.

Once the catalog recovery is completed or you have deleted the catalog, you must close and then re-open Windows Server Backup to refresh the view.

Shadow Copy (Volume Snapshot Service or Volume Shadow copy Service or VSS) is a technology included in Microsoft Windows that allows you take a snapshot of data, even if it has a lock on a specific volume at a specific point in time which would prevent from making a copy. Today, most backup software uses VSS to make backups of files within Windows.

Understanding Shadow Copies of Shared Folders

Windows Server 2003 introduces a new feature called shadow copies of shared folders, which is also used in Windows Server 2008. Shadow copies, when configured, automatically create backup copies of the data stored in shared folders on specific NTFS drive volumes at scheduled times.

Shadow copies allow users to retrieve previous versions of files and folders on their own, without requiring IT personnel to restore files or folders from backup media. Of course, you need to have sufficient disk space to store the shadow copies, at least 100 MB of free space.

 ENABLE AND CONFIGURE SHADOW COPIES

GET READY. To enable and configure Shadow Copies of Shared Folders:

1. Click Start, click Administrative Tools, and then click Computer Management.
2. In the console tree, right-click Shared Folders, click All Tasks, and click Configure Shadow Copies.
3. In Select a volume, click the volume for which you want to enable Shadow Copies of Shared Folders, and then click Enable. See Figure 4-16.

Figure 4-16

Enable Shadow Copies

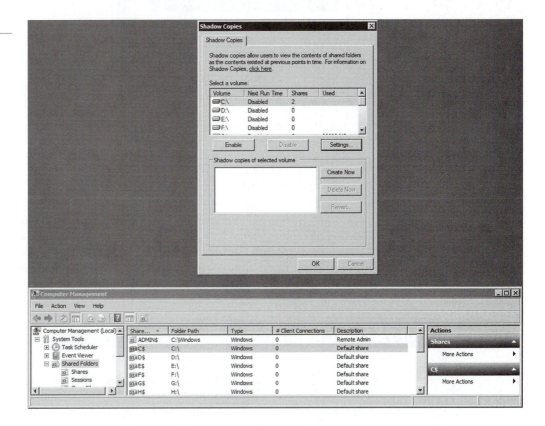

4. You will see an alert that Windows will create a shadow copy now with the current settings and that the settings might not be appropriate for servers with high I/O loads. Click Yes if you want to continue or No if you want to select a different volume or settings.
5. To make changes to the default schedule and storage area, click Settings.

Once you enable Shadow Copies of Shared Folders and start creating shadow copies, you can use the Previous Version feature to recover previous versions of files and folders, or files and folders that have been renamed or were deleted.

 RESTORE A PREVIOUS VERSION OF A FILE OR FOLDER

GET READY. To restore a previous version of a file or folder:

1. Locate the file or folder that you want to restore, right-click the file or folder, and click Properties. The Properties dialog box will appear.

2. Click the Previous Versions tab, click the version of the file that you want to restore, and then click Restore. A warning message about restoring a previous version will appear. Click Restore to complete the procedure. See Figure 4-17.

Figure 4-17

Restore a previous version

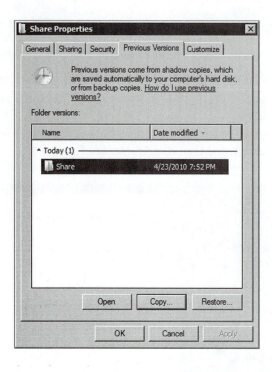

Restoring a previous version will delete the current version. If you choose to restore a previous version of a folder, the folder will be restored to its state at the date and time of the version you selected. You will lose any changes that you have made to files in the folder since that time. Instead, if you do not want to delete the current version of a file or folder, click Copy to copy the previous version to a different location.

■ Performing Server Repair

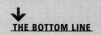

THE BOTTOM LINE

When a server does not start, there are several tools that are available to help you. Some of them have already been discussed such as booting the computer in safe mode or using the System Configuration tool. Other tools are included with the Windows installation disk.

For computers running Windows Server 2003, you can use the *Recovery Console*. The Recovery Console is a command-line tool that you can use to repair Windows if the computer does not start correctly. You can start the Recovery Console from the Windows Server 2003 CD, or at startup through the startup menu if you previously installed the Recovery Console on the computer.

➜ RUN THE RECOVERY CONSOLE

GET READY. To run the Recovery Console from the Windows CD or DVD, follow these steps:

1. Insert the Windows Server 2003 CD in the computer's CD or DVD drive and restart the computer.

2. When you receive the message that prompts you to press any key to start from the CD, press a key to start the computer from the Windows Server 2003 CD.

3. When the Welcome to Setup screen appears, press the R key to start the Recovery Console (Figure 4-18).

Figure 4-18

Press R to start the Recovery Console

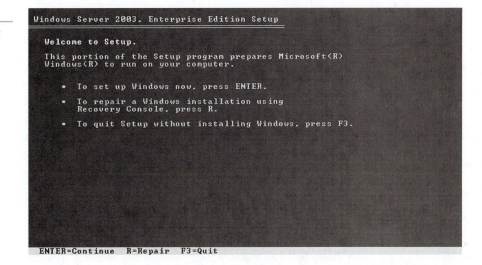

4. Select the Windows installation that you must access from the Recovery Console.
5. Follow the instructions that appear on the screen, type the Administrator password, and then press ENTER.
6. At the command prompt, type the appropriate Recovery Console commands to repair your Windows Server 2003 installation. See Figure 4-19.

Figure 4-19

Recovery Console

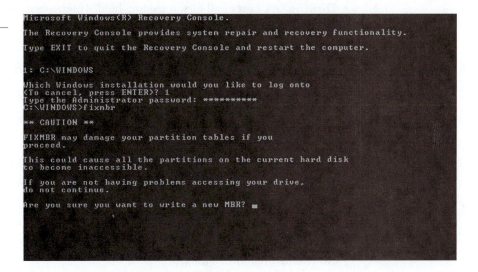

7. To quit the Recovery Console and restart the computer, type exit at the command prompt, and then press ENTER.

 INSTALL THE RECOVERY CONSOLE

GET READY. To install the Recovery Console as a startup option:

1. While Windows is running, insert the Windows Server 2003 CD in the computer's CD or DVD drive.
2. Click Start, and then click Run.

3. In the Open box, type the following line, where the drive is the drive letter of the computer's CD drive or DVD drive that contains the Windows Server 2003 CD, and then click OK:

   drive:\i386\winnt32.exe /cmdcons

4. To install Recovery Console as a startup option for Windows Server 2003 x64 edition, type the following line:

   drive:\amd64\winnt32.exe /cmdcons

5. Click Yes when the message appears, to install the Recovery Console.

6. When you receive the message that states that the Recovery Console is successfully installed, click OK.

7. To use the Recovery Console, restart the computer, and then use the ARROW keys to select Microsoft Windows Recovery Console in the Please select the operating system to start list.

Some of the commands available in Recovery Console include:

- **Attrib:** Changes attributes on one file or folder.
- **Bootcfg:** Used for boot configuration and recovery. You can use the bootcfg command to make changes to the boot.ini file.
- **CD (chdir):** Changes the current directory.
- **Chkdsk:** Checks the disk for errors.
- **Cls:** Clears the screen.
- **Copy:** Copies one file to a target location.
- **Del (delete):** Deletes one file. By default, you cannot use wildcard characters.
- **Dir:** Displays a list of all files, including hidden and system files.
- **Disable:** Disables a Windows system service or a Windows driver.
- **Diskpart:** Manages partitions on hard disk volumes.
- **Enable:** Enables a Windows system service or a Windows driver.
- **Exit:** Quits the Recovery Console and then restarts the computer.
- **Expand:** Expands a compressed file.
- **Fixboot:** Writes a new boot sector on the system partition. The fixboot command is only supported on x86-based computers.
- **Fixmbr:** Repairs the boot partition's master boot record (MBR).
- **Format:** Formats a disk. The /q switch performs a quick format. The /fs:file-system switch specifies the file system.
- **Listsvc:** Displays all available services and drivers on the computer.
- **Md (Mkdir):** Creates a directory.
- **Rd (rmdir):** Removes a directory.
- **Ren (rename):** Renames a single file.

For Windows Server 2008, you would use the WinPE disk instead of the Recovery Console. *Windows Preinstallation Environment (Windows PE)* 3.0 is a minimal Win32 operating system with limited services, built on the Windows 7 kernel. It is used to prepare a computer for Windows installation, to copy disk images from a network file server, and to initiate Windows Setup. Besides being used to deploy operating systems, it is an integral component in recovery technology with Windows Recovery Environment (Windows RE). Some of the tools included in the Windows PE disk include:

- **BCDBoot:** Used to quickly set up a system partition, or to repair the boot environment located on the system partition.

- **BCDEdit:** A command-line tool for managing the BCD Store, which describes the boot application and boot application settings such as the boot menu.
- **BootSect:** Used to restore the boot sector on your computer.
- **Deployment Image Servicing and Management (DISM):** Used to service Windows images off-line before deployment.
- **DiskPart:** Text-mode command interpreter to manage disks, partitions, and volumes.
- **DrvLoad:** Adds out-of-box drivers.
- **OscdImg:** A command-line tool for creating an image file (.iso) of a customized 32-bit or 64-bit version of Windows PE.
- **Winpeshl:** Controls whether a customized shell is loaded in Windows PE or default Command prompt window. To load a customized shell, create a file named Winpeshl. ini and place it in %SYSTEMROOT%\System32 of your customized Windows PE image.
- **WpeInit:** A command-line tool that initializes Windows PE each time Windows PE boots. It installs Plug and Play devices, processes Unattend.xml settings, and loads network resources.
- **WpeUtil:** A command-line tool that enables you to run various commands in a Windows PE session.

MORE INFORMATION

For more information about Windows PE and its tools, visit the following Web sites:

http://technet.microsoft. com/en-us/library/ cc749538(WS.10).aspx

http://technet.microsoft.com/ en-us/library/cc749055 (WS.10).aspx

http://download.microsoft. com/download/5/b/5/5b5bec 17-ea71-4653-9539-204a672f 11cf/WindowsPE_tech.doc

REPAIR THE INSTALLATION OF WINDOWS SERVER 2003

GET READY. You may be able to repair a damaged Windows Server 2003 installation by running Windows Setup from the Windows CD. To repair your installation of Windows, follow these steps:

1. Insert the Windows Server 2003 CD in the CD-ROM or DVD-ROM drive and boot from the Windows installation disk.
2. After Setup starts, press ENTER to continue the setup process.
3. Press ENTER to select the option To set up Windows now, press ENTER. Do not select the Recovery Console option.
4. Press F8 to accept the licensing agreement.
5. Setup searches for previous installations of Windows. If Setup does not find a previous installation of Windows Server 2003, you might have a hardware failure. If Setup does find a previous installation of Windows Server 2003, you may receive the following message: If one of the following Windows Server 2003 installations is damaged, setup can try to repair it. Use the up and down arrows to select an installation. To repair the selected installation, press R. To continue without repairing, press ESC.
6. Follow the on-screen instructions to repair the installation.

After you repair your Windows Server 2003, you may be required to reactivate your copy.

RUN SFC IN RECOVERY CONSOLE TO REPAIR BOOT FILES

GET READY. To run SFC in Recovery Console to repair boot files, follow these steps:

1. Boot from Windows Install Media (Windows Vista or Windows Server 2008 DVD).
2. At the Welcome to Setup screen, choose the link for repair instead of clicking OK.
3. At the repair menu, choose Command Prompt.
4. At the command prompt, type the following command:
   SFC/Scannow /OffBootDir=C:\ /OffWinDir=C:\Windows

The system file checker utility, Sfc.exe, allows administrators to scan all protected resources to verify their versions. Files critical to restart Windows that do not match the expected Windows version may be replaced with the correct versions. If a file is repaired, the corresponding registry data is also repaired. Protected files that are not critical to restart Windows are not repaired. SFC offers the following options:

- **/SCANNOW:** Scans all protected system files immediately.
- **/OFFBOOTDIR:** Use this option for off-line repairs. Specify the location of the off-line boot directory.
- **/OFFWINDIR:** Use this option for off-line repairs. Specify the location of the off-line Windows directory.

Unfortunately, Windows Server 2008 does not have a repair option similar to Windows Server 2008. Instead, you could perform an in-place upgrade or perform an upgrade.

 RECOVER A WINDOWS SERVER 2008 OPERATING SYSTEM FROM BACKUP

GET READY. If all else fails, you will have to recover your operating system using a Windows Setup disc and a backup:

1. Insert the Windows Setup disc into the CD or DVD drive and turn on the computer. If needed, press the required key to boot from the disc. The Install Windows Wizard should appear.
2. Specify language settings, and then click Next.
3. Click Repair your computer. See Figure 4-20.

Figure 4-20

Windows 2008 R2 repair

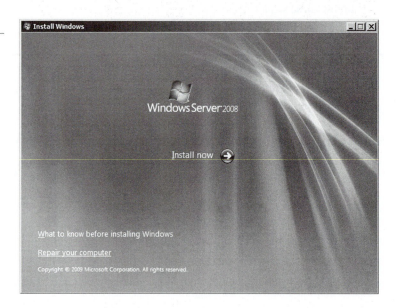

4. Setup searches the hard disk drives for an existing Windows installation and then displays the results in System Recovery Options. If you are recovering the operating system onto separate hardware, the list should be empty (there should be no operating system on the computer). Click Next.

5. On the System Recovery Options page (Figure 4-21), click System Image Recovery.

Figure 4-21

Windows 2008 System Recovery options

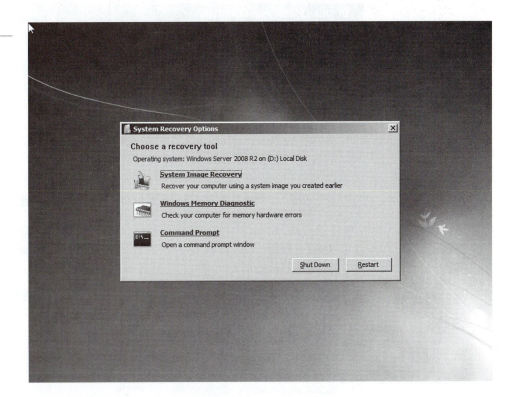

6. Do one of the following:
   • Click Use the latest available backup (recommended) and then click Next.
   • Click Restore a different backup and then click Next.
7. If you chose to restore a different backup, on the Select the location of the backup page, do one of the following:
   • Click the computer that contains the backup that you want to use, and then click Next.
   • Click Advanced to browse for a backup on the network, and then click Next.
8. On the Choose how to restore the backup page, do the following optional tasks, and then click Next:
   • Select the Format and repartition disks check box to delete existing partitions and reformat the destination disks to be the same as the backup.
   • Select the Only restore system disks check box to perform an operating system—only recovery.
   • Click Install drivers to install device drivers for the hardware that you are recovering to.
   • Click Advanced to specify whether the computer is restarted and the disks are checked for errors immediate after the recovery.
9. Confirm the details for the restoration, and then click Finish.

SKILL SUMMARY

- You need to have processes in place to plan, design, implement, monitor, and retire servers, services, and applications.
- The Information Technology Infrastructure Library (ITIL) is a set of concepts and practices for managing Information Technology (IT) services (ITSM), IT development, and IT operations.
- An effective troubleshooting methodology is to reduce the amount of guesswork and random solutions so that you can troubleshoot and fix the problem in a timely manner.
- System Information (also known as msinfo32.exe) shows details about your computer's hardware configuration, computer components, and software, including drivers.
- The Event Viewer is a Microsoft Management Console (MMC) snap-in that enables you to browse and manage event logs.
- Every time you turn on a computer, the computer goes through the Power-On Self Test (POST), which initializes hardware and finds an operating system to load.
- When you load Windows XP or Windows Server 2003, you will be loading NTLDR, NTDetect.com, NTOSKRNL.EXE, and HAL.DLL.
- When you load Windows Vista, Windows 7, or Windows Server 2008, you will be loading BOOTMGR, WINLoad, NTOSKRNL.EXE, and Boot-class device drivers.
- A master boot record (MBR) is the first 512-byte boot sector of a partitioned data storage device such as a hard disk. It is used to hold the disk's primary partition table, contains the code to bootstrap an operating system, which usually passes control to the volume boot record, and uniquely identifies the disk media.
- A volume boot record (VBR), also known as a volume boot sector or a partition boot sector, is a type of boot sector stored in a disk volume on a hard disk, floppy disk, or similar data storage device that contains code for booting an operating system such as NTLDR and BOOTMGR.
- The Windows XP and Windows Server 2003 NTLDR will read the boot.ini file to determine which operating system to load even if your system only has one operating system.
- Boot Configuration Data (BCD) is a firmware-independent database for boot-time configuration data used by Microsoft's Windows Boot Manager found with Windows Vista, Windows 7, and Windows Server 2008.
- When problems occur during boot up, you may need to take some extra steps to get the computer into a usable state so that you can fix the problem. Since the release of Windows XP, you can access the Advanced Boot Options to get to advanced troubleshooting modes, including safe mode and last known good configuration.
- To access the Advanced Boot Options screen turn your computer on and press F8 before the Windows logo appears.
- Safe mode starts Windows with a minimal set of drivers and services. If you make a change to the system and Windows no longer boots, you can try safe mode.
- Last known good configuration starts Windows with the last registry and driver configuration that worked successfully, usually marked as the last successful login.
- System Configuration (msconfig.exe) is a tool that can help identify problems that might prevent Windows from starting correctly by disabling programs and services that start automatically when Windows starts.
- Performance is the overall effectiveness of how data moves through the system.

- If your computer lacks the RAM needed to run a program or perform an operation, Windows uses virtual memory to compensate.
- When RAM runs low, virtual memory moves data from RAM to a space called a paging file. Moving data to and from the paging file frees up RAM so your computer can complete its work.
- Task Manager gives you a quick glance at performance and provides information about programs and processes running on your computer.
- Windows Performance Monitor is a Microsoft Management Console (MMC) snap-in that provides tools for analyzing system performance.
- Windows Resource Monitor is a system tool that allows you to view information about the use of hardware (CPU, memory, disk, and network) and software resources (file handlers and modules) in real time.
- As a server administrator, you need to minimize downtime by identifying potential failures and taking steps to avoid those failures and to reduce the effect of those failures.
- NIC teaming is the process of grouping together two or more physical NICs into one single logical NIC, which can be used for network fault tolerance and increased bandwidth through load balancing.
- A computer cluster is a group of linked computers that work together as one computer. Based on the technology used, clusters can provide fault tolerance (often referred to as availability), load balancing, or both.
- A failover cluster is a set of independent computers that work together to increase the availability of services and applications. The clustered servers (called nodes) are connected by physical cables and by software.
- In an active-passive cluster, both servers are configured to work as one, but only one at a time.
- Network load balancing (NLB) is when multiple computers are configured as one virtual server to share the workload among multiple computers.
- A common use of clusters would include a failover cluster for the back end servers such as a database (like SQL Server) or mail server (such as Exchange Server) and a load balancing cluster for the front end that provides the web interface to the back end servers.
- An uninterruptible power supply or UPS is an electrical device consisting of one or more batteries to provide backup power when a power outage occurs.
- A backup or the process of backing up refers to making copies of data so that these additional copies may be used to restore the original after a data-loss event.
- The best method for data recovery is back up, back up, back up.
- The Windows system state is a collection of system components that are not contained in a simple file that can be backed up easily. It includes boot files and the registry.
- Full backups back up all designated files and data.
- Full backups with incremental backups start with a full backup followed by several incremental backups. When you do a restore, you restore the last full backup and then restore each incremental backup from oldest to newest. Full backups with incremental backups offers the fastest way to back up data.
- Full backup with differential backup starts with a full backup followed by several differential backups. When you do a restore, you restore the last full backup and the last differential backup.
- Shadow copies, when configured, automatically create backup copies of the data stored in shared folders on specific NTFS drive volumes at scheduled times.

■ Knowledge Assessment

Fill in the Blank

Complete the following sentences by writing the correct word or words in the blanks provided.

1. The _____ is the first 512-byte boot sector of a partitioned data storage device such as a hard disk.

2. The _____ is a simple text file that defines which operating system to load on Windows XP and Windows Server 2003 systems.

3. The _____ starts Windows with a minimal set of drivers and servers.

4. The _____ tool can be used to easily disable individual startup programs.

5. In Windows, virtual memory uses a _____ file.

6. _____ is the combining of network cards to provide fault tolerance.

7. A _____ is a group of computers that work together as one virtual computer to provide fault tolerance or increased performance.

8. The most common failover cluster is the _____ cluster in which only one server is active at a time.

9. In a cluster, an individual computer is known as a _____.

10. A _____ is an electrical device to provide temporary power during power outages.

Multiple Choice

Circle the letter that corresponds to the best answer.

1. What publications include a set of concepts and practices for managing IT services, development, and operations?
   a. Red book
   b. IT Development Guide
   c. ITIL core books
   d. IT Transition Guidebook

2. What tool is used to view the hardware and software loaded on a Windows server?
   a. System Information
   b. System Configuration
   c. KB tool
   d. POST

3. Where would you find NTLDR or BOOTMGR on a hard drive?
   a. MBR
   b. VBR
   c. boot.ini
   d. WINNT folder

4. What determines which operating system should be loaded when running Windows Vista, Windows 7, or Windows Server 2008?
   a. RAID
   b. GUID
   c. boot.ini
   d. BCD

5. You loaded a program and rebooted Windows. Unfortunately, Windows no longer boots. What should you try first?
   a. Enable boot logging.
   b. Load last known good configuration.
   c. Disable the boot.ini file.
   d. Reinstall Windows.

6. What program gives you a quick look at system performance and the processes that are running?
   a. Task Manager
   b. Performance Monitor
   c. Resource Monitor
   d. SystemInformation

7. _____ is multiple computers configured as one virtual server to share the workload.
   a. Network load balancing
   b. Active-passive cluster
   c. SAN cluster
   d. Terminal server

8. _____ is making copies of data so that these additional copies may be used to restore the original after a data-loss event.
   a. DFS
   b. RAID
   c. Backup
   d. EMS

9. Which type of backup backs up all designated files and turns off the archive attribute?
   a. Full
   b. Differential
   c. Incremental
   d. Copy

10. Which type of backup takes the longest to restore?
    a. Full
    b. Differential
    c. Incremental
    d. Copy

True / False

Circle T if the statement is true or F if the statement is false.

T | F   1. The best method for data recovery is backup.

T | F   2. Shadow copies are only available under older file systems.

T | F   3. To view Windows log, use the Log Viewer application.

T | F   4. 99.9999 availability means that a system can be down for 4.32 minutes a year.

T | F   5. Clusters nodes will protect against faulty power supplies, faulty processors, and faulty RAM.

■ Competency Assessment

Scenario 4-1: Using a Troubleshooting Methodology

Your computer does not boot. The computer has no lights and you hear no beeps. What would the steps be in troubleshooting this problem?

Scenario 4-2: Planning a Backup Strategy

You have several servers that all include important data that changes often. Unfortunately, when you try to back up these servers, it takes about 30 hours to complete. What would you recommend as a backup strategy?

■ Proficiency Assessment

Scenario 4-3: Looking at Backups

You have setup backups and you perform full backups once a week and incremental backups Monday through Thursday. So what should you do next?

Scenario 4-4: Looking at Event Viewer

You are experiencing some problems on a server running Windows Server 2008 R2. You log in and open the Server Management console and decide to look at the System logs in the Event Viewer. Unfortunately, you see many errors and warnings. What should you have done before you had problems to get the most out of the Event Viewer.

Workplace Ready

Monitoring and Managing Servers

After a server is built and configured, it takes a lot of work to keep it working as efficiently as it should be so that it can perform its job properly. Keeping the system updated can be time consuming, especially if you have many servers to keep patched.

Therefore, you should invest in some kind of monitoring software such as the Microsoft System Center Operations Manager (SCOM), which will make sure the server is up by constantly contacting the agent running on the server. It will also constantly check the Event Viewer for errors. Finally, depending on the roles that the server has and the management packs loaded on the SCOM server, it can constantly test key components to make sure they are up and running.

Essential Services

OBJECTIVE DOMAIN MATRIX

SKILLS/CONCEPTS	MTA EXAM OBJECTIVE	MTA EXAM OBJECTIVE NUMBER
Looking at Objects Introducing Groups	Understand accounts and groups.	3.1
Introducing Domains, Trees, and Forests Introducing Organizational Units	Understand organizational units (OUs) and containers.	3.2
Introducing Directory Services with Active Directory	Understand Active Directory infrastructure.	3.3
Introducing Group Policies	Understand group policy.	3.4

KEY TERMS

Active Directory

built-in group

computer account

directory service

distribution group

domain controller

domain local group

Domain Name System (DNS)

Dynamic Host Configuration Protocol (DHCP)

Flexible Single Master Operations (FSMO) roles

forest

fully qualified domain name (FQDN)

functional level

global catalog

global group

group

group policy

hosts file

Lightweight Directory Access Protocol (LDAP)

member server

object

organizational unit

permission

right

security group

site

tree

trusts relationship

universal group

user account

Windows Internet Name Service (WINS)

You are building a new network, and you need to get things started. You figure the best place to begin is to create servers that will host essential services, including DHCP and DNS. Then, when those servers are in place, you can create a domain controller so that you can begin establishing user and computer accounts and assigning rights and permissions to those users and computers.

■ Naming Resolution

THE BOTTOM LINE

In today's networks, you assign logical addresses, such as with IP addressing. Unfortunately, these addresses tend to be hard to remember, especially in the case of newer, more complicated IPv6 addresses. Therefore, you need to use some form of naming service that will allow you to translate logical names, which are easier to remember, into logical addresses. The most common naming service is *Domain Name System (DNS)*.

There are two types of names to translate. The first type consists of hostnames, which reside in the Domain Name System and are the same names used on the Internet. When you type the name of a Web site or a server that is on the Internet, such as www.microsoft.com or www.cnn.com, you are specifying a domain/hostname. The second type of name is your computer name, also known as the NetBIOS name. If you are on a corporate network or your home network, the hostname is usually the computer name. In fact, for most computers, the hostname and the NetBIOS/computer name are the same.

Understanding HOSTS and LMHOSTS Files

Early TCP/IP networks used hosts (used with domain/hostnames associated with DNS) and lmhost (used with NetBIOS/computer names associated with WINS) files, which were text files that would list a name and its associated IP address. However, with this system, every time you needed to add or modify a name and address, you would have to go to every computer and modify the text file each required to know the address. For larger organizations, this was incredibly inefficient because it might involve hundreds if not thousands of computers and extremely large text files.

In Windows, both of these files are located in the C:\WINDOWS\system32\drivers\etc folder. The *hosts file* (see Figure 5-1) can be edited and is ready to use. The lmhosts.sam file is a sample file, and it will have to be copied as lmhosts without the .sam filename extension.

Figure 5-1

A sample hosts file

```
# Copyright (c) 1993-2009 Microsoft Corp.
#
# This is a sample HOSTS file used by Microsoft TCP/IP for Windows.
#
# This file contains the mappings of IP addresses to host names. Each
# entry should be kept on an individual line.  The IP address should
# be placed in the first column followed by the corresponding host name.
# The IP address and the host name should be separated by at least one
# space.
#
# Additionally, comments (such as these) may be inserted on individual
# lines or following the machine name denoted by a '#' symbol.
#
# For example:
#
#      102.54.94.97     rhino.acme.com        # source server
#       38.25.63.10     x.acme.com            # x client host

# localhost name resolution is handled within DNS itself.
#        127.0.0.1       localhost
#        ::1             localhost

127.0.0.1         localhost
204.52.32.33      acme.com
192.168.3.12      webserver
192.1.68.3.12     webserver.acme.com
```

Although the hosts and lmhosts files are considered legacy methods for naming resolution, they still come in handy when troubleshooting or testing because name resolution will check these two files before contacting naming servers. For example, say you just installed a new server but do not want to make it available to everyone else. In this situation, you can add an entry in your local hosts file so that when your computer resolves a certain name, it will resolve to the IP address of the new server. This avoids changing the DNS entry, which would affect all users on your organization's network, until you are ready.

Exploring DNS

DNS is short for Domain Name System. DNS is a hierarchical client/server-based distributed database management system that translates domain/hosts names to IP addresses. In other words, your organization most likely has one or more DNS servers that provide name resolution for your company. At home, your ISP provides a DNS server so that when you type in a URL or try to connect to a server over the Internet, your computer can find the hosting server's IP address. What makes DNS so powerful and scalable is that all of the DNS servers on the Internet are linked together to provide worldwide naming resolution while allowing you to manage the DNS for your organization. Because DNS servers provide name resolution, they are sometimes referred to as name servers.

The top of the tree is known as the root domain. Below the root domain, you will find top-level domains, such as .com, .edu, .org, and .net, as well as two-letter country codes, such as .uk, .ca, and .us. Below the top-level domains, you will find the registered variable name that corresponds to an organization or other registered name. The second-level domain name must be registered by an authorized party, such as www.networksolutions.com or www.godaddy.com.

For example, www.microsoft.com is registered to the Microsoft Corporation. When you search for this URL, your computer will first contact the .com DNS servers to determine the name server for microsoft.com. It will then contact the microsoft.com DNS servers to determine the address that is assigned to microsoft.com. Larger organizations may subdivide their DNS name space into subdomains, such as technet.microsoft.com, msdn.microsoft.com, or social.microsoft.com.

A hostname is a name assigned to a specific computer within a domain or subdomain to identify the TCP/IP host. Multiple hostnames can be assigned to the same IP address, although only one name can be assigned to a physical computer or virtual computer.

A *fully qualified domain name (FQDN)* describes the exact position of a host with the DNS hierarchy. Examples of FQDNs include the following:

- www.microsoft.com
- technet.microsoft.com
- server1.sales.microsoft.com

Then, within a DNS zone, there are resource records (RR) that provide name resolution. These RRs are as follows:

- **SOA (Start of Authority):** Identifies the name server that is the authoritative source of information for a DNS domain or zone. It also includes parameters for how long DNS entries should be cached in a system.
- **NS (name server):** Provides a list of names servers that are assigned to a domain.
- **A (host address):** Provides a hostname to an IPv4 address.
- **AAAA (host address):** Provides a hostname to an IPv6 address.
- **PTR:** Resolves an IP address to a hostname (reverse mapping).
- **CNAME (canonical name):** Creates an alias or alternate DNS domain name for a specified hostname. Examples include www.acme.com or ftp.acme.com, which point

to a server on the acme.com network, such as server01.acme.com. This type of RR is often used with virtual servers that point to multiple servers, such as servers that provide network load balancing so that work can be distributed.

- **SRV (service):** Locates servers that are hosting a particular service, including LDAP servers or domain controllers.
- **MX (mail exchanger):** Identifies which mail exchanger should contact a specified domain and in what order to use each mail host.

See Figure 5-2.

Figure 5-2

Resource records shown in a forward lookup zone

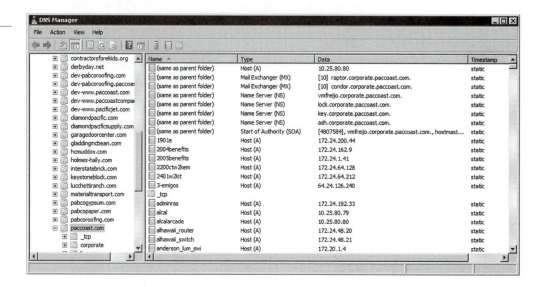

When you define DNS zones, you create the zone as either a forward lookup zone or a reverse lookup zone. The forward lookup zone (such as technet.microsoft.com or microsoft.com) has the majority of the resource records, including A and CNAME records, whereas the reverse lookup zone has PTR records. The reverse lookup zone is defined by reverse lookup format. For example, if you have a 172.24.1.x subnet, it will be shown as 1.24.172.

DNS servers use a mechanism called round-robin to share and distribute loads for a network resource. Round-robin rotates the order of resource records with the same name that point to different IP addresses.

UNIX and Linux systems used BIND implementations of DNS, which support two types of zones: a standard primary zone and a standard secondary zone. The standard primary zone is the master copy of a new zone that is replicated to standard secondary zones. Thus, if you need to make a change, that change should be made on the primary zone so that it can be replicated to the secondary zones.

Since the release of Windows Server 2000, there has also been an Active Directory integrated zone that is stored in Active Directory instead of a file. With Active Directory integrated zones, each server acts as a peer primary server, meaning you can update any server running the Active Directory integrated zones and the changes will be replicated as part of Active Directory replication to the other DNS servers. By using Active Directory integrated zones, the zones have increased fault tolerance (assuming you have two or more DNS servers with integrated Active Directory zones), have minimal traffic for zone replication, and are more secure.

DNS queries and DNS transfers between primary and secondary zones occur over TCP/UDP port 53. So, if you have any firewall between servers (including firewalls running on the servers), you will need to open port 53.

Since DNS has become the primary naming resolution tool, Dynamic DNS has been created. Dynamic DNS uses and will automatically register and update a DNS server's resource records when a host gets an IP address. For servers that have static addresses, you should add static entries.

When you configure a DNS server to handle name resolution for your organization, the DNS server is usually the authority for your organization. If you need to resolve a name for another organization, it will have to forward the request to another DNS server. You can configure DNS servers to forward requests to other specific DNS servers, such as an external DNS server that you also manage or a server provided by your ISP. You can also keep the default and let the server access the root servers to determine the address of the top-level DNS server and work its way down until it finds the authoritative server for the zone you are trying to resolve. The root hints file provides a list of IP addresses for DNS servers that are considered authoritative at the root level of the DNS hierarchy.

WINS

> **Windows Internet Name Service (WINS)** is a legacy naming service that translates from NetBIOS (computer name) to specify a network resource. A WINS sever contains a database of IP addresses and NetBIOS names that update dynamically. Unfortunately, WINS is not a hierarchy system like DNS, so it is only good for your organization; also, it functions only for Windows operating systems. Typically, other network devices and services cannot register with a WINS server. Therefore, you have to add static entries for these devices if you want name resolution using WINS.

When a WINS client starts up, it registers its name, IP address, and type of services within the WINS server database. See Figure 5-3. The type of service is designated by a hexadecimal value:

00h	workstation
03h	messenger
20h	file server

The NetBIOS name can be only up to 15 characters long, not counting the hexadecimal value.

Figure 5-3

WINS server

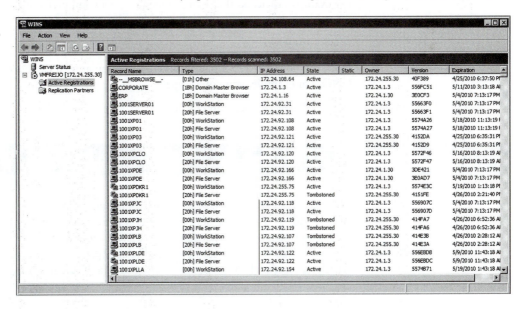

To provide fault tolerance, you should have more than one WINS server with the same WINS database. A WINS replication partner can be added and configured as either a pull partner, a push partner, or a push/pull partner. A pull partner is a WINS server that requests new database entries from its partner on a normal time interval. A push partner is a WINS server that sends update notification messages based on the number of changes to the WINS database. A push/pull partner does a push update based on the number of changes and a pull partner updates on a normal time interval.

If you configure WINS and the clients to use broadcast (known as b-node) to find a WINS server, you need to configure a WINS proxy agent to listen on remote subnets where a WINS server does not exist and forward those requests directly to a WINS server. WINS proxies are typically not needed for most networks because most clients are configured as peer node (known as p-node), which will send a packet directly to the WINS server instead of a broadcast.

DNS GLOBALNAME ZONES

Most of the time, when specifying an FQDN, you need only specify the hostname, and each client will have a DNS suffix search list that it appends to the hostname. Therefore, when you want to connect to server01, the client will append a DNS suffix search domain such as acme.com to make it server01.acme.com.

One advantage of WINS is its use of a single-label name instead of FQDNs that require the full name, including the domain. Unfortunately, NetBIOS names/single-label names are not supported with IPv6.

To help an organization retire WINS, Windows Server 2008 supports a specially named zone called GlobalNames, which allows you to define static global records with single-label names without relying on WINS. These entries will typically be used for servers that have static addresses and are managed by the network administrator.

UNIVERSAL NAMING CONVENTION

When you share a directory, drive, or printer on a PC running Microsoft Windows or on a Linux machine running Samba, you access the resource using the Universal Naming Convention (UNC), also known as Uniform Naming Convention, to specify the location of the resource. Traditionally, the UNC uses the following format:

\\computername\sharednamed\optionalpathname

For example, to access the shared directory on a computer called server1, you would type the following name:

\\server1\data

However, now that DNS has become more popular, you can also use hostnames with the UNC. For example, you could type:

\\server1.microsoft.com\data

■ DHCP Services

↓ **THE BOTTOM LINE**

As explained in an earlier lesson, it would take hours to configure every host IP configuration, including IP address, addresses of DNS and WINS servers, and any other parameters. Thus, most organizations use *Dynamic Host Configuration Protocol (DHCP)* services to automatically assign IP addresses and related parameters (including subnet mask and default gateway and length of the lease) so that a host can immediately communicate on an IP network when it starts.

A DHCP server maintains a list of IP addresses called a pool. When a DHCP client starts and needs an IP address assigned to it, it broadcasts to a DHCP server asking for a leased address. The client sends messages to UDP port 67, and the server sends messages to UDP port 68.

➡ INSTALL DHCP SERVICE ROLE

GET READY. To install the DHCP service role, perform the following steps:

1. Start Server Manager.

2. In Roles summary, click Add Roles, click the Next button, and select DHCP server. Click Next again.

3. Select the DHCP Server and click Next.

4. When the Introduction to DHCP Server page is displayed, click Next.

5. When the Select Network Connection Bindings page appears, choose the network adapter/IP address that will be used to hand out IP addresses. Click Next.

6. On the Specify IPv4 DNS Server Settings page, specify a parent domain and up to two IP addresses of DNS servers. Click Next.

7. On the Specify IPv4 WINS Server Settings page, specify the addresses of WINS servers (if necessary), and click the Next page.

8. When the Add or Edit DHCP Scopes page appears, click the Add button. Specify a Scope Name, Start IP Address, End IP address, Subnet type, a Subnet mask, and the default gateway. Also select Activate this scope. Click OK to close the Add scope dialog box. Click the Next button.

9. On the Configure DHCPv6 Stateless Mode page, click Enable DHCPv6 stateless mode for this server (if necessary). If this is not necessary, click Disable DHCPv6 stateless mode for this server. Click the Next button.

10. If you selected Enable DHCPv6 stateless mode for this server, specify the parent domain and up to two IPv6 DNS servers. Click the Next button.

11. To work on a Windows network, the DHCP server must be authorized within Active Directory. Therefore, specify a login account that has administrative permissions for Active Directory and click the Next button.

12. When the Confirm Installation Selections page appears, click the Install button.

Before your DHCP server can provide IP address leases, you have to define a scope that includes a range of IP addresses that can be distributed. See Figure 5-4. A scope will define a

Figure 5-4

DHCP console in Windows Server 2008 R2

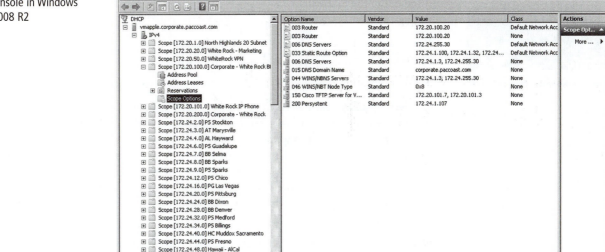

single physical subnet on your network to which DHCP services are offered. For the DHCP server to hand out addresses to a subnet, it has to be physically connected to the subnet, or you have to install a DHCP relay agent on the subnet that will relay the DHCP requests to the DHCP server. The DHCP relay agent could be a Windows server or workstation or built into a router or switch.

A DHCP server can have only one scope per subnet for each DHCP server. However, you can assign a range of addresses and excluded addresses within the scope for those addresses that are manually assigned to servers or other network devices. After you create a scope, you must activate the scope so that it will be available for lease assignments. To activate a scope in the DHCP console, right-click the console and select Activate.

When a host receives an IP address and related IP configuration from a DHCP server, it assigns them a lease time, which specifies how long the address is assigned to the host. When a DHCP lease has reached 50% of the lease time, the client will automatically attempt to renew the lease in the background. The default lease time is eight days. If, for some reason, the host cannot contact the DHCP server, it will try again and again on the remaining lease time until either it contacts the DHCP server or the lease time runs out.

If you have a client that must always use the same address, you can reserve that address using a client reservation. With a client reservation, the address is reserved for a specific host and will not be assigned to other hosts. If there are multiple DHCP servers handing out addresses, you will have to reserve the same addresses on each DHCP server.

Introducing Directory Services with Active Directory

THE BOTTOM LINE

A **directory service** stores, organizes, and provides access to information in a directory. Directory services are used for locating, managing, administering, and organizing common items and network resources, such as volumes, folders, files, printers, users, groups, devices, telephone numbers, and other objects. One popular directory service used by many organizations is Microsoft's Active Directory.

Active Directory is a technology created by Microsoft that provides a variety of network services, including the following:

• LDAP

• Kerberos-based and single sign-on authentication

• DNS-based naming and other network information

• A central location for network administration and delegation of authority

The **Lightweight Directory Access Protocol (LDAP)** is an application protocol for querying and modifying data using directory services running over TCP/IP. Within the directory, the sets of objects are organized in a logical hierarchical manner so that you can easily find and manage them. The structure can reflect geographical or organizational boundaries, although it tends to use DNS names for structuring the topmost levels of the hierarchy. Deeper inside the directory, there might be entries representing people, organizational units, printers, documents, groups of people, or anything else that represents a given tree entry (or multiple entries). LDAP uses TCP port 389.

Kerberos is a computer network authentication protocol, which allows hosts to prove their identity over a nonsecure network in a secure manner. It can also provide mutual authentication so that both the user and server verify each other's identity. For security reasons, Kerberos protocol messages are protected against eavesdropping and replay attacks.

Single sign-on (SSO) allows you to log on once and access multiple related but independent software systems without having to log in again. As you log on with Windows using Active Directory, you are assigned a token, which can then be used to sign on to other systems automatically.

Finally, Active Directory allows you to organize all of your network resources, including users, groups, printers, computers, and other objects, so that you can assign passwords, permissions, and rights to the users on your network. You can also assign who can manage a group of objects.

Introducing Domains, Trees, and Forests

Active Directory domains, trees, and forests are logical representations of your network organization, which allow you to organize them in the best way to manage them. To identify domains, trees, and forests, Active Directory is closely tied to DNS.

As mentioned earlier, a Windows domain is a logical unit of computers and network resources that define a security boundary. A domain uses a single Active Directory database to share its common security and user account information for all computers within the domain, allowing centralized administration of all users, groups, and resources on the network.

Because some organizations contain thousands of users and thousands of computers, it might make sense to break an organization into more than one domain. An Active Directory forest contains one or more transitive, trust-linked trees, with each tree linked in a transitive trust hierarchy, so that users and computers from one domain can access resources in another domain. Active Directory is very closely tied to DNS and, in fact, requires it.

A *tree* is made of one or more domains (although most people think of a tree as two or more domains) with contiguous name space. For example, you could have one domain assigned to an organization's developers and another domain assigned to its salespeople:

Developers.microsoft.com

Sales.microsoft.com

The Developers and Sales domains would both be child domains of the microsoft.com domain.

A *forest* is made of one or more trees (although most people think of a forest as two or more trees). A forest differs from a tree because it uses disjointed namespaces between the trees. For example, in a forest, you could have microsoft.com as the root for one tree. Say that Microsoft then purchases another company called Acme (acme.com), and acme.com then becomes the root of another tree. Both trees could be combined into a forest, yet each tree's identity could be kept separate.

To allow users in one domain to access resources in another domain, Active Directory uses *trust relationships*. As mentioned earlier, domains with a tree and forest are automatically created as two-way transitive trusts. A transitive trust is based on the following concept:

If domain A trusts domain B, and domain B trusts domain C, then domain A trusts domain C.

However, if you have a partnership with another company and you need users from one domain within one organization to access resources in another domain, you can configure an explicit nontransitive trust to be either one way or two way.

Introducing Sites and Domain Controllers

Although domains, trees, and forests are logical representations of your organization, sites and domain controllers represent the physical structure of your network.

A *site* is one or more IP subnets that are connected by a high-speed link, typically defined by a geographical location. For example, say you have a four-story office building. Although the building includes several subnets, all of the computers within the building use layer-2 and layer-3 switches to communicate with each other. If you have multiple sites, each site is connected to other sites over a much slower WAN link (at least slower than the LAN speeds you would find within an individual site). You can then define various network traffic patterns based on how the sites are defined.

When a user logs on, Active Directory clients locate an Active Directory server (using the DNS SRV resource records) known as a domain controller in the same site as the computer. Each domain has its own set of domain controllers to provide access to the domain resources, such as users and computers.

For fault tolerance, a site should have two or more domain controllers. That way, if one domain controller fails, the other domain controller can still service the clients. Note that whenever an object (such as a username or password) is modified, it is automatically replicated to the other domain controllers within a domain.

A *domain controller* is a Windows server that stores a replica of the account and security information for the domain and defines the domain boundaries. To make a computer running Windows Server 2008 a domain controller, you must install the Active Directory Domain Services and execute the dcpromo (short for dc promotion) command.

After you have promoted a computer to a domain controller, you can use several MMC snap-in consoles to manage Active Directory. These consoles are as follows:

- **Active Directory Users and Computers:** Used to manage users, groups, computers, and organizational units.
- **Active Directory Domains and Trusts:** Used to administer domain trusts, domain and forest functional levels, and user principal name (UPN) suffixes.
- **Active Directory Sites and Services:** Used to administer replication of directory data among all sites in an Active Directory Domain Services (AD DS) forest (Figure 5-5).

Figure 5-5

Active Directory Sites and Services console

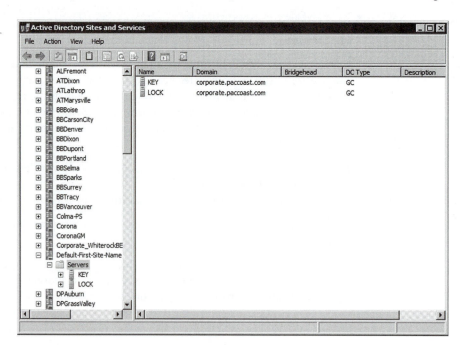

- **Active Directory Administrative Center:** Used to administer and publish information in the directory, including managing users, groups, computers, domains, domain controllers, and organizational units. Active Directory Administrative Center is new in Windows Server 2008 R2.
- **Group Policy Management Console (GPMC):** Provides a single administrative tool for managing Group Policy across the enterprise. GPMC is automatically installed in Windows Server 2008 and subsequent domain controllers but must be downloaded and installed on Windows Server 2003 domain controllers.

Although these tools are installed on domain controllers, they can also be installed on client PCs so that you can manage Active Directory without logging on to a domain controller.

A server that is not running as a domain controller is known as a *member server*. To demote a domain controller to a member server, you would rerun the dcpromo program.

The replication path, or site topology, within a site is automatically managed by a service called the Knowledge Consistency Checker (KCC). Typically, replication within sites happens more quickly than replication between sites. The Active Directory Sites and Services MMC snap-in allows you to control intersite replication. You can use it to create site-link bridge objects and to configure replication patterns.

Within Active Directory, you need to define each subnet. Once you have done this, Active Directory can figure out the best way to replicate information locally and between sites.

To minimize traffic across a WAN link, bridgehead servers perform directory replication between two sites, whereas only two designated domain controllers talk to each other. If you have domain controllers from multiple domains, you will have a bridgehead server for each domain.

FLEXIBLE SINGLE MASTER OPERATIONS

Active Directory uses multimaster replication, which means that there is no master domain controller, commonly referred to as a primary domain controller within Windows NT domains. However, because there are certain functions that can be handled by only one domain controller at a time, Active Directory uses *Flexible Single Master Operations (FSMO) roles*, also known as operations master roles. See Table 5-1 and Figure 5-6.

Table 5-1

FSMO roles

Role Name	Scope	Description
Schema Master	1 per forest	Controls and handles updates/modifications to the Active Directory schema.
Domain Naming Master	1 per forest	Controls the addition and removal of domains from the forest if present in root domain.
PDC Emulator	1 per domain	PDC is short for Primary Domain Controller, which was the main domain controller used with Windows NT. The PDC emulator provides backwards compatibility for NT4 clients. It also acts as the primary server for password changes and as the master time server within the domain.
RID Master	1 per domain	Allocates pools of unique identifiers to domain controllers for use when creating objects.
Infrastructure Master	1 per domain	Synchronizes cross-domain group membership changes. The infrastructure master cannot run on a global catalog server unless all DCs are also GCs.

Figure 5-6

Domain-level FMSO roles

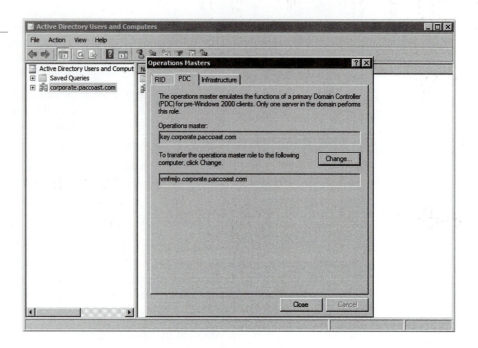

LOOKING AT GLOBAL CATALOGS

Because the domain controller only has information for the domain and does not store a copy of the objects for other domains, you still need a way to find and access objects in other domains within your tree and forest. A *global catalog* replicates the information of every object in a tree and forest. However, instead of storing the entire object, it stores just those attributes that are most frequently used in search operations, such as a user's first and last name, computer name, and so forth. By default, a global catalog is created automatically on the first domain controller in the forest, but any domain controller can be made into a global catalog. See Figure 5-7.

Figure 5-7

Configuring a domain controller as a global catalog

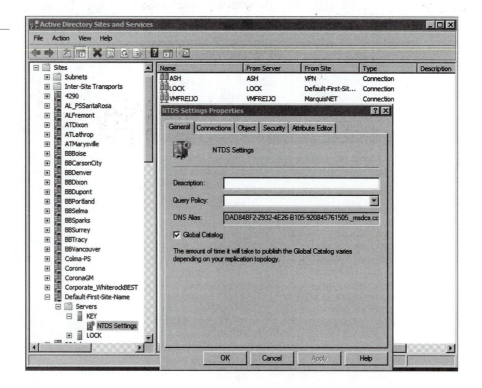

Beyond being used to find objects in a forest, global catalogs are also used during user authentication as follows:

- In Windows 2000 native mode and above domain functional levels, domain controllers must request universal group membership enumeration from a global catalog server.
- When a user principal name (UPN) is used at logon and the forest has more than one domain, a global catalog server is required to resolve the name. A UPN follows the same format as an email address (i.e., username@domainname.ext).

Last, a global catalog is needed for universal group membership caching. In a forest that has more than one domain, and in sites that have domain users but no global catalog server, universal group membership caching can be used to enable caching of logon credentials so that the global catalog does not have to be contacted for subsequent user logons. This feature eliminates the need to retrieve universal group memberships across a WAN link from a global catalog server in a different site. Besides having a global catalog in each geographical site, it is a best practice to enable universal group membership caching in each geographic site.

DEFINING FUNCTIONAL LEVELS

In Active Directory, you can have domain controllers running different versions of Windows servers, such as Windows 2000, Windows Server 2003, or Windows Server 2008. The *functional level* of a domain or forest depends on which Windows Server operating system versions are running on the domain controllers in that domain or forest. The functional level also controls which advanced features are available in the domain or forest. To get all of the features available with Active Directory, you must have the latest version of the Windows Server operating system, and you have to use the highest forest and domain functional level. Of course, you must take care before migrating to the higher functional level because doing so may close out some legacy features that were only available with the older functional levels. Upgrading to a higher functional level is a one-way process that cannot be reversed.

The six domain functional levels available at the time of this writing include:

- Windows 2000 mixed (the default in Windows Server 2003)
- Windows 2000 native
- Windows Server 2003 interim
- Windows Server 2003
- Windows Server 2008
- Windows Server 2008 R2

Setting the functional level for a domain enables features that affect the entire domain and that domain only. If all domain controllers in a domain are running Windows Server 2008 R2 and the functional level is set to Windows Server 2008 R2, all domain-wide features are available.

The five forest functional levels available at the time of this writing include:

- Windows 2000 (the default in Windows Server 2003 and Windows Server 2008)
- Windows Server 2003 interim
- Windows Server 2003 (the default in Windows Server 2008 R2)
- Windows Server 2008
- Windows Server 2008 R2

Setting the functional level for a forest enables features across all the domains within the forest. Also, if all domain controllers in a forest are running Windows Server 2008 R2

+ MORE INFORMATION
For a list of functions available with each domain and forest functional level, visit the following Web site:

http://technet.microsoft.com/ en-us/library/understanding-active-directory-functional-levels (WS.10).aspx

and the functional level is set to Windows Server 2008 R2, all forest-wide features are available.

For example, although Windows 2000 mixed mode can support Windows NT 4.0 backup controllers, if you upgrade to Windows 2000 native, you can use universal security groups, group nesting (groups inside other groups), and security identifier (SID) history capabilities. Windows Server 2003 domain functional level supports the LastLogonTimestamp attribute, which is updated with the last logon time of the user or computer. This attribute is replicated within the domain. By running in Windows Server 2008 R2 domain functional level, Active Directory supports a Recycle Bin to undelete deleted objects.

Introducing Organizational Units

CERTIFICATION READY
What is the best way to assign users to manage other users and computers in Active Directory?
3.2

As mentioned earlier, a single organization might have thousands of users and thousands of computers. With Windows NT, a domain could only handle a limited number of objects before you encountered some performance issues. With later versions of Windows, the size of the domain was dramatically increased. Although you may have required several domains with Windows NT to define your organization, you could now have just one domain to represent a large organization. However, you still need a way to organize and manage the objects within that domain.

To help organize objects within a domain and minimize the number of domains you require, you can use *organizational units*, commonly known as OUs. OUs can be used to hold users, groups, computers, and other organizational units. See Figure 5-8. An organizational unit can only contain objects that are located in a domain. Although there are no restrictions on how many nested OUs (an OU inside of another OU) you can have, you should strive to design a shallow hierarchy for better performance.

Figure 5-8

Active Directory organizational unit

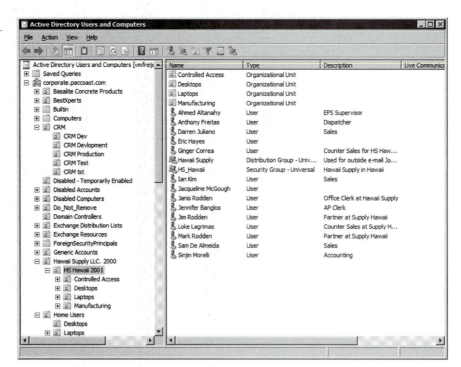

When you first install Active Directory, there are several organizational units already created. They include computers, users, domain controllers, and built-in OUs. Unlike the OUs that you create, these OUs do not allow you to delegate permissions or assign group policies to them. (Group policies will be explained later.) Another OU worth mentioning is the domain controller, which holds the default domain controllers policy.

Containers are objects that can store or hold other objects. They include the forest, tree, domain, and organizational unit. To help manage your objects, you can delegate authority to a container, particularly the domain or organizational unit.

For example, let's say that you have your domain divided by physical location. You can assign a site administrator authoritative control to the OU that represents a physical location so that the user will only have administrative control to the objects within that OU. You can also structure your OUs by function or areas of management. For example, you might create a Sales OU to hold all of your sales users. You might also create a Printers OU to hold all of the printer objects and assign a printer administrator.

By delegating administration, you can assign a range of administrative tasks to the appropriate users and groups. For instance, you can assign basic administrative tasks to regular users or groups and leave domain-wide and forest-wide administration to members of the Domain Admins and Enterprise Admins groups. By delegating administration, you allow groups within your organization to take more control of their local network resources. You also help secure your network from accidental or malicious damage by limiting the membership of administrator groups.

You can delegate administrative control to any level of a domain tree by creating organizational units within a domain and delegating administrative control for specific organizational units to particular users or groups.

 DELEGATE CONTROL

GET READY. To delegate control of an organizational unit, perform the following steps:

1. Open Active Directory Users and Computers.
2. In the console tree, right-click the organizational unit for which you want to delegate control.
3. Click Delegate control to start the Delegation of Control Wizard, and then follow the instructions onscreen.

Looking at Objects

An *object* is a distinct, named set of attributes or characteristics that represent a network resource. Common objects used within Active Directory are computers, users, groups, and printers. Attributes have values that define the specific object. For example, a user could have the first name John, the last name Smith, and the login name jsmith, all of which identify the user.

CERTIFICATION READY
Why is it important to define users within Active Directory?
3.1

When working with objects, administrators use the names of the objects, such as usernames. However, Active Directory objects are assigned a 128-bit unique number called a globally unique identifier (GUID), sometimes referred to as a security identifier (SID), to uniquely identify an object. Therefore, if a user changes his or her name, you can change his or her username yet he or she will still be able to access all objects and have all of the rights he or she had previously because these are assigned to the GUID.

GUIDs also provide some security. In particular, if a user is deleted, you cannot create a new user account with the same username and expect to have access to all of the objects and rights the previous user had access to. Thus, if you decide to let someone go within your organization but you plan to replace that person, you can disable the account, hire the new person, rename the user account, change the password, and re-enable the account so that the new person can access all resources and have all of the rights that the previous user had.

The schema of Active Directory defines the format of each object and the attributes or fields within each object. The default schema contains definitions of commonly used objects, such as user accounts, computers, printers, and groups. For example, the schema defines that a user account has the user's first name, last name, and telephone number.

To allow Active Directory to be flexible so that it can support other applications, you can extend the schema to include additional attributes. For example, you could add badge number or employee identification number to the user object. Indeed, when you install some applications, such as Microsoft Exchange, they will extend the schema, usually by adding additional attributes or fields so that the schema can support the application.

LOOKING AT USERS

A *user account* enables a user to log on to a computer and domain. As a result, it can be used to prove the identity of a user, and this identity information can then be used to determine what the user can access and what kind of authorization he or she has. It can also be used for auditing so that if there is a security problem in which something was accessed or deleted, the person who accessed or deleted the object can be determined.

On today's Windows networks, there are two types of user accounts:

- Local user accounts
- Domain user accounts

A user account allows users to log on and access resources on the computer in which the account was created. The local user account is stored in the Security Account Manager (SAM) database on the local computer. The only Windows computer that does not have a SAM database is the domain controller. The administrator local user account is the only account that is both created and enabled by default in Windows. Although this account cannot be deleted, it can be renamed.

The only other account created (but not enabled) by default is the guest account. This account was created for the occasional user who needs access to network resources on a low-security network. Use of the guest account is not recommended, and this account is disabled by default.

A domain user account is stored on the domain controller and allows you to gain access to resources within the domain, assuming you have been granted permissions to access those objects. The administrator domain user account is the only account that is created and enabled by default in Windows when you first create a domain. Although the administrator domain user account cannot be deleted, it can be renamed.

When you create a domain user account, you must supply a first name, last name, and user logon name. The user logon name must be unique within the domain. See Figure 5-9. After the user account is created, you can then open the user account properties and configure a person's username, logon hours, telephone numbers, and addresses; which computers the user can log on to; what groups the person is a member of, and so on. You can also specify whether a password expires, whether the password can be changed, and whether the account

Figure 5-9

User Account in Active
Directory

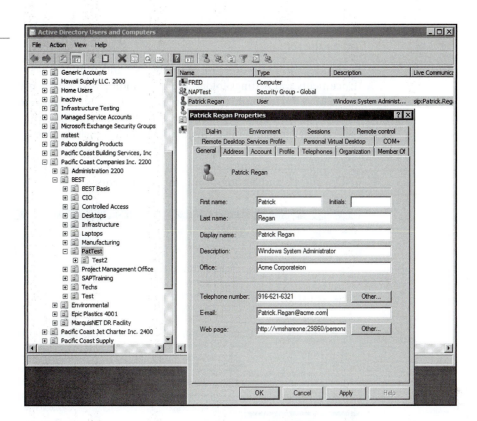

is disabled. Last, in the Profile tab, you can define the user's home directory, logon script, and
profile path. See Figure 5-10.

Figure 5-10

Profile tab

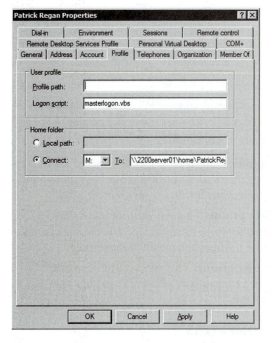

Associated with a user account is the user profile, which is a collection of folders and data
that store the user's current desktop environment and application settings. A user profile
also records all network connections that are established so that when a user logs on to a
computer, it will remember the mapped drives to shared folders. Thus, when a user logs on to

a particular computer, he or she will get the same desktop environment he or she previously had on the computer.

By default, the user profiles for Windows XP and Windows Server 2003 are stored in the C:\Documents and Settings folder under the individual's username. For example, if jsmith logs in, his or her user profile folder would be C:\Documents and Settings\jsmith. For Windows Vista, Windows 7, and Windows Server 2008, user profiles are stored in the C:\Users folder. In each user's folder, some of the available folders include Desktop, My Documents, Start Menu, and Favorites. See Figure 5-11. So, when jsmith directly accesses his or her Desktop or My Documents, jsmith is really accessing C:\Documents and Settings\jsmith\desktop or C:\Documents and Settings\jsmith\my documents.

Figure 5-11

A user's profile folder

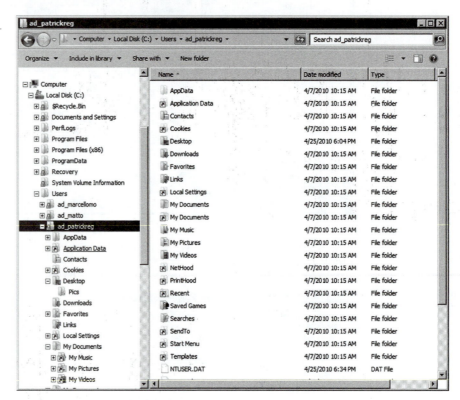

There are three types of user profiles:

- **Local user profile:** This type of profile is stored on the local hard drive of the computer the user is logging on to. Thus, if the user logs on to a different computer, he or she will get the default settings for that computer.

- **Roaming user profile:** This type of profile is created and stored on a shared folder on a server over the network. Therefore, no matter what computer the user logs on to within the domain, he or she will have the same settings.

- **Mandatory user profile:** This type of profile is used as a roaming profile in which the settings can be changed but, when the user logs on again, all settings are reset back to their default values.

LOOKING AT COMPUTERS

Like user accounts, Windows *computer accounts* provide a means for authenticating and auditing a computer's access to a Windows network and access to domain resources. Each Windows computer to which you want to grant access must have a unique computer account. See Figure 5-12. A computer account can also be used for auditing purposes, specifying what system was used when something was accessed.

Figure 5-12

Computer account

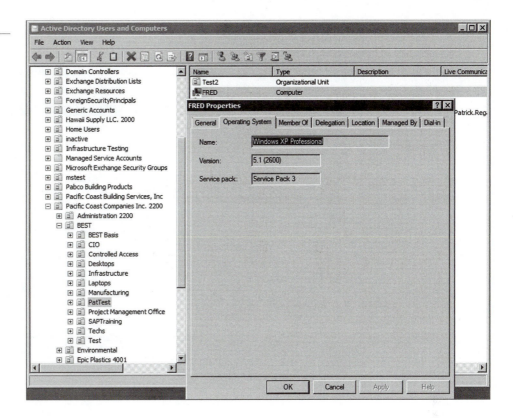

Introducing Groups

A *group* is a collection or list of user accounts or computer accounts. Different from a container, a group does not store user or computer information; rather, it just lists it. The advantage of using groups is that they simplify administration, especially when assigning rights and permissions.

A group is used to group users and computers together so that when you assign rights and permissions, you assign them to the entire group rather than to each user individually. Users and computers can be members of multiple groups, and in some instances, a group can be assigned to another group.

COMPARING GROUP TYPES

In Windows Active Directory, there are there are two types of groups: security and distribution. A *security group* is used to assign rights and permissions and gain access to network resources. It can also be used as a distribution group. A *distribution group* is used only for nonsecurity functions, such as distributing email, and it cannot be used to assign rights and permissions. See Figure 5-13.

COMPARING GROUP SCOPES

Any group, whether a security group or a distribution group, is characterized by a scope that identifies the extent to which the group is applied in the domain tree or forest. The three group scopes (also described in Table 5-2) are as follows:

- *Domain local group:* A domain local group contains global groups and universal groups, even though it can also contain user accounts and other domain local groups. It is usually in the domain with the resource to which you want to assign permissions or rights.

Figure 5-13

Active Directory group

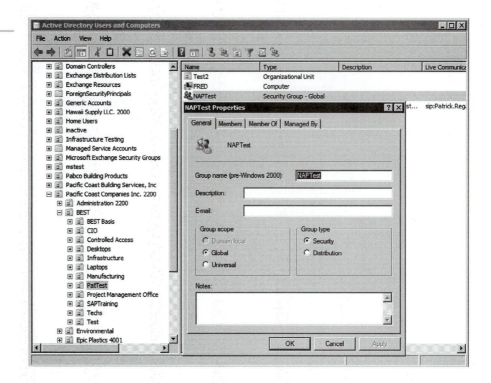

Table 5-2

Group Scopes

Scope	Group can include as members...	Group can be assigned permissions in . . .	Group scope can be converted to...
Universal	Accounts from any domain within the forest in which the universal group resides; global groups from any domain within the forest in which the universal group resides; universal groups from any domain within the forest in which the universal group resides	Any domain or forest	Domain local Global (as long as no other universal groups exist as members)
Global	Accounts from the same domain as the parent global group; global groups from the same domain as the parent global group	Any domain	Universal (as long as it is not a member of any other global groups)
Domain local	Accounts from any domain; global groups from any domain; universal groups from any domain; domain local groups but only from the same domain as the parent domain local group	Only the same domain as the parent domain local group	Universal (as long as no other domain local groups exist as members)

- **Global group:** Global groups can contain user accounts and other global groups. Global groups are designed to be "global" for the domain. After you place user accounts into global groups, the global groups are typically placed into domain local groups or local groups.

- **Universal group:** This group scope is designed to contain global groups from multiple domains. Universal groups can contain global groups, other universal groups, and user accounts. Because global catalogs replicate universal group membership, you should limit the membership to global groups. This way, if you change a member within a global group, the global catalog will not have to replicate the change.

When assigning rights and permissions, you should always try to arrange your users into groups and assign the rights and permissions to the group instead of the individual users. To effectively manage the use of groups when assigning access to a network resource using global groups and domain local groups, remember the mnemonic AGDLP (Accounts, Global, Domain Local, Permissions):

- Add the user account (A) into the global group (G) in the domain in which the user exists.
- Add the global group (G) from the user domain into the domain local group (DL) in the resource domain.
- Assign permissions (P) on the resource to the domain local group (DL) in its domain.

If you are using universal groups, the mnemonic is expanded to AGUDLP:

- Add the user account (A) into the global group (G) in the domain in which the user exists.
- Add global groups (G) from the user domain into the universal group (U).
- Add universal group (U) to the domain local group (DL).
- Assign permissions (P) on the resource to the domain local group (DL) in its domain.

LOOKING AT BUILT-IN GROUPS

Similar to the administrator and guest accounts, Windows has default groups called *built-in groups*. These default groups are granted specific rights and permissions to get you started. Various built-in groups are as follows:

- **Domain Admins:** Members of this group can perform administrative tasks on any computer within the domain. The default, the Administrator account, is a member.
- **Domain Users:** Windows automatically adds each new domain user account to the Domain Users group.
- **Account Operators:** Members of this group can create, delete, and modify user accounts and groups.
- **Backup Operators:** Members of this group can backup and restore all domain controllers by using Windows Backup.
- **Authenticated Users:** This group includes all users with a valid user account on the computer or in Active Directory. Use the Authenticated Users group instead of the Everyone group to prevent anonymous access to a resource.
- **Everyone:** This group includes all users who access a computer, even if a particular user does not have a valid account.

> **+ MORE INFORMATION**
>
> For more information on available groups, visit the following Web site: http://technet.microsoft.com/en-us/library/cc756898(WS.10).aspx

Introducing Group Policy

> **CERTIFICATION READY**
> What is Group Policy, and how does it help you manage your network?
> 3.4

Group Policy is one of the most powerful features of Active Directory that controls the working environment for user accounts and computer accounts. Group Policy provides centralized management and configuration of operating systems, applications, and user settings in an Active Directory environment. For example, you can use Group Policy to specify how often a user has to change his or her password, what the background image on a person's computer is, or whether spell checking is required before a user can send an email.

There are literally thousands of settings that can be used to restrict certain actions, make a system more secure, or standardize a working environment. A setting can control a computer registry, NTFS security, audit and security policy, software installation, folder redirection, offline folders, or log on and log off scripts. *Group Policy* is one of the most powerful features of Active Directory that controls the working environment for user accounts and computer accounts. Group Policy (see Figure 5-14) provides the centralized management and configuration of operating systems, applications, and user settings in an Active Directory environment. As each server version is released, Microsoft usually adds additional parameters.

Figure 5-14

Group Policy Editor

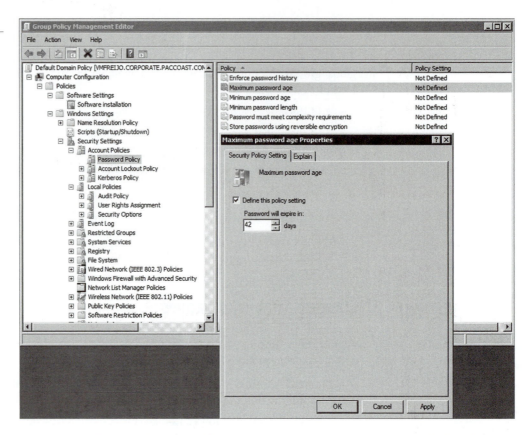

Group Policy objects (GPOs) are collections of user and computer settings including the following:

- **System settings:** Application settings, desktop appearance, and behavior of system services.
- **Security settings:** Local computer, domain, and network security settings.
- **Software installation settings:** Management of software installation, updates, and removal.
- **Scripts settings:** Scripts for when a computer starts or shuts down and for when a user logs on and off.
- **Folder redirection settings:** Storage for users' folders on the network.

USING LOCAL POLICIES

If you expand Computer Configuration, Policies, Windows Settings, and Security Settings, you will find Local Policy. Local Policy contains the following folders:

- **Audit policy:** Determines whether security events are written to the security log in Event Viewer on the computer. Some examples would be log successful attempts, failed login attempts, and failed attempts of accessing designated objects, such as files or user accounts. Auditing is discussed in Lesson 6.
- **User rights assignment:** Determines which users or groups have logon rights or privileges on the computer. User rights are explained later in this section.
- **Security options:** Enables or disables security policy settings for the computer. Examples would include the renaming of Administrator and Guest accounts, prevent access to floppy disk drives or CD drives, enforcement of various authentication methods or encryption methods, logon prompts, User Account User Control settings, digital signing of data, driver installation, and logon prompts.

APPLYING GROUP POLICY

Group Policy can be set locally on a workstation or set at different levels (site, domain, or organizational unit) within Active Directory. Generally speaking, you will not find as many settings locally as you will at the site, domain, or OU level. When group policies are applied, they are applied in the following order:

1. Local
2. Site
3. Domain
4. OU

If you configure a Group Policy setting at the site, domain, or OU level and that setting contradicts a setting configured at the local policy level; the local policy setting will be overridden. Generally speaking, if you have a policy setting that conflicts with a previous executed setting, the more recent executed setting remains in effect (Figure 5-15). For a local computer, security settings can be accessed by opening the Local Security Policy MMC from Administrative Tools.

Figure 5-15

Group Policy Management Console

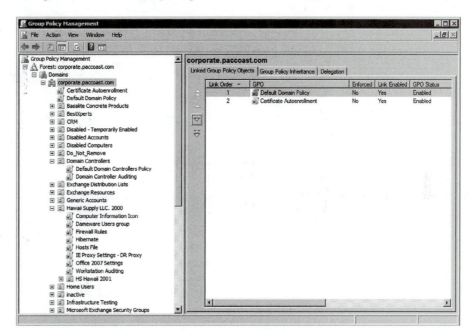

ACCESS THE LOCAL GROUP POLICY EDITOR

GET READY. You can open the Local Group Policy Editor by using gpedit.msc at a command line or by using the Microsoft Management Console (MMC). To open the Local Group Policy Editor from the command line, perform the following steps:

1. Open MMC. (Click Start, click in the Start Search box, type mmc, and then press ENTER.)
2. On the File menu, click Add/Remove Snap-in.
3. In the Add or Remove Snap-in dialog box, click Group Policy Object Editor, and then click Add.
4. In the Select Group Policy Object dialog box, click Browse.
5. Click This computer to edit the Local Group Policy object, or click Users to edit Administrator, Non-Administrator, or per-user Local Group Policy objects.
6. Click Finish.

Most times, you only need to access the security settings that you found in the local policy. This can be done by opening the Local Security Policy from Administrative Tools.

COMPARING RIGHTS AND PERMISSIONS

Precisely what a user can or cannot do on a system or to a resource is determined by two things:

- Rights
- Permissions

A *right* authorizes a user to perform certain actions on a computer, such as logging on to a system interactively or backing up files and directories on a system. User rights are assigned through local policies or Active Directory Group Policy. See Figure 5-16.

Figure 5-16

Group Policy user rights assignment

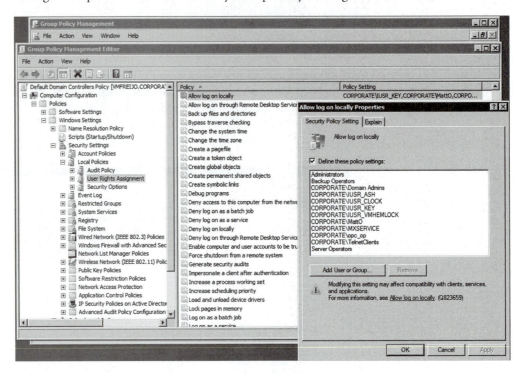

A *permission* defines the type of access that is granted to an object (an object can be identified with a security identifier) or object attribute. The most common objects assigned permissions are NTFS files and folders, printers, and Active Directory objects. Which users can access an object and what actions those users are authorized to perform are recorded in the access control list (ACL), which lists all users and groups that have access to the object. NTFS and printer permissions will be discussed in the next lesson.

SKILL SUMMARY

IN THIS LESSON YOU LEARNED:

- Besides becoming the standard for the Internet, DNS, short for Domain Name System, is a hierarchical client/server-based distributed database management system that translates domain/hosts names to IP addresses.

- A fully qualified domain name (FQDN) describes the exact position of a host within a DNS hierarchy.

- The legacy naming service is Windows Internet Name Service or WINS, which translates from NetBIOS (computer name) to specify a network resource.

- When you share a directory, drive, or printer on a PC running Microsoft Windows or on a Linux machine running Samba, you can access the resource by using the Universal Naming Convention (UNC), also known as Uniform Naming Convention, to specify the location of the resource.

- Dynamic Host Configuration Protocol (DHCP) services automatically assign IP addresses and related parameters (including subnet mask and default gateway and length of the lease) so that a host can immediately communicate on an IP network when it starts.

- The Lightweight Directory Access Protocol, or LDAP, is an application protocol for querying and modifying data using directory services running over TCP/IP.

- Active Directory domains, trees, and forests are logical representations of network organization, which allow you to organize them in the best way to manage them.
- Sites and domain controllers represent the physical structure of a network.
- A site is one or more IP subnets that are connected by a high-speed link, typically defined by a geographical location.
- A domain controller is a Windows server that stores a replica of the account and security information for the domain and defines the domain boundaries.
- A server that is not running as a domain controller is known as a member server.
- To minimize traffic across a WAN link, bridgehead servers perform directory replication between two sites, whereas only two designated domain controllers talk to each other.
- Active Directory uses multimaster replication, which means that there is no master domain controller.
- Because there are certain functions that can only be handled by one domain controller at a time, Active Directory uses Flexible Single Master Operations (FSMO) roles.
- A global catalog holds replicate information of every object in a tree and forest.
- The functional level of a domain or forest controls which advanced features are available in the domain or forest.
- To help organize objects within a domain and minimize the number of domains, you can use organizational units, commonly known as OUs.
- You can delegate administrative control to any level of a domain tree by creating organizational units within a domain and delegating administrative control for specific organizational units to particular users or groups.
- A user account enables a user to log on to a computer and domain. As a result, it can used to prove the identity of a user, and this information can then be used to determine what a user can access and what kind of access he or she will have (authorization).
- Windows computer accounts provide a means for authenticating and auditing a computer's access to a Windows network and to domain resources.
- A group is a collection of user accounts or computer accounts.
- Group Policy provides the centralized management and configuration of operating systems, applications, and user settings in an Active Directory environment.
- A right authorizes a user to perform certain actions on a computer.
- A permission defines the type of access that is granted to an object (an object can be identified with a security identifier) or object attribute.

Knowledge Assessment

Fill in the Blank

Complete the following sentences by writing the correct word or words in the blanks provided.

1. The file that is used to resolve hostnames to IP addresses is _____ .

2. The resource record used in DNS to resolve IP address to hostnames is _____ .

3. The _____ automatically assigns IP addresses and other IP configuration to a host.

4. _____ is a popular directory service with objects in a logical hierarchical manner.

5. The _____ are roles that provide certain functions that can only be handled by one domain controller.

6. A(n) _____ is used to organize the objects within a domain.

7. Printers, users, and computers are examples of _____ in Active Directory.

8. The local security database found on a member server is known as the _____ .

9. A collection or list of users is known as _____ .

10. The _____ built-in group is used to create, delete, and modify user accounts and groups.

Multiple Choice

Circle the letter that corresponds to the best answer.

1. The primary naming service used in Windows is _____ .
   a. AD
   b. WINS
   c. DNS
   d. DHCP

2. What is the resource record that translates from hostname to IP address in DNS?
   a. PTR
   b. H
   c. IP
   d. A

3. _____ is a legacy naming system used to translate Computer Names/NetBIOS names to IP addresses.
   a. AD
   b. WINS
   c. DNS
   d. DHCP

4. What is the master time server?
   a. Schema Master
   b. Domain Naming Master
   c. PDC Emulator
   d. RID Master

5. What holds replica information of every object in a tree and forest?
   a. Infrastructure Master
   b. Schema Master
   c. Global Catalog
   d. PDC Emulator

6. Which group scope is meant to be used to assign permissions to a local resource?
   a. Distribution group
   b. Domain local
   c. Global
   d. Captured

7. Which group scope can contain global groups from multiple domains?
   a. Emulation
   b. Domain local
   c. Global
   d. Universal

8. What can be used to specify how many times a user can enter a login with an incorrect password before the account is disabled?
   a. User profile
   b. Group policy
   c. Software policy
   d. User account collection

9. To which of the following can a group policy not be directly applied?
   a. Group
   b. Site
   c. Domain
   d. OU

10. What authorizes a user to perform certain actions on a computer?
    a. Permission
    b. UNC
    c. Right
    d. Task

True / False

Circle T if the statement is true or F if the statement is false.

T | F   1. A collection is two or more trees.

T | F   2. A site and domain controllers are the physical aspects of the network.

T | F   3. A member server is running Active Directory domain services.

T | F   4. Higher domain and forest functional levels will enhance the functionality of Active Directory.

T | F   5. Active Directory is closely tied to DNS.

■ Competency Assessment

Scenario 5-1: Designing Active Directory

You have ten sites throughout the country and five major departments. How would you design your Active Directory structure?

Scenario 5-2: Designing AD Physical Structure

How do you define how the domain controllers will replicate data to the other domain controllers?

■ Proficiency Assessment

Scenario 5-3: Installing Active Directory

Install Active Directory services and promote your computer to a domain controller with the domain name of domain *xx* where *xx* is your student number. If you do not have a student number, use 01.

Scenario 5-4: Managing a Domain

Next, create three users in each OU. Then create a group in each OU that contains the members of the OU. Create a user called JSmith in the Engineering OU. Add JSmith to the Engineers group.

✳ Workplace Ready

User Administrator and Service Accounts

Active Directory is a major part of many corporations and is central to authentication, authorization, and auditing. However, you must sometimes think a bit out of the box to get everything possible out of Active Directory, including making your network as secure as you can.

Running your system as an administrator gives you great power and responsibility. Because you have access to so much, you can accidentally or unknowingly cause problems. For example, if your system is infected with malware, such as a virus, this malware can spread to other computers because you have permission to access those computers. As a safety precaution, you should consider creating two accounts for administrators. The "normal" user account should be used for performing day-to-day tasks, such as accessing a person's personal files, checking email, or running reports. The "administrator" account should be used for accessing servers and applications that need to be managed or reconfigured. You can even login as the "normal" account and temporarily switch your context by executing the runas command at the command prompt, using the run option, or right-clicking an executable and selecting Run as Administrator.

Some applications and services need to run as administrator or with administrative permissions. Therefore, you can create a user account and assign the minimum permissions needed for the application to run properly. As a side note, it is not recommended that you use "normal" user accounts to run application or services because people leave from time to time. If you disable an account that an application or service is running, the application or service will fail to run.

File and Print Services

OBJECTIVE DOMAIN MATRIX

SKILLS/CONCEPTS	MTA EXAM OBJECTIVE	MTA EXAM OBJECTIVE NUMBER
Introducing NTFS Sharing Drives and Folders Looking at Printers Enabling Auditing	Understand file and print services.	2.4

KEY TERMS

administrative shares	NTFS permissions
auditing	owner
effective permissions	print device
Encrypted File System (EFS)	print job
encryption	printer
explicit permission	printer permissions
inherited permission	share permission
Internet printing	shared folder

Say you have multiple servers running Windows Server 2008 R2. You want to centralize your document storage and printing so that users can easily access files while providing an efficient way to back up data files. In addition, you want to buy two large, fast color printers that will be centrally located to handle many large print jobs.

■ Introducing NTFS

THE BOTTOM LINE

In Lesson 3, you learned that NTFS is the preferred file system in part because it supports much larger hard disks and a higher level of reliability. In addition, NTFS offers better security through permissions and encryption.

CERTIFICATION READY
Why is NTFS the preferred file system?
2.4

In this lesson, a permission is defined as the type of access that is granted to an object, such as NTFS files and folders. When files and folders are created on an NTFS volume, a security descriptor known as an Access Control List (ACL) is created. This descriptor includes information that controls which users and groups can access the file or folder, as well as what type of access is granted to particular users and groups. Each assignment of permissions to a user or group is represented as an access control entry (ACE).

159

TAKE NOTE *

NTFS permissions are managed using Windows Explorer (explorer.exe).

TAKE NOTE *

While List Folder Contents and Read & Execute appear to have the same special permissions, these permissions are inherited differently. List folder Contents is inherited by folders but not files while Read & Execute is inherited by both files and folders.

Setting NTFS Permissions

NTFS permissions allow you to control which users and groups can gain access to files and folders on an NTFS volume. The advantage of NTFS permissions is that they affect local users as well as network users.

Usually, when assigning NTFS permissions, you would assign the following standard permissions:

- **Full control:** This is permission to read, write, modify, and execute files in a folder; change attributes and permissions; and take ownership of a folder or the files within it.
- **Modify:** This is permission to read, write, modify, and execute files in a folder, as well as change attributes of the folder or the files within it.
- **Read & execute:** This is permission to display a folder's contents; display the data, attributes, owner, and permissions for files within the folder; and run files within the folder.
- **List folder contents:** This is permission to display a folder's contents; display the data, attributes, owner, and permissions for files within the folder; and run files within the folder.
- **Read:** This is permission to display a file's data, attributes, owner, and permissions.
- **Write:** This is permission to write to a file, append to the file, and read or change the file's attributes.

To manage NTFS permissions, right-click a drive, folder, or file and select Properties, then select the Security tab. As shown in Figure 6-1, you should see the group and users who have been given NTFS permissions and their respective standard NTFS permissions. To change the permissions, click the Edit button.

Figure 6-1

NTFS permissions

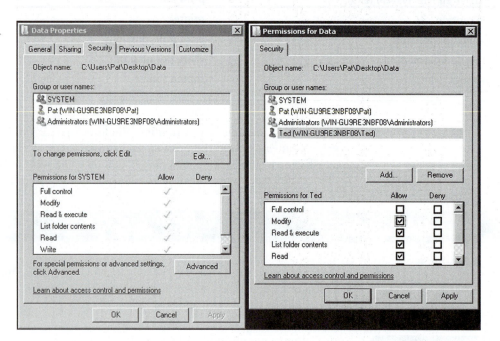

Each of the standard permissions consists of a logical group of special permissions. The available special permissions are as follows:

- **Traverse folder/Execute file:** Traverse folder allows or denies moving through folders to reach other files or folders, even if the user has no permissions for the traversed folders.

By default, the Everyone group is granted the Bypass traverse checking user right. (This applies to folders only.) Execute file allows or denies running program files. (This applies to files only.) Setting the Traverse folder permission on a folder does not automatically set the Execute file permission on all files within that folder.

- **List folder/Read data:** List folder allows or denies viewing filenames and subfolder names within a folder. List folder affects the contents of that folder only and does not affect whether the folder you are setting the permission on will be listed. (This applies to folders only.) Read data allows or denies viewing data in files. (This applies to files only.)
- **Read attributes:** Read attributes allows or denies viewing the attributes of a file or folder, such as read-only and hidden.
- **Read extended attributes:** This permission allows or denies viewing the extended attributes of a file or folder. Extended attributes are defined by programs and may vary by program.
- **Create files/Write data:** Create files allows or denies creating files within a folder. (This applies to folders only.) Write data allows or denies making changes to a file and overwriting existing content. (This applies to files only.)
- **Create folders/Append data:** Create folders allows or denies creating folders within a folder. (This applies to folders only.) Append data allows or denies making changes to the end of a file but not changing, deleting, or overwriting existing data. (This applies to files only.)
- **Write attributes:** Write attributes allows or denies changing the attributes of a file or folder, such as read-only or hidden. The Write attributes permission does not imply creating or deleting files or folders; it only includes the permission to make changes to the attributes of a file or folder. To allow (or deny) create or delete operations, see Create files/Write data, Create folders/Append data, Delete subfolders and files, and Delete.
- **Write extended attributes:** This permission allows or denies changing the extended attributes of a file or folder. Extended attributes are defined by programs and may vary by program. The Write extended attributes permission does not imply creating or deleting files or folders; it only includes the permission to make changes to the attributes of a file or folder. To allow (or deny) create or delete operations, see Create folders/Append data, Delete subfolders and files, and Delete.
- **Delete subfolders and files:** This permission allows or denies deleting subfolders and files, even if the Delete permission has not been granted on the subfolder or file.
- **Delete:** This allows or denies deleting the file or folder. If you do not have Delete permission on a file or folder, you can still delete it if you have been granted Delete subfolders and files permission on the parent folder.
- **Read permissions:** This allows or denies reading the permissions of a file or folder, such as full control, read, and write.
- **Change permissions:** This allows or denies changing the permissions of a file or folder, such as full control, read, and write.
- **Take ownership:** This permission allows or denies taking ownership of a file or folder. The owner of a file or folder can always change permissions on it, regardless of any existing permissions on the file or folder.
- **Synchronize:** This allows or denies different threads to wait on the handle for a file or folder and synchronize with another thread that may signal it. This permission applies only to multithreaded, multiprocess programs.

Table 6-1 shows the special permissions assigned to each standard NTFS permission. If for some reason you need more granular control, you can assign special permissions. To assign special permissions, right-click a drive, folder, or file, click on Properties, and select the Security tab. Then click the Advanced button to open the Advanced Security Settings, click the Change Permissions button, and click the Add, Edit, or Remove button. See Figure 6-2.

Table 6-1

NTFS permissions

SPECIAL PERMISSIONS	FULL CONTROL	MODIFY	READ & EXECUTE	LIST FOLDER CONTENTS (FOLDERS ONLY)	READ	WRITE
Traverse folder/Execute file	X	X	X	X		
List folder/Read data	X	X	X	X	X	
Read attributes	X	X	X	X	X	
Read extended attributes	X	X	X	X	X	
Create files/Write data	X	X				X
Create folders/Append data	X	X				X
Write attributes	X	X				X
Write extended attributes	X	X				X
Delete subfolders and files	X					
Delete	X	X				
Read permissions	X	X	X	X	X	X
Change permissions	X					
Take ownership	X					
Synchronize	X	X	X	X	X	X

Figure 6-2

Advanced Security Settings

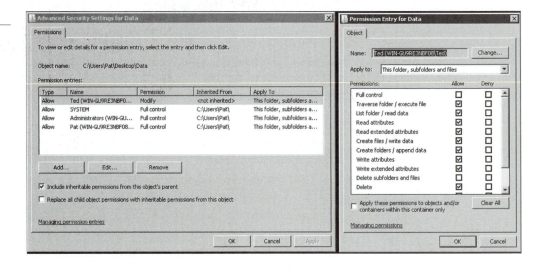

Groups or users that are granted full control permission on a folder can delete any files in that folder regardless of the permissions protecting the file. In addition, the List folder contents permission is inherited by folders but not files, and it should only appear when you view folder permissions. In Windows Server 2008, the Everyone group does not include the Anonymous Logon group by default, so permissions applied to the Everyone group do not affect the Anonymous Logon group.

To simplify administration, you can grant permissions using groups. By assigning NTFS permissions to a group, you are granting permissions to one or more people simultaneously, reducing the number of entries in each access list, as well as the amount of effort required to grant multiple people access to certain files or folders.

Looking at Effective NTFS Permissions

> The folder/file structure on an NTFS drive can be complicated, with many folders and nested folders. In addition, because you can assign permissions to groups and at different levels on an NTFS volume, figuring out the effective permissions of a particular folder or file for a particular user can be tricky.

There are two types of permissions used in NTFS:

- *Explicit permissions:* Permissions granted directly to a file or folder.
- *Inherited permissions:* Permissions that are granted to a folder (parent object or container) that flow into child objects (subfolders or files inside the parent folder).

When assigning permissions to a folder, by default, the permissions apply to both the folder and the subfolders and files within it. To stop permissions from being inherited, you can select the "Replace all existing inheritable permissions on all descendants with inheritable permissions from this object" check box in the Advanced Security Settings dialog box. You will then be asked whether you are sure you want to proceed. You can also clear the "Allow inheritable permissions from parent to propagate to this object" check box. When this check box is clear, Windows will respond with a Security dialog box. When you click on the Copy button, the explicit permission will be copied from the parent folder to the subfolder or file. You can then change the subfolder's or file's explicit permissions. If you click the Remove button, you will remove the inherited permission altogether.

By default, any objects within a folder inherit the permissions from that folder when they are created (Table 6-2). However, explicit permissions take precedence over inherited permissions (Table 6-3). So, if you grant different permissions at a lower level, the lower-level permissions take precedence.

Table 6-2

Inherited permissions

OBJECT	NTFS PERMISSIONS
Data	Grant Allow full control (explicit)
Folder1	Allow full control (inherited)
Folder2	Allow full control (inherited)
File1	Allow full control (inherited)

Table 6-3

Explicit permissions overwrite inherited permissions

OBJECT	NTFS PERMISSIONS
Data	Grant Allow full control (explicit)
Folder1	Allow full control (explicit)
Folder2	Allow full control (inherited)
File1	Allow full control (inherited)

For example, say you have a folder called Data. Within the Data folder, you have Folder1, and within Folder1, you have Folder2. If you grant Allow full control to a user account, the Allow full control permission will flow down to the subfolders and files within the Data folder.

In comparison, if you grant Allow full control on the Data folder to a user account and you grant Allow read permission to Folder1, the Allow read permission will overwrite the inherited permissions and will then flow down to Folder2 and File1.

If a user has access to a file, he or she will still be able to gain access to the file even if he or she does not have access to the folder containing the file. Of course, because the user doesn't have access to the folder, the user cannot navigate or browse through the folder to get to the file. Therefore, the user will have to use the universal naming convention (UNC) or local path to open the file.

When you view permissions, they will be one of the following:

- **Checked:** Here, permissions are explicitly assigned.
- **Cleared (unchecked):** Here, no permissions are assigned.
- **Shaded:** Here, permissions are granted through inheritance from a parent folder.

Besides granting the Allow permissions, you can also grant the Deny permission. The Deny permission always overrides other permissions that have been granted, including when a user or group has been given Full control. For example, if a group has been granted Read and Write permission yet one person within the group has been denied the Write permission, that user's effective rights would be the Read permission.

When you combine applying Deny versus Allowed with explicit versus inherited permissions, the hierarchy of precedence of permission is as follows:

1. Explicit Deny
2. Explicit Allow
3. Inherited Deny
4. Inherited Allow

Because users can be members of several groups, it is possible for them to have several sets of explicit permissions for a particular folder or file. When this occurs, the permissions are combined to form the *effective permissions*, which are the actual permissions when logging in and accessing a file or folder. These consist of explicit permissions plus any inherited permissions.

When you calculate effective permissions, you must first calculate the explicit and inherited permissions for an individual or group and then combine them. When combining user and group permissions for NTFS security, the effective permission is the cumulative permission. The only exception is that Deny permissions always apply.

For example, say you have a folder called Data. Within the Data folder, you have Folder1, and within Folder1, you have Folder2. If User 1 is a member of Group 1 and Group 2 and you assign the Allow write permission to the Data folder to User 1, the Allow read permission to Folder1 to Group 1, and the Allow modify permission to Folder2 to Group 2, then User 1's effective permissions would be as shown in Table 6-4.

Table 6-4

Calculating effective permissions

Object	User 1 NTFS Permissions	Group 1 Permissions	Group 2 Permissions	Effective Permissions
Data	Allow Write (explicit)			Allow Write
Folder1	Allow Write (inherited)	Allow Read (explicit)		Allow Read and Write
Folder2	Allow Write (inherited)	Allow Read (inherited)	Allow Modify* (explicit)	Allow Modify*
File1	Allow Write (inherited)	Allow Read (inherited)	Allow Modify* (inherited)	Allow Modify*

*The Modify permission includes the Read and Write permissions.

As another example, say you have a folder called Data. Within the Data folder, you have Folder1, and within Folder1, you have Folder2. If User 1 is a member of Group 1 and Group 2 and you assign the Allow Write permission to the Data folder to User 1, the Allow Read permission to Folder1 to Group 1, and the Deny Modify permission to Folder2 to Group 2, User 1's effective permissions would be as shown in Table 6-5.

Table 6-5

Effective permissions affected by Deny permissions

Object	User 1 NTFS Permissions	Group 1 Permissions	Group 2 Permissions	Effective Permissions
Data	Allow Write (explicit)			Allow Write
Folder1	Allow Write (inherited)	Allow Read (explicit)		Allow Read and Write
Folder2	Allow Write (inherited)	Allow Read (inherited)	Deny Modify (explicit)	Deny Modify
File1	Allow Write (inherited)	Allow Read (inherited)	Deny Modify (inherited)	Deny Modify

 VIEW NTFS EFFECTIVE PERMISSIONS

GET READY. To view the NTFS effective permissions for a file or folder, perform the following steps:

1. Right-click the file or folder and select Properties.
2. Select the Security tab.
3. Click the Advanced button.
4. Click the Effective Permissions tab (Figure 6-3).

Figure 6-3

NTFS Effective Permissions tab

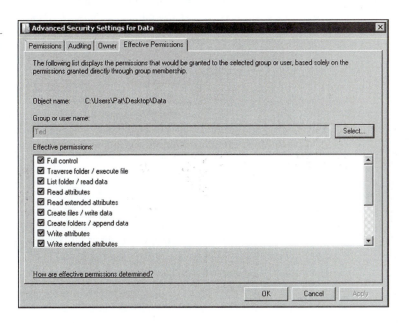

5. Click the Select button and type in the name of the user or group you want to view. Click the OK button.

Copying and Moving Files

When you move or copy files from one location to another, you need to understand what happens to the files' NTFS permissions.

When copying and moving files, the following three scenarios can result:

- If a folder or file is copied, the new folder or file will automatically acquire the permissions of the drive or folder to which it is being copied.
- If a folder or file is moved within the same volume, the folder or file will retain the same permissions that were already assigned.
- If a folder or file is moved from one volume to another volume, the folder or file will automatically acquire the permissions of the drive to which it is being moved.

Looking at Folder and File Owners

The *owner* of an object controls how permissions are set on the object and to whom permissions are granted. If for some reason you have been denied access to a file or folder, you need to reset the permissions by taking ownership of the file or folder and modifying the permissions. All administrators automatically have the Take ownership permission of all NTFS objects.

 TAKE OWNERSHIP OF A FILE OR FOLDER

GET READY. To take ownership of a file or folder, perform the following steps:

1. Open Windows Explorer, then locate the file or folder you want to take ownership of.
2. Right-click the file or folder, click Properties, and then click the Security tab.
3. Click Advanced, and then click the Owner tab.
4. Click Edit, then do **one** of the following:
   - To change the owner to a user or group that *is not* listed: click Other users and groups and, in Enter the object name to select (examples), type the name of the user or group. Then click OK.
   - To change the owner to a user or group that *is* listed: in the Change owner to box, click the new owner.
5. To change the owner of all subcontainers and objects within the tree, select the Replace owner on subcontainers and objects check box.

Encrypting Files with NTFS

Encryption is the process of converting data into a format that cannot be read by another user. Once a user has encrypted a file, it automatically remains encrypted when stored on disk. Decryption is the process of converting data from an encrypted format back to its original format. Once a user has decrypted a file, the file remains decrypted when stored on disk.

If a hard drive were stolen from a system, the thief could install the hard drive on a Windows system for which he or she is an administrator. As an administrator, the thief could then take ownership and access every file and folder on the disk. This is one reason why your servers must have physical security. To help protect your data in situations like this one, you can use encryption.

Encrypting File System (EFS) is a core file encryption technology used to store encrypted files on NTFS file system volumes. Encrypted files cannot be used unless a user has access to the keys required to decrypt the information. After a file has been encrypted, you do not have to manually decrypt that file before you can use it. Rather, once you encrypt a file or folder, you can work with that file or folder just as you would with any other file or folder.

TAKE NOTE*

Encryption can also be used to protect data on laptops, which have a much greater chance of being stolen because they are mobile devices. On Windows 7, EFS can be used to encrypt individual folders or files and BitLocker can be used to encrypt entire volumes.

 ENCRYPT A FOLDER OR FILE USING EFS

TAKE NOTE*

You cannot encrypt a file with EFS while compressing a file with NTFS. You can only do one or the other.

GET READY. To encrypt a folder or file, perform the following actions:

1. Right-click the folder or file you want to encrypt, and then click Properties.
2. Click the General tab. Next, click Advanced.
3. Select the Encrypt contents to secure data check box, click OK, and then click OK again. See Figure 6-4.

Figure 6-4

Encrypting content using EFS

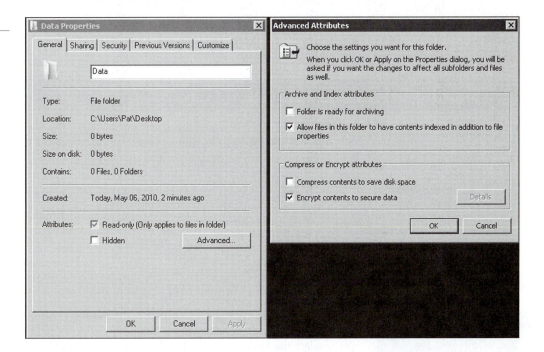

 DECRYPT A FOLDER OR FILE

GET READY. To decrypt a folder or file, perform the following actions:

1. Right-click the folder or file you want to decrypt, and then click Properties.
2. Click the General tab. Next, click Advanced.
3. Clear the Encrypt contents to secure data check box, click OK, and then click OK again.

The first time you encrypt a folder or file, an encryption certificate is automatically created. If your certificate and key are lost or damaged and you don't have a backup, you won't be able to use the files that you have encrypted. Therefore, you should back up your encryption certificate.

BACK UP EFS CERTIFICATE

GET READY. To back up your EFS certificate, perform the following actions:

1. Execute the certmgr.msc command. If you are prompted for an administrator password or confirmation, type your password or provide confirmation.
2. In the left pane, double-click Personal.
3. Click Certificates.
4. In the main pane, click the certificate that lists Encrypting File System under Intended Purposes. If there is more than one EFS certificate, you should back up all of them.
5. Click the Action menu, point to All Tasks, and then click Export.
6. In the Certificate Export wizard, click Next, click Yes, export the private key; and then click Next.
7. Click Personal Information Exchange, and then click Next.
8. Type the password you want to use, confirm it, and then click Next. The export process will create a file to store the certificate.
9. Type a name for the file and the location (include the whole path), or click Browse, navigate to a location, type a filename, and then click Save.
10. Click Next, and then click Finish.

You should then place the certificate in a safe place.

■ Sharing Drives and Folders

THE BOTTOM LINE

Most users are not going to log onto a server directly to access their data files. Instead, a drive or folder will be shared (known as a ***shared folder***), and they will access the data files over a network. To help protect against unauthorized drive or folder access, you should use share permissions along with NTFS permissions (assuming the shared folder is on an NTFS volume). When a user needs to access a network share, he or she will use the UNC, which is \\servername\sharename.

 SHARE A FOLDER

GET READY. To share a drive or folder, perform these steps:

CERTIFICATION READY
How do you make a folder available to others over a network?
2.4

1. In Windows Server 2003, right-click the desired drive or folder and select Sharing and security. In Windows Server 2008, right-click the drive or folder, select Properties and select the Sharing tab, then click the Advanced Sharing button. Then follow these steps:
2. Select Share this folder.
3. Type in the name of the shared folder.
4. If necessary, specify the maximum number of people that can access the shared folder at the same time.
5. Click the Permissions button.
6. By default, Everyone is given the Allow Read shared permission. You can then remove Everyone, expand the Read shared permission, or add additional people.
7. After users and groups have been added with the proper permissions, click the OK button to close the Permissions dialog box. See Figure 6-5.
8. Click OK to close the Properties dialog box.

Figure 6-5

Sharing a folder

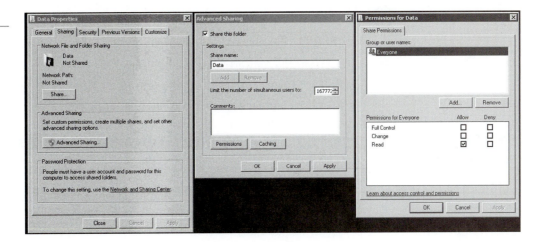

The *share permissions* that are available are as follows:

- **Full control:** Users who are allowed this permission have Read and Change permissions, as well as additional capabilities to change file and folder permissions and take ownership of files and folders.
- **Change:** Users who are allowed this permission have Read permission and the additional capability to create files and subfolders, modify files, change attributes on files and subfolders, and delete files and subfolders.
- **Read:** Users with this permission can view file and subfolder names, access the subfolders of the share, read file data and attributes, and run program files.

As with NTFS, you can allow or deny each share permission. To simplify managing share and NTFS permissions, Microsoft recommends giving everyone Full control at the share level, then controlling access using NTFS permissions. In addition, because a user can be member of several groups, it is possible for a particular user to have several sets of permissions to a shared drive or folder. The effective share permissions are a combination of the user's permissions and the permissions of all groups of which the user is a member.

When a person logs onto the server and accesses files and folders without using the UNC, only the NTFS permissions apply, not the share permissions. When a person accesses a shared folder using the UNC, you must combine the NTFS and share permissions to see what a user can do. To figure overall access, first calculate the effective NTFS permissions. Then determine the effective shared permissions. Finally, apply the more-restrictive permissions between the NTFS and shared permissions.

Network Discovery and Browsing

In Windows Server 2003, you need only two services to provide and access shared folders. The Workstation service allows you to access shared folders and printers, and the Server service allows you to provide shared folders and printers. Starting with Windows Server 2008, you also have to enable network services under the Advanced Sharing setting in the Network and Sharing Center.

When you use servers, you should only enable those services that you need to reduce the surface area of the server, which reduces the ability to exploit vulnerabilities. Therefore, to provide services on a network, the server should be discoverable on the network.

ENABLE NETWORK DISCOVERY

GET READY. To enable network discovery, perform these actions:

1. Open the Network and Sharing Center.
2. Click Change advanced sharing settings.
3. Select Turn on network discovery. See Figure 6-6.

Figure 6-6

Network discovery

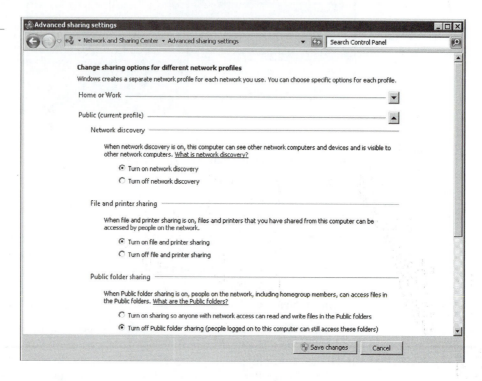

4. Click the Save changes button.

The network services configurable under advanced sharing settings are as follows:

- **Network discovery:** Allows this computer to see other network computers and devices and be visible to other network computers.
- **File and printer sharing:** Allows files and printers that you have shared from this computer to be accessed by people on the network.
- **Public folder sharing:** Allows people on the network to access files in the public folder.
- **Media streaming:** Allows people and devices on the network to access pictures, music, and videos on the computer. In addition, this permits the computer to find media on the network.
- **Password protected sharing:** Allows only people who have a user account and password on the computer to access shared files, printers attached to the computer, and the public folders. To give other people access, you must turn off password-protected sharing.

Looking at Special and Administrative Shares

In Windows, there are several special shared folders that are automatically created by Windows for administrative and system use. Different from regular shares, these shares do not show when a user browses computer resources using Network Neighborhood, My Network Place, or similar software. In most cases, special shared folders should not be deleted or modified. For Windows Servers, only members of the Administrators, Backup Operators, and Server Operators groups can connect to these shares.

An *administrative share* is a shared folder typically used for administrative purposes and usually hidden. To make any shared folder or drive hidden, the share name must have a $ at the end of it. Because the share folder or drive cannot be seen during browsing, you have to use a UNC name to find the folder or drive, which includes the share name (including the $). By default, all hard drive volumes with drive letters automatically have administrative shares (C$, D$, E$, and so on). Other hidden shares can be created as needed for individual folders.

Besides the administrative shares for each drive, you also have the following special shares:

- **ADMIN$:** A resource used by the system during remote administration of a computer. The path of this resource is always the path to the Windows 2008 system root (the directory in which Windows 2008 is installed; for example, C:\Windows).
- **IPC$:** A resource sharing the named pipes that are essential for communication between programs. It is used during remote administration of a computer and when viewing a computer's shared resources.
- **PRINT$:** A resource used during remote administration of printers.
- **NETLOGON:** A resource used by the Net Logon service of a Windows 2008 Server computer while processing domain logon requests.

Looking at Printers

 THE BOTTOM LINE

One basic network service is network printing, in which multiple users can share the same printer. This is a cost-effective solution when you have multiple employees in different locations.

CERTIFICATION READY
How do you limit printing to expensive printers?
2.4

As an administrator, you can install two types of printers: local and network. Today, most local printers are connected using USB ports, although some legacy printers may use parallel or serial ports. Network printers can be shared local printers or printers that connect directly to a network with built-in network cards or expandable jet-direct cards.

When you install a physical printer, which Microsoft refers to as a *print device*, you must first connect the printer and turn it on. Next, you need to create a logical printer (Microsoft refers to this as the *printer*), which will provide a software interface between the print device and the applications. When you create the printer, you also load a print driver that acts as a translator for Windows and the programs running on Windows so that they do not have to worry about the specifics of the printer's hardware and printer language.

When you print a document in Windows, the printer uses the logical printer and printer driver to format the document into a form that is understood by the printer, including rendering it into a printer language such as HP's Printer Control Language or Adobe's Postscript to create an enhanced metafile (EMF). The *print job* is then sent to the local spooler, which provides background printing, allowing you to print and queue additional documents while your first document is being printed.

If a print job is being sent to the local print device, it will temporarily save it to the local hard drive's spool file. When the printer is available, it will then send the print job to the local print device. If Windows determines that the job is for a network print device, Windows sends the job to the print server's spooler. The print server's spooler will save it to the print server's hard drive spool file. Then, when the network print device becomes available, the job will print on the network print device.

Installing Printers

If you have the correct permissions to add a local printer or a remote shared printer, you can use the Add Printer Wizard to install the printer. After the printer is installed, it will appear in the Devices and Printers folder as well as in the Device Manager.

➜ ADD A LOCAL PRINTER

GET READY. To add a local printer to a Windows Server 2008, perform these actions:

1. Click the Start button and open the Control Panel.
2. Under Hardware and Sound, click View Devices and Printers.
3. To start the Add Printer Wizard, click Add a printer.
4. Select Add a Local Printer.
5. When the Add Printer dialog box appears, specify the port to which the printer is connected. See Figure 6-7. If the port already exists, such as an LPT1 or a network port specified by an IP address, select the port from the Use an existing port drop-down list. If the port does not exist, click Create a New Port, select Standard TCP/IP Port, and click Next. For the device type, you can select either Auto detect, TCP/IP device, or Web services device. Then specify the IP address or DNS name of the printer and the Port Name. If you type the address in hostname or IP address box, it will populate the IP address in the port name. It will then try to communicate with the printer using the address you specified.

Figure 6-7

Adding a local printer

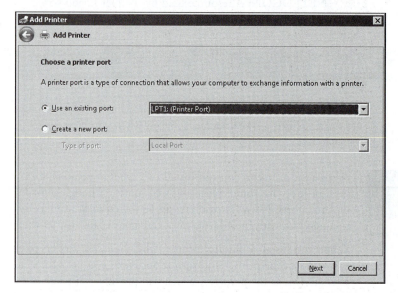

6. If Plug and Play does not detect and install the correct printer automatically, you will be asked to specify the printer driver (printer manufacturer and printer model). If the printer is not listed, you will have to use the Have Disk option.
7. When the Type a Printer Name dialog box appears, specify the name of the printer. If you want this to be the default printer for the system, select the Set as the default printer option. Click the Next button.
8. In the Printer Sharing dialog box, specify the share name. You can also specify the Location or Comments. Although Windows Server 2008 supports long printer names and share names (including spaces and special characters), it is best to keep names short, simple, and descriptive. The entire qualified name, including the server name (for example, \\Server1\HP4100N-1), should be 32 characters or fewer.
9. When the printer is successfully added, you can print the standard Windows test page by clicking the Print a test page button. Click the Finish button.

TAKE NOTE*

The TCP/IP printer port uses host port 9100 to communicate.

➜ ADD A NETWORK PRINTER

GET READY. To add a network printer to Windows Server 2008, perform these steps:

1. Click the Start button and open the Control Panel.
2. Under Hardware and Sound, click View Devices and Printers.
3. To start the Add Printer Wizard, click Add a printer.

4. Select Add a Network, Wireless, or Bluetooth printer.

5. If the printer is not automatically found, click The Printer that I want isn't listed option.

6. If you have a printer published in Active Directory (assuming you are part of a domain), choose Find a printer in the directory, based on location or feature. If you know the UNC, choose Select a shared printer by name. If you know the TCP/IP address, choose the last option. Click the Next button.

7. In the Type a printer name dialog box, specify the printer name. If you want this to be the default printer for the system, select Set as the default printer option. Click the Next button.

8. When the printer is successfully added, you can print the standard Windows test page by selecting the Print a test page button. Click the Finish button.

Windows Servers can provide a driver to the clients if the driver is loaded on the server. For example, because Windows Server 2008 R2 is only available in 64-bit versions, it will have a 64-bit print driver so that the server can print to the printer. However, most computers used within organizations today will most likely be 32-bit clients that need to use 32-bit print drivers. Therefore, you would load both 64-bit and 32-bit print drivers on the server so that it can hand out either driver as needed.

 ADD ADDITIONAL PRINT DRIVERS

GET READY. To add additional print drivers in Windows Server 2008 R2, perform these steps:

1. Open Devices and Printers.

2. Click the Print Server button.

3. Select the Drivers tab.

4. Click the Change Driver Settings.

5. Click the Add button.

6. When the Welcome to the Add Printer Driver Wizard screen appears, click the Next button. See Figure 6-8.

Figure 6-8

Add Printer Driver Wizard

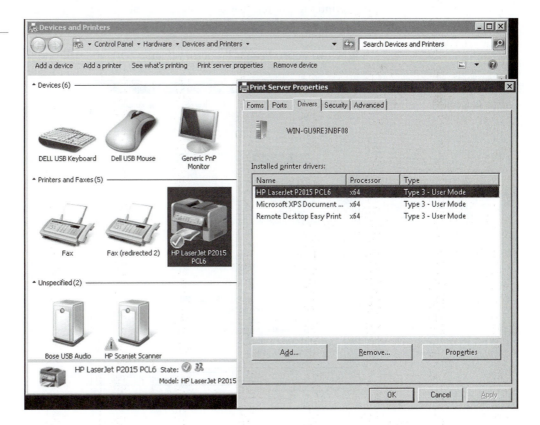

7. Select the appropriate processor and operating system drivers and click the Next button.
8. If necessary, provide a path for the printer driver and click the OK button.
9. When the wizard is complete, click the Finish button.

Network printers are usually used by more than one user. If you have a high volume of print jobs, the printer can become congested and users will have to wait for the documents to print. Either you can purchase a faster printer or you can create a group of printers called a printer pool that acts as a single virtual printer with a single print queue. Users print to a single printer, and the print jobs are distributed among the printers within the pool.

To create a printer pool, you must have two or more printers that are the same model and use the same printer driver. They can use the same type of ports or different ports. Because you don't know which print job will go to which printer, it is recommended that you place all pooled printers in the same physical location.

CREATE A PRINTER POOL

GET READY. To create a printer pool, perform these steps:

1. In the Control Panel, open the Printers and Faxes folder, right-click the appropriate printer, and click Properties.
2. On the Ports tab, select the Enable printer pooling check box.
3. In the list of ports, select the check boxes for the ports connected to the printers that you want to pool.
4. Repeat steps 2 and 3 for each additional printer to be included in the printer pool.

If you want to ensure that documents are first sent to faster printers, add the faster printers to the pool first and the slower printers last. Print jobs are routed in the order in which you create the ports.

Looking at Printer Properties

With most printers, you have a wide range of options. Although these options vary from printer to printer, they are easily accessible by right-clicking the printer in the Devices and Printers folder and selecting Printer Properties.

When you open Printer Properties (Figure 6-9), you will find the following options:

Figure 6-9

Printer Properties

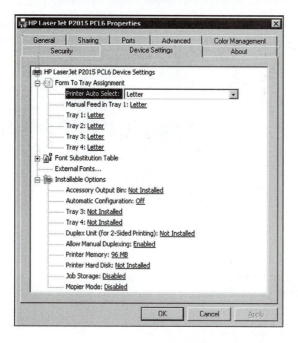

- **General tab:** Allows you to configure the printer name, location, and comments and to print a test page. In addition, if you click the Printing Preferences button on the General tab, the default paper size, paper tray, print quality/resolution, pages per sheet, print order (such as front to back or back to front), and number of copies will display. The actual options that are available will vary depending on your printer.
- **Sharing tab:** Allows you to share a printer. You can also publish the printer in Active Directory if you chose the List in the directory option. Because a printer on a server can be used by other clients connected to the network, you can add additional drivers by clicking the Additional Drivers button.
- **Ports tab:** Allows you to specify which port (physical or TCP/IP) the printer will use, as well as to create new TCP/IP ports.
- **Advanced tab:** Allows you to configure the driver to use with the printer, the priority of the printer, when the printer is available, and how print jobs are spooled.
- **Security tab:** Allows you to specify the permissions for the printer.
- **Device Settings tab:** Allows you to configure the trays, font substitution, and other hardware settings.

Setting Printer Permissions

Printers are considered objects. Therefore, as with NTFS files and folders, you can assign permissions to a printer so that you can specify who can use the printer, who can manage the printer, and who can manage the print jobs.

Windows Server 2008 provides three levels of *printer permissions* (Figure 6-10):

- **Print:** Allows users to send documents to the printer.
- **Manage this printer:** Allows users to modify printer settings and configurations, including the ACL itself.
- **Manage documents:** Provides the ability to cancel, pause, resume, or restart a print job.

Figure 6-10

Printer permissions

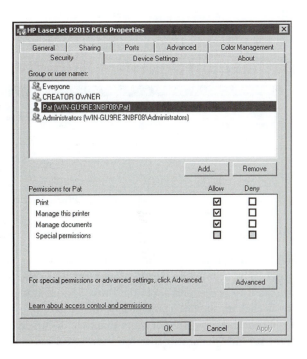

By default, the Print permission is assigned to the Everyone group. If you need to restrict who can print to the printer, you will need to remove the Everyone group and add another group or user and assign the Allow print permission to the user or group. Of course, it is still recommended that you use groups instead of users. As with file permissions, you can also deny print permissions.

Managing Print Jobs

> The print spooler is an executable file that manages the printing process, which includes retrieving the location of the correct print driver, loading the driver, creating the individual print jobs, and scheduling the print jobs for printing.

On occasion, a print job may have been sent that was not intended, or you may decide it is not necessary to print a job. Therefore, you need to delete the print job from the print queue.

 VIEW THE PRINT QUEUE

GET READY. To view the print queue, perform these steps:

1. Open the Devices and Printers folder.
2. Double-click the printers for which you want to view the print jobs waiting to print.
3. To view the print queue, Click Printer: Ready or # document(s) in queue. See Figure 6-11.

Figure 6-11

Viewing the print queue

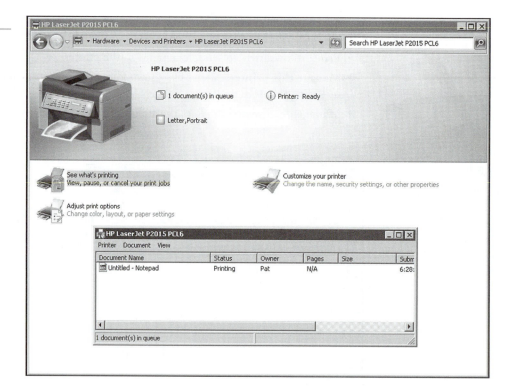

The print queue shows information about a document, such as print status, owner, and number of pages to be printed. To pause a document, open the print queue, right-click on the document you want to pause, and select the Pause option. If you want to stop printing the document, right-click on the document that you want to stop printing and select the Cancel option. You can cancel the printing of more than one document by holding down the Ctrl key and clicking on each document that you want to cancel.

By default, all users can pause, resume, restart, and cancel their own documents. To manage documents that are printed by other users, however, you must have the Allow manage documents permissions.

When the print device is available, the spooler retrieves the next print job and sends it to the print device. By default, the spool folder is located at C:\Windows\\System32\Spool\Printers. If you have a server that handles a large number of print jobs or several large print jobs, make sure the drive where the spool folder is has sufficient disk space.

CHANGE THE LOCATION OF THE SPOOL FOLDER

GET READY. To change the location of the spool folder in Windows Server 2008 R2, perform these steps:

1. Open the Devices and Printers folder.
2. Click a printer and select the Print server properties.
3. Click the Advanced tab.
4. Click the Change Advanced Settings button.
5. Specify the new location and click the OK button.

On occasion, the print spooler may freeze or become unresponsive. You can restart the print spooler by following these steps:

1. Open the Services console located in Administrative Tools.
2. Right-click Print Spooler, and select Restart.

You can also stop and start the service.

Configuring Internet Printing

To enable *Internet Printing* on a computer running Windows Server 2008, you just need to install the Internet Printing role service.

To install the Internet Printing Client in Windows Server 2008, click Add Features in Server Manager, select the Internet Printing Client check box, and then click OK. To manage a server by using the Web site created by Internet Printing, open a web browser and navigate to http://servername/printers.

■ Enabling Auditing

THE BOTTOM LINE

Security can be divided into three areas. Authentication is used to prove the identity of a user. Authorization gives access to the user that was authenticated. To complete the security picture, you need to enable *auditing* so that you can have a record of the users who have logged in and what the user accessed or tried to access.

CERTIFICATION READY
What are the steps in enabling auditing for an NTFS folder?
2.4

It is important that you protect your information and service resources from people who should not have access to them, and at the same time make those resources available to authorized users. Along with authentication and authorization, you can also enable auditing so that you can have a record of:

- Who has successfully logged in
- Who has attempted to log in but failed
- Who has changed accounts in Active Directory
- Who has accessed or changed certain files

Figure 6-12

Audit events in the local
security policy

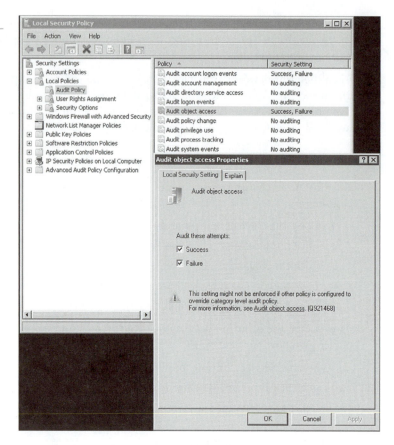

- Who has used a certain printer
- Who restarted a system
- Who has made some system changes

Auditing is not enabled by default. To enable auditing, you specify what types of system events to
audit using Group Policy or the local security policy (Security Settings\Local Policies\Audit Policy).
See Figure 6-12. Table 6-6 shows the basic events to audit that are available in Windows Server
2003 and 2008. Windows Server 2008 has additional options for more granular control. After you
enable logging, you then open the Event Viewer security logs to view the security events.

Table 6-6

Audit events

EVENT	EXPLANATION
Account logon	Determines whether the OS audits each time the computer validates an account's credentials, such as account login.
Account management	Determines whether to audit each event of account management on a computer including changing passwords and creating or deleting user accounts.
Directory service access	Determines whether the OS audits user attempts to access Active Directory objects.
Logon	Determines where the OS audits each instance of a user attempting to log on to or log off his or her computer.
Object access	Determines whether the OS audits user attempts to access non-Active Directory objects including NTFS files and folders and printers.
Policy change	Determines whether the OS audits each instance of an attempt to change user rights assignments, auditing policy, account policy, or trust policy.

Table 6-6 *(continued)*

EVENT	EXPLANATION
Privilege use	Determines whether to audit each instance of a user exercising a user right.
Process tracking	Determines whether the OS audits process-related events such as process creation, process termination, handle duplication, and indirect object access. This is usually used for troubleshooting.
System	Determines whether the OS audits if the system time is changed, if the system is started or shut down, if there is an attempt to load extensible authentication components, if there is a loss of auditing events due to auditing system failure, and if the security log is exceeding a configurable warning threshold level.

 **WARNING** Enabling auditing of successful events can affect server performance, in particular for busy folders.

Auditing NTFS files, NTFS folders, and printers is a two-step process. You must first enable Object Access using Group Policy. Then you must specify which objects you want to audit.

 AUDIT FILES AND FOLDERS

GET READY. To audit files and folders, perform these steps:

1. Open Windows Explorer.
2. Right-click the file or folder that you want to audit, click Properties, and then click the Security tab.
3. Click Edit, and then click Advanced.
4. In the Advanced Security Settings for <object> dialog box, click the Auditing tab.
5. Click the Edit button.
6. Do **one** of the following:
   - To set up auditing for a new user or group, click Add. In Enter the object name to select, type the name of the user or group that you want, and then click OK. See Figure 6-13.

Figure 6-13

Auditing an NTFS folder

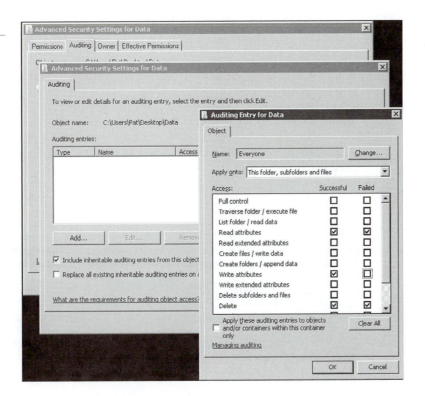

- To remove auditing for an existing group or user, click the group or username, click Remove, click OK, and then skip the rest of this procedure.

  - To view or change auditing for an existing group or user, click its name, and then click Edit.

7. In the Apply onto box, click the location where you want auditing to take place.

8. In the Access box, indicate what actions you want to audit by selecting the appropriate check boxes:

  - To audit successful events, select the Successful check box.

  - To stop auditing successful events, clear the Successful check box.

  - To audit unsuccessful events, select the Failed check box.

  - To stop auditing unsuccessful events, clear the Failed check box.

  - To stop auditing all events, click Clear All.

9. If you want to prevent subsequent files and subfolders of the original object from inheriting these audit entries, select the Apply these auditing entries to objects and/or containers within this container only check box.

10. Click OK to close the Advanced Security Settings dialog box.

11. Click OK to close the Properties dialog box.

→ AUDIT PRINTING

GET READY. To audit printing in Windows Server 2008, perform these steps:

1. Right-click the printer in Devices and Printers, and select Printer Properties.

2. Select the Security tab, and click the Advanced button.

3. Select the Auditing tab.

4. Click the Add button and

  - To set up auditing for a new user or group, click Add. In Enter the object name to select, type the name of the user or group that you want, and then click OK.

  - To remove auditing for an existing group or user, click the group or username, click Remove, click OK, and then skip the rest of this procedure.

  - To view or change auditing for an existing group or user, click its name, and then click Edit.

5. Click OK to close the Advanced Security Settings dialog box.

6. Click OK to close the Properties dialog box.

Because the security log is limited in size, select only those objects that you need to audit and consider the amount of disk space that the security log will need. The maximum size of the security log is defined in Event Viewer by right-clicking Security Log and selecting the Properties option.

SKILL SUMMARY

IN THIS LESSON YOU LEARNED:

- NTFS permissions allow you to control which users and groups can gain access to files and folders on an NTFS volume.

- Each of the standard permissions consists of a logical group of special permissions.

- Explicit permissions are permissions granted directly to the file or folder.

- Inherited permissions are permissions that are granted to a folder (parent object or container) and that flow into child objects (subfolders or files inside the parent folder).
- The Deny permission always overrides the permissions that have been granted, including when a user or group has been given the full control permission.
- Effective permissions are the actual permissions when logging in and accessing a file or folder. They consist of explicit permissions plus any inherited permissions as a user or from any groups that user is a member of.
- If a file or folder is copied, the new file or folder automatically acquires the permissions of the drive or folder to which it is being copied.
- If a file or folder is moved within the same volume, the file or folder retains the same permissions that were already assigned to it.
- If a file or folder is moved from one volume to another volume, it automatically acquires the permissions of the drive or folder to which it is being copied.
- The owner of the object controls how permissions are set on the object and to whom permissions are granted.
- If, for some reason, you have been denied access to a file or folder, you need to reset the permissions by taking ownership of a file or folder and modifying the permissions.
- Encryption is the process of converting data into a format that cannot be read by another user.
- Encrypting File System (EFS) is a core file encryption technology used to store encrypted files on NTFS file system volumes.
- Most users are not going to log on to a server directly to access their data files. Instead, a drive or folder will be shared (known as a shared folder), and they will access the data files over the network.
- Like NTFS, you can allow or deny each share permission.
- To simplify managing share and NTFS permissions, Microsoft recommends giving everyone full control, and then controlling access using NTFS permissions.
- An administrative share is a shared folder typically used for administrative purposes.
- Microsoft refers to the printer itself as a print device.
- A printer in Windows is a logical printer, which will provide a software interface between the print device and applications.
- A printer pools to act as a single virtual printer with a single print queue, but it contains two or more physical printers.
- Since printers are considered objects, you can assign permissions to a printer. You can specify who can use the printer, who can manage the printer, and who can manage the print jobs.
- By default, the Print permission is assigned to the everyone group.
- The print queue shows information about a document such as print status, owner, and number of pages to be printed.
- When you use Internet Printing, you can print or manage documents from a web browser using the Internet Print Protocol (IPP), which is encapsulated in the Hypertext Transfer Protocol (HTTP).
- Auditing provides a record of the users that have logged in and what the user accessed or tried to access.
- Auditing is not enabled by default. To enable auditing, you specify what types of system events to audit using group policies or the local security policy.
- To audit NTFS files, NTFS folders, and printers is a two-step process. You must first enable Object Access using group policies. Then you must specify which objects you want to audit.

■ Knowledge Assessment

Fill in the Blank

Complete the following sentences by writing the correct word or words in the blanks provided.

1. To print to a printer, you need the _____ permission.

2. The NTFS special permission that allows you to move through a folder to reach lower files or folders is _____.

3. The Windows component that allows you to manage shares and NTFS permissions is _____.

4. Permissions that flow from a parent object to a child object are called _____.

5. The _____ are the actual permissions when a user logs in and accesses a file or folder.

6. The encrypting technology included in NTFS is _____.

7. For Windows Server 2008 to be seen on the network, you must enable _____.

8. A(n) _____ share is not seen when browsed.

9. When some has removed all users from a folder, you can _____ of the folder.

10. The default location of the spool folder is _____.

Multiple Choice

Circle the letter that corresponds to the best answer.

1. What is the standard NTFS permission needed to change attributes of a NTFS folder?
   a. Write
   b. Read
   c. Modify
   d. Full Control

2. Which permission takes precedence?
   a. Explicit Deny
   b. Explicit Allow
   c. Inherited Deny
   d. Inherited Allow

3. Which of the following is NOT a share permission?
   a. Full Control
   b. Write
   c. Change
   d. Read

4. TCP/IP printers use port _____.
   a. 443
   b. 23
   c. 9100
   d. 3000

5. What is a single virtual printer with a single print queue that consist of two or more printers?
   a. Print collection
   b. Direct printers
   c. Printer group
   d. Printer pool

6. What symbol makes an administrative share not seen when browsed?
    a. #
    b. *
    c. !
    d. $

7. When enabling Internet Printing, you need to install _____.
    a. DFS
    b. IIS
    c. GPO Manager
    d. Task Manager

8. What is the minimum share permission that allows you to change file and folder permissions?
    a. Full Control
    b. Change
    c. Read
    d. Manage

9. When you copy files from one folder to another folder within the same volume, you get the _____.
    a. Same permissions as the source
    b. Same permissions as the target
    c. No permissions are set
    d. Everyone has full permission

10. You are an administrator on a computer. Unfortunately, there is a folder that you cannot access because you have do not have permissions to the folder. What can you do?
    a. Take ownership of the folder.
    b. Delete the folder and recreate it.
    c. Turn off the deny attribute.
    d. Grant the allow everyone full permission.

True / False

Circle T if the statement is true or F if the statement is false.

T | F **1.** If Full Control is assigned to a parent object for a user, the Full Control permission will overwrite explicit permissions at a child object.

T | F **2.** To see who accesses a file over time, you only have to turn on object access audit events.

T | F **3.** When you are looking at NTFS permissions that are grayed out, it means that you don't have the permissions needed to modify the NTFS permissions.

T | F **4.** You can encrypt and compress a file within NTFS at the same time.

T | F **5.** When calculating the NTFS and share permissions, you would apply the more restrictive permissions between the NTFS and shared permission.

■ Competency Assessment

Scenario 6-1: Creating a Shared Folder

You have a Data folder that you need to share so that all managers have access and can make changes, but no one else can access it. What should you do to set this folder up?

Scenario 6-2: Auditing the Managers folder

You just created a Data folder for your Managers and you need to verify that it is not getting accessed by anyone who is not supposed to access the files and if someone deletes or makes changes to a system. What should you do?

■ Proficiency Assessment

Scenario 6-3: Managing a Folder

1. Create a Data folder. In the Data folder, create a Manager folder and Sales folder.
2. Share the Data folder and assign everyone Allow Full Control.
3. Modify the NTFS permissions for the Manager folder so that only the Managers group and Administrators group have access to the Managers folder. Grant Allow Modify NTFS permission to the Manager group.
4. Modify the NTFS permissions for the Sales folder so that only the Sales and Managers groups and Administrators groups have access to the Managers folder. Grant Allow Modify NTFS permission to the Manager and Sales group.

Scenario 6-4: Managing Printers

1. Install a local printer on your server.
2. Share the printer.
3. Configure the permissions so that the Managers group is the only group that can print to the printer.

✳ Workplace Ready

Distributed File Systems

Distributed File Systems (DFS) is an extension of file services. DFS namespaces allows you to create a share of shares. It allows you to take multiple shared folders and place them under a single shared folder even if the shared folders exist among multiple servers, making it easier for users to find and access those shares.

DFS replication uses File Replication Service (FRS) to duplicate a share folder between two computers. You can use it as a redundancy to provide access to those files when one of the servers is no longer accessible. You can also use it to centralize files that may be spread out between sites so that you can back them up more easily.

Popular Windows Network Services and Applications

OBJECTIVE DOMAIN MATRIX

SKILLS/CONCEPTS	MTA EXAM OBJECTIVE	MTA EXAM OBJECTIVE NUMBER
Introducing the Web Server Understanding Remote Access Introducing Remote Administration	Understand web services.	2.2
Understanding Server Virtualization	Understand server virtualization.	2.5

KEY TERMS

application

application pool

digital certificate

File Transfer Protocol (FTP)

HyperText Markup Language (HTML)

hypervisor

Internet Information Services (IIS)

physical-to-virtual (P2V) conversion

Remote Assistance

Remote Desktop Services

Secure Sockets Layer (SSL)

Simple Mail Transfer Protocol (SMTP)

snapshot

virtual directory

virtual machine

virtual private network (VPN)

web server

World Wide Web (WWW)

You have installed several servers running Windows Server 2008 R2 to form a new network, and you have set up Active Directory and DNS. Now you need to install a web server that will host HR forms. Therefore, you are ready to take one of your computers running Windows Server 2008 R2 and configure it as a web server. You also need an FTP server to provide files to users throughout your organization. However, you want to keep the two servers isolated while minimizing cost. Therefore, you decide to install Hyper-V to create a virtual server for the web server and a virtual server for the FTP server.

■ Introducing the Web Server

THE BOTTOM LINE

The Internet is a global WAN consisting of interconnected networks that use the Internet Protocol Suite (TCP/IP). It is a network of networks that consists of millions of computers, including home, corporation, public, academic, and government computers. The Internet allows users to access a vast array of information resources and services, including web servers that make up the World Wide Web (WWW) and support sending and receiving email. It has also changed the newspaper publishing industry as Web sites, blogging, and web feeds have grown in popularity and newspaper circulation has declined. Last, streaming media, Voice over Internet Protocol (VoIP), and IPTV have become common.

CERTIFICATION READY
How do you create a web server on Windows server?
2.2

The *World Wide Web (WWW)* is a system of interlinked hypertext documents known as web pages that can be viewed with a web browser such as Internet Explorer. Web pages may contain text, images, videos, and other multimedia that you can navigate between by using hyperlinks, and they are usually found by using a search engine such as Bing or Google.

HyperText Markup Language (HTML) is the predominant markup language interpreted by browsers for web pages. It may include text, headings, paragraphs, lists, and hyperlinks. It can also contain embedded objects such as images and videos. It is flexible enough to include scripts and other languages such as JavaScript.

TAKE NOTE *
Because Web sites using HTML have become common on the Internet and it is readily available on any computer with a browser, this technology is often used within an organization to access internal applications.

Traditional web pages consisted of static pages that do not change content without being manually changed. Active Server Pages (ASP) is a technology that enables you to make dynamic and interactive web pages. Instead of using .htm or .html, ASP pages use the .asp extension. The default scripting language used for writing ASP is VBScript, although you can use other scripting languages like JScript (Microsoft's version of JavaScript).

When you view web pages, you are connecting to the *web server* using TCP port 80. However, the content is not encrypted and could be read by anyone who can access the data stream. Since personal information can be sent over the Internet, including credit card numbers, a supplemental protocol was developed called SSL. *Secure Sockets Layer (SSL)* uses TCP port 443, which uses a digital certificate to encrypt the packet so that it cannot be read by anyone else except the source and target. When you are using SSL, the browser URL starts with https (e.g., https://www.acme.com).

Another traditional service provided over the Internet is FTP. *File Transfer Protocol (FTP)* is a standard network protocol used to transfer a file from one host to another over a TCP/IP-based network. Different from HTTP, it uses two TCP ports to operate—ports 20 and 21. FTP can be used with user-based password authentication or with anonymous user access. Unfortunately, the username, password, and data transfers are sent unencrypted. Therefore, when encryption is needed, you should use SFTP (SSH File Transfer Protocol), or FTPS (FTP over SSL), which adds SSL or TLS encryption.

For emails to travel over the Internet, email servers (or any server or client that sends email directly out) use *Simple Mail Transfer Protocol (SMTP)* as an outgoing mail transport. SMTP uses TCP port 25.

Managing Web Sites with IIS

Microsoft's web server/application server is *Internet Information Services (IIS)*. Windows Server 2008 R2 includes IIS 7.5; Windows Server 2008 includes IIS 7.0; and Windows Server 2003 includes IIS 6.0. IIS 7.0 and 7.5 support FTP, FTPS, SMTP, and HTTP/HTTPS, while IIS 6.0 supports FTP, SMTP, and HTTP/HTTPS.

INSTALL IIS IN WINDOWS SERVER 2008 R2

GET READY. To install IIS in Windows Server 2008 R2:

1. Click Start, point to Administrative Tools, and then click Server Manager.
2. In Roles Summary, click Add Roles.
3. Use the Add Roles Wizard to add the web server role.
4. To open IIS Manager, click the Start button. Then select All programs, select Administrative Tools, and click Internet Information Services (IIS) Manager. See Figure 7-1.

Figure 7-1

IIS Manager

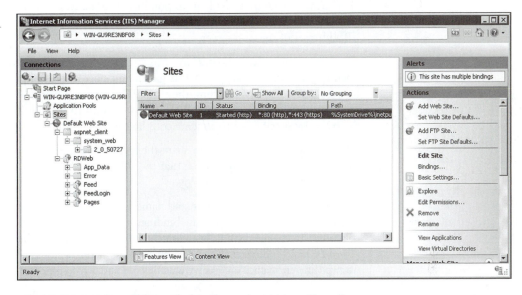

CREATING WEB SITES AND VIRTUAL DIRECTORIES

When IIS is installed, the server will only have a default Web site. IIS was designed to handle multiple Web sites. Therefore, if your organization represents several subsidiaries, each with its own Web site, or you are a company that hosts web services for other companies, you would create multiple sites within IIS.

 CREATE A WEB SITE

GET READY. To create additional Web sites:

1. Open IIS Manager.
2. In the Connections pane, right-click the Sites node in the tree, and then click Add Web Site.
3. In the Add Web Site dialog box, type a friendly name for your Web site in the Web site name box.
4. Click Select if you want to select a different application pool than the one listed in the Application Pool box. In the Select Application Pool dialog box, select an application pool from the Application Pool list and then click OK. Application pools will be discussed a little bit later.
5. In the Physical path box, type the physical path of the Web site's folder, or click the browse button (. . .) to navigate to the file system to find the folder.
6. If the physical path that you entered in step 5 is to a remote share, click Connect to specify credentials that have permission to access the path. If you do not use specific credentials, select the Application user (pass-thru authentication) option in the Connect As dialog box.
7. Select the protocol for the Web site from the Type list.

8. The default value in the IP address box is All Unassigned. If you must specify a static IP address for the Web site, type the IP address in the IP address box.

9. Type a port number in the Port text box.

10. Optionally, type a host header name for the Web site in the Host Header box.

11. If you do not have to make any changes to the site, and you want the Web site to be immediately available, select the Start Web site immediately check box.

12. Click OK.

The default Web site is made to respond to all IP addresses assigned to server port 80 and port 443. In addition, the web server will respond to any name that corresponds to one of the IP addresses of the web server.

To support multiple Web sites, you can assign additional IP addresses and assign a Web site to each IP address. You can also define a different port instead of port 80 or 443. When a user tries to access http://acme.com, they are really accessing http://acme.com:80. The :80 means port 80. If you want to make a Web site to respond to port 8080, you would then access the Web site by specifying http://acme.com:8080.

One method that allows you to share the same IP address and port is to use host headers, which are used to specify a name that the Web site will respond to rather than all names that point to the address.

To configure the IP address, port, and name a Web site will respond to, you need to configure the site binding. To change the site bindings, right-click the site in IIS Manager and select Edit Bindings. To change the binding, click the binding you want to change and click the Edit button. To add a new binding, click the Add button. See Figure 7-2. If you want the Web site to respond to two different names such as www.acme.com and acme.com, you need to add two bindings.

Figure 7-2

Creating a site

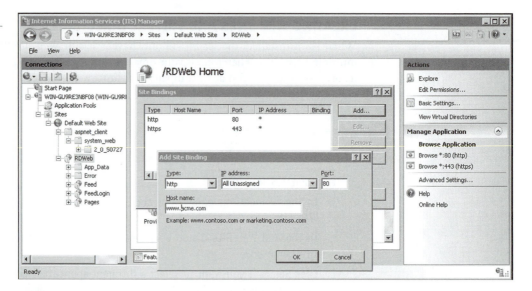

When you create a Web site, you specify a folder that represents the root of the Web site. Within that folder, you can create subfolders. For example, you have a Web site for acme.com. When you access http://acme.com, it goes to the root of the folder to access the default web pages. You can then create a subfolder called sales. Type in a URL similar to http://acme.com/sales or click on a hyperlink on the home page that points to the http://acme.com/sales folder and execute a default web page in the sales folder.

A *virtual directory* is a directory used in a Web site that corresponds to a physical directory elsewhere on the server, on another server, or on a Web site. This allows you to reuse the same folder for multiple sites or to connect to content without physically moving it.

ADD A VIRTUAL DIRECTORY

GET READY. To add a virtual directory within your Web site:

1. Open IIS Manager.
2. In the Connections pane, expand the Sites node in the tree and click to select the site in which you want to create a virtual directory.
3. In the Actions pane, click View Virtual Directories.
4. On the Virtual Directories page in the Actions pane, click Add Virtual Directory.
5. In the Add Virtual Directory dialog box, type a name in the Alias text box. This alias is used to access the content from a URL.
6. In the Physical path text box, type the physical path of the content folder or click Browse to navigate through the file system to find the folder.
7. Optionally, click Connect As to specify credentials that have permission to access the physical path. If you do not use specific credentials, select the Application user (pass-thru authentication) option in the Connect As dialog box.
8. Optionally, click Test Settings to verify the settings that you specified for the virtual directory.
9. Click OK.

EXPLORING APPLICATIONS AND APPLICATION POOLS

An *application* is a grouping of content on a Web site that is defined at the root level or in a separate folder that has specific properties, such as the application pool in which the application runs and the permissions that are granted on the folder. Each site must have at least one application named the root application or default application.

An *application pool* is a set of resources (a worker process or a set of worker processes) used by a Web site or application that defines the memory boundaries for the Web site. Forcing each application to have its own application pool ensures that one Web site does not interfere with another Web site on the same server, which ensures application performance and improved application availability. Therefore, if one application has a memory leak or crashes, it will not affect the other sites.

 CREATE AN APPLICATION IN IIS

GET READY. To create an application:

1. Open IIS Manager.
2. In the Connections Pane, expand the Sites node.
3. Right-click the site for which you want to create an application and click Add Application.
4. In the Alias box, type a value for the application URL, such as sales.
5. Click Select if you want to select a different application pool than the one listed in the Application Pool box. In the Select Application Pool dialog box, select an application pool from the Application Pool List and click OK.
6. In the Physical Path box, type the physical path of the application's folder or click Browse to navigate the file system to find the folder.
7. Optionally, click Connect As to specify credentials that have permission to access the physical path. If you do not use specific credentials, select the Application user (pass-thru authentication) option in the Connect As dialog box.
8. Optionally, click Test Settings to verify the settings that you specified for the application.
9. Click OK.

CREATE AN APPLICATION POOL

GET READY. To create an application pool:

1. Open IIS Manager.
2. In the Connections pane, expand the server node and click Application Pools.
3. On the Application Pools page in the Actions pane, click Add Application Pool.
4. On the Add Application Pool dialog box, type a friendly name for the application pool in the Name box.
5. From the .NET Framework version list, select the version of the .NET Framework required by your managed applications, modules, and handlers, or select No Managed Code if the applications that you run in this application pool do not require the .NET Framework.
6. From the Managed pipeline mode list, select **one** of the following options:
   - Integrated if you want to use the integrated IIS and ASP.NET request-processing pipeline.
   - Classic if you want to use IIS and ASP.NET request-processing modes separately. In classic mode, managed code is processed using Aspnet_isapi.dll instead of the IIS 7 integrated pipeline.
7. Select Start application pool immediately to start the application pool whenever the WWW service is started. By default, this is selected.
8. Click OK.

 CHANGE AN APPLICATION POOL

GET READY. To change an application pool for an application:

1. Open IIS Manager.
2. In the Connections pane, expand the server node and click Application Pools.
3. On the Application Pools page, select the application pool that contains the application that you want to change.
4. In the Actions pane, click View Applications.
5. Select the application whose application pool you want to change and click Change Application Pool in the Actions pane.
6. In the Select Application Pool dialog box, select an application pool from the Application pool list and click OK.

If you have a problematic application and you cannot easily correct the code that causes the problems, you can limit the extent of these problems by periodically recycling the worker process that services the application.

 RECYCLE A WORKER PROCESS MANUALLY

GET READY. To manually recycle a worker process:

1. Open IIS Manager.
2. In the Connections pane, expand the server node and click Application Pools.
3. On the Application Pools page, select the application pool you want to recycle immediately.
4. In the Actions pane, click Recycle and then click Yes.

Rather than manually recycling a worker process, you can choose to configure an application pool to recycle at a scheduled time.

CONFIGURE AN APPLICATION POOL TO RECYCLE AT A SCHEDULED TIME

GET READY. To configure an application pool to recycle at a scheduled time:

1. Open IIS Manager.
2. In the Connections pane, expand the server node and click Application Pools.
3. On the Application Pools page, select an application pool and click Recycling in the Actions pane.
4. Select Specific time(s) and, in the corresponding box, type a time at which you want the application pool to recycle daily. For example, type 11:30 AM or 11:30 PM. You can also specify time intervals such as every 60 minutes.
5. Click Next, select the events that should be logged when an application pool recycles, and click Finish.

EXPLORING DEFAULT DOCUMENTS AND DIRECTORY LISTINGS

By default, when you type in a Web site's URL such as http://acme.com, it will go to the root folder designed for acme.com and first look for one of the following files:

1. Default.htm
2. Default.asp
3. Index.htm
4. Index.html
5. Isstart.htm
6. Default.aspx

The Default Documents feature allows you to configure the list of default documents that will automatically be presented to a browser if a document is not specified, such as http://acme.com/start.html. Therefore, it will first look for http://acme.com/default.htm. If it does not find default.htm, it will then try http://acme.com/default.asp, and so on. You can change the order of default documents or add additional default documents by clicking the Web site or folder and double-clicking Default Document under IIS in the left pane. To change the order, click the file you want to change and click the Move Up or Move Down arrows in the Actions pane. If you want to add a new default document, click the Add option in the Actions pane.

In some instances, you may just want to provide a directory listing of files so that users can quickly download those files. Use the Directory Browsing feature page to modify the content settings for browsing a directory on the web server. When you configure directory browsing, all subdirectories use the same settings unless you override them at a lower level.

USING IIS SECURITY

Since Web sites are designed to provide information, some of which may be sensitive, there will be times when you have to protect that data. You can protect it by limiting who can access the Web site, how users authenticate, and/or by encrypting the content when a request is made.

You can grant or deny specific computers, groups of computers, or domains access to sites, applications, directories, or files on your server by using Authorization rules.

 VIEW URL AUTHORIZATION RULES

GET READY. To view the URL authorization rules using IIS Manager:

1. Open IIS Manager and navigate to the level you want to manage.
2. In Features View, double-click Authorization Rules.

CREATE A NEW AUTHORIZATION RULE

GET READY. To create a new authorization rule using IIS Manager:

1. Open IIS Manager and navigate to the level you want to manage.
2. In Features View, double-click Authorization Rules.
3. In the Actions pane, click Add Allow Rule.
4. In the Add Allow Authorization Rule dialog box, select **one** of the following types of access:
   - **All users:** Specifies that all users, whether they are anonymous or identified, can access the content.
   - **All anonymous users:** Specifies that anonymous users can access the content.
   - **Specified roles or user groups:** Specifies that only members of certain roles or user groups can access the content. Type the role or user group in the text box.
   - **Specified users:** Specifies that only certain users can access the content. Type the user IDs in the text box.
5. Optionally, check Apply this rule to specific verbs if you want to further stipulate that the users, roles, or groups allowed to access the content can only use a specific list of HTTP verbs or actions. Type those verbs in the text box.
6. Click OK.

To create a Deny Rule, select Add Deny Rule instead of selecting Add Allow Rule.

 LIMIT ACCESS TO WEB SITE BY ADDRESS AND DOMAIN

GET READY. To limit access to the Web site by IPv4 address and domain:

1. Open IIS Manager and navigate to the level you want to manage.
2. In Features View, double-click IPv4 Address and Domain Restrictions.
3. In the Actions pane, click Add Allow Entry.
4. In the Add Allow Restriction Rule dialog box, select Specific IPv4 address, IPv4 address range, or Domain name, add the IPv4 address, range, mask, or domain name, and click OK.

Use the Edit IP and Domain Restrictions dialog box to define access restrictions for unspecified clients or to enable domain name restrictions for all rules.

Authentication is used to confirm the identity of clients who request access to your sites and applications. IIS 7.0 supports the following forms of authentication:

- **Anonymous:** Allows access without providing a username and password.
- **ASP.NET Impersonation:** Allows you to run ASP.NET applications under a context other than the default ASP.NET account.
- **Basic Authentication:** Requires that users provide a valid username and password to gain access to content. Since basic authentication transmits passwords across the network in clear text, you should use it with a digital certificate to encrypt usernames and passwords being sent over the network.
- **Digest Authentication:** Uses a Windows domain controller to authenticate users who request access to content on your server.
- **Forms Authentication:** Uses client-side redirection to forward unauthenticated users to an HTML form where they can enter their credentials, which are usually a username and password.
- **Windows Authentication:** Uses NTLM or Kerberos protocols to authenticate clients.

Popular Windows Network Services and Applications | **193**

- **AD Client Certificate Authentication:** Allows you to use the Active Directory service features to map users to client certificates for authentication.

To configure authentication for a Web site, application, or virtual folder, click the site, application, or virtual folder and double-click Authentication. The default setting for Windows authentication is Negotiate. This setting means that the client can select the appropriate security support provider.

EXPLORING SECURE SOCKETS LAYER AND DIGITAL CERTIFICATES

When you use SSL to encrypt web traffic, you are using asymmetric encryption, which involves a private key and a public key. The public key is provided to anyone who wants to access the web server, and the private key is kept secret, usually by the web server that you are trying to protect. The public key is used to encrypt data, which only the private key can decrypt.

To enable SSL, you must obtain and install a valid server certificate on the web server from a recognized certificate authority (CA) or use a self-signed certificate. The CA can be your internal Windows domain or a trusted third-party public CA such as Entrust or Verisign. While the self-signed certificate is not a trusted certificate, it can still be used for troubleshooting, testing, or application development.

When you visit an SSL Web site using Internet Explorer, you will notice a lock icon at top of the IE window. To view the ***digital certificate***, click the lock and select View Certificates. The most common type of digital certificate is the X.509 digital certificate. See Figure 7-3.

Figure 7-3

Digital certificate

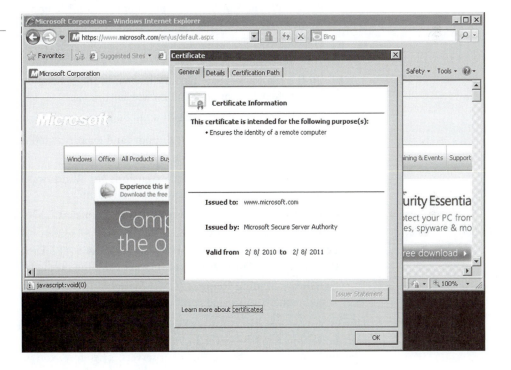

→ ACQUIRE A DIGITAL CERTIFICATE

GET READY. To acquire a digital certificate using IIS 7:

1. Request an Internet server certificate from the IIS server. To request an Internet server certificate, click the server from within IIS Manager and double-click Server Certificates in Features View. Then click Create Certificate Request from the Actions Pane.
2. Send the generated certificate request to the CA, usually using the vendor's Web site.

3. Receive a digital certificate from the CA and install it on the IIS server. Again, open IIS Manage, double-click the server from within IIS Manager, and double-click Server Certificates in Features View. Then select the Complete Certificate Request.

4. On the Distinguished Name Properties page of the Request Certificate Wizard, type the following information and click Next.

   - In the Common name text box, type a name for the certificate.
   - In the Organization text box, type the name of the organization in which the certificate will be used.
   - In the Organizational unit text box, type the name of the organizational unit in the organization in which the certificate will be used.
   - In the City/locality text box, type the unabbreviated name of the city or locality where your organization or organizational unit is located.
   - In the State/province text box, type the unabbreviated name of the state or province where your organization or organizational unit is located.
   - In the Country/region text box, type the name of the country or region where your organization or organizational unit is located.

5. On the Cryptographic Service Provider Properties page, select either Microsoft RSA SChannel Cryptographic Provider or Microsoft DH SChannel Cryptographic Provider from the Cryptographic service provider drop-down list. By default, IIS 7 uses the Microsoft RSA SChannel Cryptographic Provider.

6. In the Bit length drop-down list, select a bit length that can be used by the provider. By default, the RSA SChannel provider uses a bit length of 1024. The DH SChannel provider uses a bit length of 512. A longer bit length is more secure, but it can affect performance.

7. Click Next.

8. On the File Name page, type a filename in the Specify a file name for the certificate request text box, or click the browse button (. . .) to locate a file, and click Finish.

9. Send the certificate request to a public CA.

From time to time, you may need to import and export digital certificates. The common formats used today are:

- **X509 format (.cer and .crt file extensions for Windows):** A widely supported digital certificate that represents the individual certificate.
- **Cryptographic Message Syntax—PKCS #7 Format (.p7b file extension for Windows):** Used to export the complete chain of digital certificates.
- **Personal Information Exchange Syntax—PKCS #12 Format (.pfx and .p12 file extensions for Windows):** Used for exporting the public/private key pair.
- **Certificate Signing Request (CSR) Syntax—PKCS #10 Format:** Used in generating signed requests to trusted certificate signing authorities.

If you have a farm that consists of multiple web servers, you need to install the digital certificate from the first server and then export the digital certificate to a .pfx format to copy the public and private key to the other servers. Therefore, you will need to export the key from the first server and import to the other servers.

 EXPORT A DIGITAL CERTIFICATE

GET READY. To export a digital certificate:

1. Open IIS Manager and navigate to the level you want to manage.

2. In the Features View, double-click Server Certificates.

3. In the Actions pane, click Export.

4. In the Export dialog box, type a filename in the Export to box or click the browse button to navigate to the name of a file in which to store the certificate for exporting.

5. Type a password in the Password box if you want to associate a password with the exported certificate. Retype the password in the Confirm password box.

6. Click OK.

 IMPORT A DIGITAL CERTIFICATE

GET READY. To import a digital certificate:

1. Open IIS Manager and navigate to the level you want to manage.

2. In the Features View, double-click Server Certificates.

3. In the Actions pane, click Import.

4. In the Import Certificate dialog box, type a filename in the certificate file box or click the browse button to navigate to the name of a file where the exported certificate is stored. Type a password in the Password box if the certificate was exported with a password.

5. Select Allow this certificate to be exported if you want to be able to export the certificate, or clear Allow this certificate to be exported if you do not want to allow additional exports of this certificate.

6. Click OK

Managing FTP with IIS

> With IIS 7.5, you manage FTP through IIS Manager. While Windows Server 2008 includes IIS 7.0, you still manage FTP through IIS 6.0.

The majority of FTP sites are used primarily to download files. In most of these situations, FTP uses anonymous authentication where username and password are not required.

 INSTALL FTP

GET READY. To install FTP on Windows Server 2008 R2:

1. On the taskbar, click Start, point to Administrative Tools, and click Server Manager.

2. In the Server Manager hierarchy pane, expand Roles and click Web Server (IIS).

3. In the Web Server (IIS) pane, scroll to the Role Services section and click Add Role Services.

4. On the Select Role Services page of the Add Role Services Wizard, expand FTP Server.

5. Select FTP Service. (Note: To support ASP.NET Membership or IIS Manager authentication for the FTP service, you will also need to select FTP Extensibility.)

6. Click Next.

7. On the Confirm Installation Selections page, click Install.

8. On the Results page, click Close.

 CONFIGURE FTP

GET READY. To configure an FTP site for anonymous access:

1. Open IIS 7 Manager. In the Connections pane, click the Sites node in the tree.

2. Create a folder at "%SystemDrive%\inetpub\ftproot."

3. Set the permissions to allow anonymous access by opening a command and typing the following command:

   ICACLS "%SystemDrive%\inetpub\ftproot"/Grant IUSR:R/T

4. Close the command prompt.

5. Right-click the Sites node in the tree and click Add FTP Site, or click Add FTP Site in the Actions pane.

6. When the Add FTP Site wizard appears, enter "My New FTP Site" in the FTP site name box, then navigate to the %SystemDrive%\inetpub\ftproot folder that you created in the Prerequisites section. Note that if you choose to type in the path to your content folder, you can use environment variables in your paths. Click Next.

7. On the Binding and SSL Settings page, fill in the following:

   • Choose an IP address for your FTP site from the IP Address drop-down, or choose to accept the default selection of "All Unassigned."

   • Enter the TCP/IP port for the FTP site in the Port box. For this walk-through, choose to accept the default port of 21.

   • For this example, do not use a host name. Make sure that the Virtual Host box is blank.

   • Make sure that the Certificates drop-down is set to "Not Selected" and that they Allow SSL option is selected.

     Click the Next button.

8. On the Authentication and Authorization Information page, select Anonymous for the Authentication settings. For the Authorization settings, choose "Anonymous users" from the Allow access to drop-down, and select Read for the Permissions option. Click Finish.

■ Understanding Remote Access

THE BOTTOM LINE

Today, it is very common for an organization to use a remote access server (RAS). This enables users to connect remotely to a network using various protocols and connection types. By connecting to the RAS over the Internet, users can connect to their organization's network so that they can access data files, read email, and access other applications just as if they were sitting at work.

Virtual private networks (VPNs) links two computers through a wide-area network such as the Internet. To keep the connection secure, the data sent between the two computers is encapsulated and encrypted. In one scenario, a client connects to the RAS server to access internal resources from off-site. Another scenario is to connect two remote sites together by creating a VPN tunnel between an RAS server located at each site.

The three types of tunneling protocols used with a VPN/RAS server running on Windows Server 2008 include:

• **Point-to-Point Tunneling Protocol (PPTP):** A VPN protocol based on the legacy Point-to-Point protocol used with modems. Unfortunately, PPTP is easy to set up but is considered to use weak encryption technology.

• **Layer 2 Tunneling Protocol (L2TP):** Used with IPSec to provide security. L2TP is the industry standard when setting up secure tunnels.

• **Secure Socket Tunneling Protocol (SSTP):** Introduced with Windows Server 2008, which users the HTTPS protocol over TCP port 443 to pass traffic through firewalls and web proxies that might block PPTP and L2TP/IPSec.

When using VPNs, Windows 7 and Windows Server 2008 support the following forms of authentication:

• **Password Authentication Protocol (PAP):** Uses plain text (unencrypted passwords). PAP is the least secure authentication and is not recommended.

- **Challenge Handshake Authentication Protocol (CHAP):** A challenge-response authentication that uses the industry standard md5 hashing scheme to encrypt the response. CHAP was an industry standard for years and is still quite popular.
- **Microsoft CHAP version 2 (MS-CHAP v2):** Provides two-way authentication (mutual authentication). MS-CHAP v2 provides stronger security than CHAP.
- **Extensible Authentication Protocol (EAP-MS-CHAPv2):** A universal authentication framework that allows third-party vendors to develop custom authentication schemes including retinal scans, voice recognition, fingerprint identifications, smart cards, Kerberos, and digital certificates. It also provides a mutual authentication method that supports password-based user or computer authentication.

 ### LOAD REMOTE ACCESS AND ROUTING

GET READY. To make a computer running Windows Server 2008 load Remote Access and Routing:

1. Start the Add Roles Wizard using Server Manager or the Initial Configuration Tasks window.
2. On the Before You Begin page, click Next.
3. On the Select Server Roles page, select Network Policy and Access Services and click Next twice.
4. On the Select Role Services page, select Routing and Remote Access Services.
5. On the Confirm Installation Selections page, click Install.
6. On the Installation Results page, review the status and click Close.

CONFIGURE A VPN SERVER

GET READY. To enable RRAS and configure it as a VPN server:

1. Open the RRAS MMC Snap-in.
2. Right-click the server name for which you want to enable routing and then click Configure and Enable Routing and Remote Access. If you are using Server Manager, right-click Routing and Remote Access and then click Configure and Enable Routing and Remote Access.
3. On the Welcome page, click Next.
4. On the Configuration page, click Remote Access (dial-up or VPN) and then click Next.
5. On the Remote Access page, select VPN and click Next.
6. On the VPN Connection page, select the network interface that is connected to the public Internet from which remote VPN clients will connect to this server.
7. To configure packet filters that restrict network access through the specified public network adapter to only the ports required by VPN clients, select Enable security on the selected interface by setting up static packet filters.
8. On the Network Selection page, select the private network to which remote VPN clients are to be granted access. The network adapter and its IP address are displayed to help you determine which to select.
9. On the IP Address Assignment page, specify the way in which the RRAS server will acquire IP addresses for the remote VPN clients. If you have a DHCP server with a range of addresses available, click Automatic. If you want the RRAS server to manage the IP addresses, click From a specified range of addresses.
10. If you did not select Automatic on the Address Range Assignment page, click New and type starting and ending IP addresses to create the range from which remote VPN clients are assigned addresses. You can enter multiple ranges if required. Click Next when you have created the address ranges.

11. On the Managing Multiple Remote Access Servers page, select whether you want to use a centralized RADIUS server for authentication of your network clients. If you select No, then RRAS uses its local account database or, if the RRAS server is joined to an Active Directory domain, the RRAS server uses the domain account database. Note: To use Active Directory Domain Services (AD DS), you must join the RRAS server to a domain and add the computer account of this server to the RAS and IAS Servers security group in the domain of which this server is a member. The domain administrator can add the computer account to the RAS and IAS Servers security group by using Active Directory Users and Computers or by using the netsh ras add registeredserver command.

12. On the Completing page, click Finish.

 CREATE A VPN TUNNEL

GET READY. To create a VPN tunnel on a computer running Windows 7 so you can connect to a Remote Access Server:

1. From the Control Panel, select Network and Internet to access the Network and Sharing Center.
2. From the Network and Sharing Center, choose Set up a new connection or wizard.
3. On the Set Up a Connection or Network page, choose Connect to a workplace.
4. On the Connect to a Workplace page, answer the question "Do you want to use a connection that you already have?" Choose to create a new connection or choose an existing connection.
5. On the next page, choose Use my Internet connection (VPN).
6. On the next screen, choose your VPN connection or specify the Internet Address for the VPN Server and a Destination Name. You can also specify the options to use a Smart card for authentication; Allow other people to use this connection; or Don't connect now, just set up so I can connect later.

You may need to do additional configuration to your VPN connection, such as specifying the type of protocol, authentication protocol, and the type of encryption.

To connect using the VPN once the VPN connection is created and configured, open the Network and Sharing Center and click Manage Network Connections. Then, right-click your VPN connection and click the Connect button. See Figure 7-4.

Figure 7-4

VPN connection

By default, when you connect to a VPN using the previous configuration, all web browsing and network traffic goes through the default gateway on the Remote Network unless you are communicating with local home computers. Having this option enabled helps protect the corporate network because all traffic also goes through firewalls and proxy servers, which prevents a network from being infected or compromised.

If you wish to route your Internet browsing through your home Internet connection rather than going through the corporate network, you can disable the "Use Default Gateway on Remote Network" option. Disabling this option is called using a split tunnel.

 ENABLE A SPLIT TUNNEL

GET READY. To enable a split tunnel:

1. Right-click a VPN connection and click Properties.
2. Click the Networking tab.
3. Double-click the Internet Protocol Version 4 (TCP/IPv4).
4. Click the Advanced button.
5. Deselect the Use default gateway on remote network.

If you have to configure multiple clients to connect to a remote server, it can be a lot of work, and it can be easy to make an error. To help simplify the administration of the VPN client into an easy-to-install executable, you could use the Connection Manager Administration Kit (CMAK), which can also be installed as a feature in Windows Server 2008.

■ Introducing Remote Administration

THE BOTTOM LINE

With early networks, users utilized dumb terminals (systems consisting of a monitor and keyboard without a processor) to connect to a mainframe. Later, computers could use telnet to connect to a server and execute commands at a command prompt. *Remote Desktop Services*, formerly known as Terminal Services, is one of the components of Microsoft Windows that allows a user to access applications and data on a remote computer over a network.

CERTIFICATION READY
Can you list and describe the various ways to manage a server remotely?
2.2

By default, Windows Servers are configured to use Remote Desktop for Administration licensing mode, which supports up to two remote sessions (three if you count the console session, which is the session that you use when you log on to the computer directly), and is primarily used to connect to a server to manage it. However, if you want to run applications that require more than the standard two remote sessions, you will need to first load and configure the computer running Windows Server 2008 R2 as a Remote Desktop Session Host server role. You will also need an RD licensing manager to keep track of the licenses used, and you will have to purchase and install terminal server licenses.

To access a computer running Remote Desktop Services, you would use Remote Desktop Connections to access a computer's graphical user interface including the desktop, start menu, and programs just as if you were sitting in front of the computer. See Figure 7-5. Two technologies that allow you to remotely access a computer's desktop are Remote Desktop and *Remote Assistance* over TCP port 1389.

Figure 7-5

Remote Desktop connection

To connect to a remote computer:

- The computer must be turned on.
- It must have a network connection.
- Remote Desktop must be enabled in the System Properties.
- You must have permission to connect (be a member of the administrators group or the Remote Desktop Users group).

 ENABLE REMOTE DESKTOP

GET READY. To enable Remote Desktop:

1. Click the Start button. Right-click Computer and select Properties.
2. Click Remote Settings and select one of the following options:
   - Allow connections from computer running any version of Remote Desktop (less secure).
   - Allow connections only from computers running Remote Desktop with Network Level Authentication (more secure) options.
3. If you are prompted for an administrator password or confirmation, type the password or provide confirmation.
4. Click Select Users. If you are enabling Remote Desktop for your current user account, your name will automatically be added to this list of remote users and you can skip the next two steps.
5. In the Remote Desktop Users dialog box, click Add. This will add users to the Remote Desktop Users group.
6. In the Select Users dialog box, enter the user's name and click OK.

 ACCESS REMOTE DESKTOP

GET READY. To start Remote Desktop on the computer you want to work from:

1. Open Remote Desktop Connection by clicking the Start button, selecting Accessories, and selecting Remote Desktop Connection. You could also run the mstsc.exe command.

2. In Computer, type the name of the computer that you want to connect to and click Connect. (You can also type the IP address instead of the computer name if you want.)

For more advanced options before the connection, click the Options button. See Figure 7-6.

Figure 7-6

Configuring Remote Desktop connections

TAKE NOTE*

If for some reason the Explorer taskbar is not available, you can also press the Ctrl+Alt+End keys to open the same window in Task Manager, from which you can start explorer.exe.

RemoteApp (or TS RemoteApp) is a special mode of Remote Desktop Services that allows you to run an application in its own window instead of opening a session with Remote Desktop Connection. For the most part, the application looks like a normal application running on your local computer but in reality it is running remotely on a server. A RemoteApp can be packaged either as a .rdp file or distributed via an .msi Windows Installer package.

Besides using a VPN tunnel, you can use a Remote Desktop Gateway (RD Gateway) role service to enable authorized remote users to connect to resources on an internal private network over the Internet using a Remote Desktop Connection (RDC) client. RD Gateway uses the Remote Desktop Protocol (RDP) over HTTPS to establish a secure, encrypted connection between remote users on the Internet and the internal network resources on which their productivity applications run.

■ Understanding Server Virtualization

THE BOTTOM LINE

Virtualization has become quite popular during the last few years. By using *virtual machine* technology, you can run multiple operating systems concurrently on a single machine, which allows separation of services while keeping cost to a minimum. It can also be used to create Windows test systems in a safe, self-contained environment. Microsoft Hyper-V is a hypervisor-based virtualization system for x64 computers starting with Windows Server 2008. The *hypervisor* is installed between the hardware and the operating system and is the main component that manages the virtual computers.

CERTIFICATION READY
What are the advantages of using virtual servers?
2.5

To run several virtual machines on a single computer, you need to have sufficient processing power and memory to handle the load. However, since most servers often sit idle, virtualization utilizes the server's hardware more efficiently.

To keep each virtual server secure and reliable, each server is placed in its own partition. A partition is a logical unit of storage in which operating systems execute. Each virtual machine accesses the hypervisor, which handles interrupts to the processor and redirects them to the respective partition.

In Hyper-V, each virtual machine uses a maximum of one processor; however, it may share the processor it is using with other virtual machines, depending on the number of processors on the physical computer and the number of running virtual machines. In addition, each virtual machine requires enough memory to run the operating system and applications, plus approximately 32 MB for the emulated video RAM and code cache. A motherboard and BIOS that supports virtualization are also required.

By default, Hyper-V stores all the files that make up a virtual machine in one folder with the same name as the virtual server for simple management and portability. Renaming a virtual machine does not rename the virtual machine folder. By default, these folders are located in the Shared Virtual Machines folder, which is located in Documents and Settings\All Users\Documents\Shared Virtual Machines.

In Hyper-V, each virtual machine uses the following files:

- A virtual machine configuration (.vmc) file in XML format that contains the virtual machine configuration information, including all settings for the virtual machine.
- One or more virtual hard disk (.vhd) files to store the guest operating system, applications, and data for the virtual machine. So if you create a 12-GB partition for the virtual machine's hard drive, the virtual hard disk file will be 12 GB.

In addition, a virtual machine may also use a saved-state (.vsv) file, if the machine has been placed into a saved state.

To install Hyper-V, you need:

- An x64 version of Windows Server 2008.
- 64-bit processors and BIOS that support hardware-assisted virtualization (Intel VT or AMD-V) technology.
- Hardware Data Execution Prevention (DEP), which Intel describes as eXecuted Disable (XD) and AMD describes as No eXecute (NS) it is a technology used in CPUs to segregate areas of memory for use by either storage of processor instructions or for storage of data.

TAKE NOTE*

In future versions of Windows, virtualization may not require the processor and motherboard supporting the hardware-assisted virtualization technology.

INSTALL HYPER-V

GET READY. To add the Hyper-V role:

1. Click Start and then click Server Manager.
2. In the Roles Summary area of the Server Manager main window, click Add Roles.
3. On the Select Server Roles page, click Hyper-V.
4. On the Create Virtual Networks page, click one or more network adapters if you want to make their network connection available to virtual machines.
5. On the Confirm Installation Selections page, click Install.
6. Restart the computer to complete the installation. Click Close to finish the wizard and then click Yes to restart the computer.
7. After you restart the computer, log on with the same account you used to install the role. After the Resume Configuration Wizard completes the installation, click Close to finish the wizard.

Creating Virtual Machines

After installing Hyper-V, you are ready to create some virtual machines and install the operating system on each virtual machine that you create.

 CREATE VIRTUAL MACHINES IN HYPER-V

GET READY. To create and set up a virtual machine:

1. Open Hyper-V Manager from the Administrative Tools. See Figure 7-7.

Figure 7-7

Hyper-V Manager

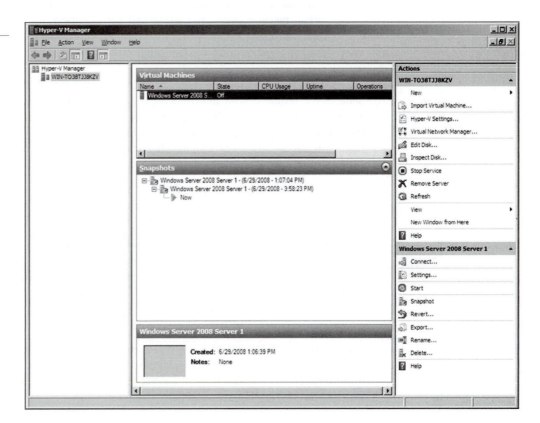

2. From the Action pane, click New and then click Virtual Machine.

3. From the New Virtual Machine Wizard, click Next.

4. On the Specify Name and Location page, specify what you want to name the virtual machine and where you want to store it.

5. On the Memory page, specify enough memory to run the guest operating system you want to use on the virtual machine.

6. On the Networking page, connect the network adapter to an existing virtual network if you want to establish network connectivity at this point. If you want to use a remote image server to install an operating system on your test virtual machine, select the external network.

7. On the Connect Virtual Hard Disk page, specify a name, location, and size to create a virtual hard disk so you can install an operating system on it.

8. On the Installation Options page, choose the method you want to use to install the operating system:

   • Install an operating system from a boot CD/DVD-ROM. You can use either physical media or an image file (.iso file).

- Install an operating system from a boot floppy disk.
- Install an operating system from a network-based installation server. To use this option, you must configure the virtual machine with a network adapter connected to the same network as the image server.

9. Click Finish.

 INSTALL THE OPERATING SYSTEM ON A VIRTUAL MACHINE

GET READY. To install the operating system:

1. From the Virtual Machines section of the results pane, right-click the name of the virtual machine you just created and click Connect. The Virtual Machine Connection tool will open.
2. From the Action menu in the Virtual Machine Connection window, click Start.
3. Proceed through the installation.

Some of the Windows built-in drivers do not run efficiently under a virtual environment. Therefore, you need to install Integration Services, which includes some basic drivers. To install the integration components, open the Action menu of Virtual Machine Connection and click Insert Integration Services Setup Disk. If Autorun does not start the installation automatically, you can start it manually by executing the %windir%\support\amd64\setup.exe command.

You are now ready to configure and manage the virtual server just as if you were working on a physical server. This would include configuring the IP, enabling remote desktop, installing the appropriate roles and features, installing additional software, and so forth.

In many organizations, you may want to consolidate several physical servers to one machine running multiple virtual servers. Microsoft System Center Virtual Machine Manager (VMM) allows you to convert existing physical computers into virtual machines through a process known as *physical-to-virtual (P2V) conversion*. VMM simplifies P2V by providing a task-based wizard to automate much of the conversion process. Since the P2V process is completely scriptable, you can initiate large-scale P2V conversions through the Windows PowerShell command line.

While many companies use virtual servers to consolidate their servers, there may be an occasional need to convert a virtual server to a physical server. However, Hyper-V does not include any tools to convert a physical server to a virtual server (known as virtual-to-physical (V2P) conversion). Instead, you will have to use a third party tool.

Managing Virtual Machines

When you work with physical servers, there may be times where you have to add a network card, add or expand a hard drive, or move a network card cable from one switch to another. Virtual servers have the same needs, but you must perform these tasks virtually.

MANAGING DISKS

When you create a virtual hard drive, you can define the virtual hard disks as:

- **Fixed size virtual hard disks:** Take up the full amount of disk space when created, even if there is no data using parts of the hard disk.
- **Dynamically expanding hard disks:** Expands as it needs space up to its full space.

One of the strengths of virtual servers is the ability to take snapshots. A *snapshot* is a point in time image of a virtual machine that you can return to. So, if you make a change to the system, such as loading a component or installing an update, that causes problems, you can use the snapshot to quickly revert back to the point before the change was made.

The snapshot files consist of:

- A copy of the VM configuration .xml file.
- Any saved state files.
- A differencing disk (.avhd) is the new working disk for all writes and is a child of the working disk prior to the snapshot.

With Hyper-V, you can create 10 levels of snapshot per virtual server.

To create a snapshot in Hyper-V, select Snapshot from the Action menu or panel or by clicking on the snapshot button in the toolbar. When you create a snapshot, a dialog box will appear that allows you to enter a name for the snapshot. You can dismiss this dialog and have the snapshot use an auto-generated name if you prefer. This auto-generated name will consist of the name of the virtual machine followed by the date and time when the snapshot was taken.

MANAGING VIRTUAL NETWORKS AND NETWORK CARDS

Virtual networks consist of one or more virtual machines configured to access local or external network resources. The virtual network is configured to use a network adapter in the physical computer.

If a network adapter in the physical computer is selected, then any virtual machines attached to the virtual network can access the networks to which that physical adapter is connected. If the virtual network is configured not to use a network adapter, then any virtual machine attached to the virtual network becomes part of the internal virtual machine network. An internal virtual machine network consists of all virtual machines attached to a virtual network that is configured to use a network adapter. Each internal virtual machine network is completely isolated from all other internal virtual machine networks.

 ADD A VIRTUAL NETWORK

GET READY. To add a virtual network:

1. Open Hyper-V Manager.
2. From the Actions menu, click Virtual Network Manager. See Figure 7-8.

Figure 7-8

Virtual Network Manager

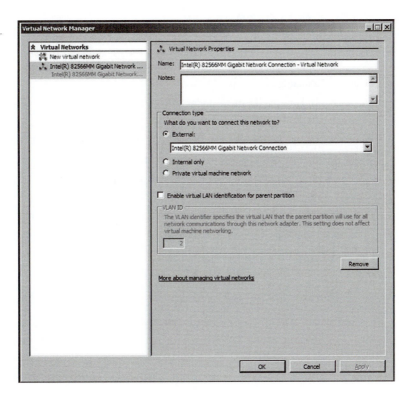

3. Under Create virtual network, select the type of network you want to create.

4. Click Add. The New Virtual Network page appears.

5. Type a name for the new network. Review the other properties and modify them if necessary.

6. Click OK to save the virtual network and close Virtual Network Manager, or click Apply to save the virtual network and continue using Virtual Network Manager.

 MODIFY A VIRTUAL NETWORK

GET READY. To modify a virtual network:

1. Open Hyper-V Manager.

2. From the Actions menu, click Virtual Network Manager.

3. Under Virtual Networks, click the name of the network you want to modify.

4. Under Virtual Network Properties, edit the appropriate properties to modify the virtual network.

5. Click OK to save the changes and close Virtual Network Manager, or click Apply to save the changes and continue using Virtual Network Manager.

 REMOVE A VIRTUAL NETWORK

GET READY. To remove a virtual network:

1. Open Hyper-V Manager.

2. From the Actions menu, click Virtual Network Manager.

3. Under Virtual Networks, click the name of the network you want to remove.

4. Under Virtual Network Properties, click Remove.

5. Click OK to save the changes and close Virtual Network Manager, or click Apply to save the changes and continue using Virtual Network Manager.

ADD A NETWORK ADAPTER

GET READY. To add a network adapter:

1. Open Hyper-V Manager. Click Start, point to Administrative Tools, and click Hyper-V Manager.

2. In the results pane under Virtual Machines, select the virtual machine that you want to configure.

3. In the Action pane under the virtual machine name, click Settings.

4. In the navigation pane, click Add Hardware.

5. On the Add Hardware page, choose a network adapter or a legacy network adapter.

6. Click Add. The Network Adapter or Legacy Network Adapter page appears.

7. Under Network, select the virtual network you want to connect to.

8. If you want to configure a static MAC address or virtual LAN identifier, specify the numbers you want to use.

9. Click OK.

+ MORE INFORMATION

For more information about Hyper-V, visit the following Web site: http://technet.microsoft.com/en-us/virtualization/default.aspx

SKILL SUMMARY

- When you view web pages, you are connecting to the web server using TCP port 80.
- SSL, short for Secure Sockets Layer, uses TCP port 443, which uses a digital certificate to encrypt data sent to and from a Web site so that it cannot be read by anyone except the source and target. When you are using SSL, the browser URL will start with https.
- File Transfer Protocol (FTP) is a standard network protocol used to transfer a file from one host to another over a TCP/IP-based network.
- Microsoft's web server/application server is Internet Information Services (IIS).
- To support multiple Web sites, you can assign additional IP addresses and assign a site to each IP address by using different ports for each site or host headers.
- To configure the IP address, port, and name a Web site will respond to, you must configure the site binding.
- A virtual directory is a directory used in a Web site that corresponds to a physical directory elsewhere on the server, on another server, or on a Website.
- An application is a grouping of content on a Web site that is defined at the root level or in a separate folder that has specific properties, such as the application pool in which the application runs and the permissions that are granted on the folder.
- An application pool is a set of resources (a worker process or a set of worker processes) used by a Web site or application that defines the memory boundaries for the Web site.
- The Default Documents feature allows you to configure the list of default documents that will automatically be presented to a browser if a document is not specified.
- A virtual private network (VPN) links two computers through a wide-area network such as the Internet. To keep the connection secure, the data sent between the two computers is encapsulated and encrypted.
- To access a computer running Remote Desktop Services, you use Remote Desktop Connections to access a computer's graphical user interface including the desktop, start menu, and programs just as if you were sitting in front of the computer.
- Remote assistance is similar to remote desktop except it is used to connect to another user's session so that you can see what the user is seeing and interact with that session.
- By using virtual machine technology, you can run multiple operating systems concurrently on a single machine, which allows separation of services while keeping cost to a minimum.
- The hypervisor is installed between the hardware and the operating system and is the main component that manages virtual computers.
- Some of the Windows built-in drivers do not run efficiently under a virtual environment. Therefore, you need to install Integration Services, which includes some basic drivers.
- Microsoft System Center Virtual Machine Manager (VMM) allows you to convert existing physical computers into virtual machines through a process known as physical-to-virtual (P2V) conversion.
- A snapshot is a point in time image of a virtual machine that you can return to.

Knowledge Assessment

Fill in the Blank

Complete the following sentences by writing the correct word or words in the blanks provided.

1. The _____ is a system of interlinked hypertext documents known as web pages that are browsed with a web browser.

2. The predominant markup language for web pages is _____.

3. Microsoft's web server is known as _____.

4. In IIS, a _____ is a directory used in a Web site that corresponds to a physical directory elsewhere on the server, on another server, or on a Web site.

5. HTTPS uses port _____.

6. _____ is the most widely used digital certificate.

7. Microsoft's newest virtual machine technology is _____.

8. A _____ is a point in time image of a virtual machine that you can return to.

9. You typically use _____ to remotely connect and manage a server, which allows you to run programs directly on the desktop.

10. _____ is a special mode of Remote Desktop Services that allows you to run an application in its own window.

Multiple Choice

Circle the letter that corresponds to the best answer.

1. Which protocol is used to transfer files between computers?
   a. DNS
   b. HTTP
   c. FTP
   d. Telnet

2. Which port does SMTP use?
   a. 21
   b. 25
   c. 80
   d. 443

3. Which port does HTTP use?
   a. 21
   b. 25
   c. 80
   d. 443

4. A(n) _____ defines a set of resources used by a Web site or application that defines the memory boundaries of a Web site.
   a. Virtual directory
   b. Root directory
   c. Application pool
   d. Port forwarder

5. Which authentication sends username and password that is not encrypted?
   a. Anonymous
   b. Basic authentication
   c. Digest authentication
   d. Windows authentication

6. When configuring VPN, L2TP uses _____ for encryption.
   a. SSTP
   b. PPTP
   c. MPE
   d. IPSec

7. Which authentication method used with VPN clients can be used with retinal scan and fingerprint identifications?
   a. PAP
   b. CHAP
   c. MS-CHAPv2
   d. EAP-MS-CHAPv2

8. By using _____ technology, you can run multiple operating systems concurrently on one machine.
   a. Virtual machine
   b. Virtual directory
   c. Terminal server
   d. Remote access

9. After you create a virtual server in Hyper-V and install the operating system, you then need to install _____ so that the virtual server can run more efficiently.
   a. VMWare client tools
   b. Remote Desktop tools
   c. Integration Services Setup
   d. P2V Disk tools

10. Which protocol is used to send out email?
    a. POP2
    b. IMAP
    c. HTTP
    d. SMTP

True / False

Circle T if the statement is true or F if the statement is false.

T | F **1.** When typing in a URL that does not specify a directory, your browser will always return a 404 error.

T | F **2.** If you are using Basic Authentication, you should use digital certificates to encrypt.

T | F **3.** To copy a digital certificate that includes the public and private key pair, use CSR.

T | F **4.** Today, PTTP is the recommended VPN tunneling protocol.

T | F **5.** The .vhd file holds the virtual machine configuration information.

▪ Competency Assessment

Scenario 7-1: Allowing Work from Home

You just started working as a system administrator for the Acme Corporation. Your company decides that as a benefit to its employees, some employees can work from home one day a week. Explain what can you do to help make this happen, what key technology you would use, and how would you configure it.

Scenario 7-2: Isolating Server Applications

You have two network applications—a network accounting application and a network HR application—that are not processor hungry. Both of these applications must be kept totally isolated, and both will access a centralized database server. What do you recommend?

▪ Proficiency Assessment

Scenario 7-3: Creating a Web Site

1. Install IIS.
2. Create a Web site that responds to contoso.com and www.contoso.com using port 80 that points to c:\Inetpub\wwwroot\contoso.
3. Add an entry in the host file that points contoso.com to the IP address of your server.
4. Create a folder called virtual in the c:\inetpub folder.
5. Create a virtual directory that points to c:\inetpub\virtual.
6. Create an application pool called contoso.
7. Change the contoso Web site to use the contoso application pool.

Scenario 7-4: Using Remote Desktop

1. Make sure remote desktop is enabled on your computer.
2. Connect to another windows computer using Remote Desktop.

Workplace Ready

Exchange and SQL Server

This lesson covered popular network application and services that are included with Windows Server 2008 R2. However, Microsoft and many other companies have created other applications or services that use or depend on the applications and services that come with Windows Server 2008 R2. For example, Microsoft Exchange depends on Active Directory for authentication, authorization, and name resolution for mailboxes. It also uses IIS to allow access to web-based versions of Microsoft Outlook and to allow mobile devices such as smart phones to sync email including calendar items and tasks. SQL Server also uses Active Directory and IIS to access and run reports. As you get deeper into being a system administrator, you will see that you are just getting started.

Appendix A
Windows Server Administration Fundamentals: Exam 98-365

Objective Domain	Skill Number	Lesson Number
Understanding Server Installation		
Understand device drivers.	1.1	2
Understand services.	1.2	2
Understand server installation options.	1.3	1
Understanding Server Roles		
Identify application servers.	2.1	1
Understand web services.	2.2	7
Understand remote access.	2.3	2
Understand the file and print services.	2.4	6
Understand server virtualization.	2.5	1, 7
Understanding Active Directory		
Understand accounts and groups.	3.1	5
Understand organizational units and containers.	3.2	5
Understand Active Directory infrastructure.	3.3	5
Understand group policy.	3.4	5
Understanding Storage		
Identify storage technologies.	4.1	3
Understand RAID.	4.2	3
Understand disk types.	4.3	3
Understanding Server Performance Management		
Identify major server hardware components.	5.1	1
Understand performance monitoring.	5.2	4
Understand logs and alerts.	5.3	4
Understanding Server Maintenance		
Identify steps in the startup process.	6.1	4
Understand business continuity.	6.2	4
Understand updates.	6.3	1
Understand troubleshooting methodology.	6.4	4

Appendix B
Understanding TCP/IP

TCP/IP

↓
THE BOTTOM LINE

Because the Internet has become so popular, so has the TCP/IP protocol suite that the Internet runs on. One of the two main protocols mentioned in the name—the IP protocol—is responsible for addressing and routing packets between hosts. Just like when sending a letter through your post office to a specific street address located within a city or zip code, each host must have its own unique IP address so that it can send and receive packets.

A **host** is any device that connects directly to a network. Although most hosts are computers, they can include network printers, routers, layer 3 switches, managed switches, and any other device that has a network card or interface.

An **Internet Protocol (IP) address** is a logical address and numerical label that is assigned to device connected to a computer network. Although you have to follow certain guidelines based on the TCP/IP protocol suite, they are logical addresses that you assign as needed.

Today, most IP addresses are based on traditional IPv4 addresses, which are based on 32-bit numbers. Unfortunately, since the Internet has grown in popularity, the 4 billion addresses used on an IPv4 network are almost depleted. Therefore, there are designs to migrate the Internet to IPv6 addresses, which are based on 128-bit addresses. Since each bit doubles the number of available addresses, the 128-bit addresses allow up to 3.403×10^{38} addresses.

IPv4 Networks

Today, most networks will be IPv4 networks. Although the IPv4 allows 2^{32} or 4,294,867,296 addresses, IPv4 has matured through the years and various techniques were invented to utilize the addresses more efficiently.

As mentioned before, IPv4 addresses are based on 32-bits. When expressed, an IPv4 address is expressed in dot-decimal notation consisting of four numbers (a.b.c.d), each ranging from 0 to 255. Each number is called an octet because it is based on 8 bits. Examples of IPv4 addresses are:

192.168.1.1

16.23.212.214

127.0.0.1

The earliest IPv4 addresses were based on a Classful network design where the first three bits of the first octet would define the class: class A, B, and C. By looking at Table 2-1, you can create 128 class A networks, 16,384 class B networks, and 2,097,151 class C networks. Although a single class A network can have over 16 million hosts, a class C can have only 254 hosts. Of course, for you to create all of these networks, you have to have your own large network that is not shared with the Internet. Most of these addresses are already in use.

212

Table A-1

IPv4 Classful network

Class	Range of First Octet	Default Subnet Mask	Network ID	Host ID	Number of Networks	Number of Addresses per Network
A	0–127	255.0.0.0	a	b.c.d	128	16,777,214
B	128–191	255.255.0.0	a.b	c.d	16,384	65,534
C	192–223	255.255.255.0	a.b.c	d	2,097,151	254

The *subnet masks* specify which bits are network bits and which bits are host bits. When you have a subnet mask of 255.0.0.0, it means that the first 8 bits are used to describe the network bits, whereas the last 24 bits are used for the host bits. Therefore, if you have a 12.212.34.5 address with a subnet mask of 255.0.0.0, you have a 12.0.00 network address and 0.212.34.5 host address.

Class A, B, and C addresses are known as unicast addresses that specify a single network device. Packets sent to a unicast address are delivered to the single node containing the interface identified by the address.

Class D addresses are defined from 224.0.0.0 to 239.255.255.255 used for multicast addresses. A multicast address is a single address that refers to multiple network devices. You can think of a multicast address as a group address that can be used to cut down traffic by sending one set of data packets meant for multiple hosts.

When using a Classful network address, you automatically know which bits are assigned to define the network and which bits define the host on the network. For example, if you have a 130.34.34.2, the default subnet mask is 255.255.0.0. Therefore, for a Classful network, the 130.34.0.0 would be the network address and the host address would be 0.0.34.2.

Unfortunately, with a Classful network, many addresses were wasted. For example, although you might assign a class A network to a single network, most of the 16 million addresses were not used. Therefore, classless inter-domain routing (CIDR) was developed to utilize the networks more efficiently. Instead of using the pre-defined subnet masks, CIDR is based on variable-length subnet masking (VLSM) where you can take a network and subdivide the network into smaller subnets.

For example, you could take a class B network (130.5.0.0), which could be assigned to large corporation. Every host within the corporation must begin with 130.5.0.0. You then assign a network address 130.5.1.0 to the first subnet or site and 130.5.2.0 to the second subnet or site. Each address located at the first subnet must start with 130.5.1.

CIDR notation uses a syntax of specifying the IP address followed by a slash followed by the number of masked bits. For example, if you have an IPv4 address of 12.23.52.120 with a subnet mask of 255.255.0.0, you would write the address as 12.23.52.120/16.

Private Networks and NAT

Although CIDR helped use the IPv4 addresses more efficiently, additional steps had to prevent the exhaustion of IPv4 addresses. *Network Address Translation (NAT)* is used with masquerading to hide an entire address space behind a single IP address. In other words, it allows multiple computers on a network to connect to the Internet through a single IP address.

NAT enables a local-area network (LAN) to use one set of IP addresses for internal traffic and a second set of addresses for external traffic. The NAT box is usually a router (including routers made for home and small-office Internet connections) or a proxy server. As a result, NAT serves two main purposes:

- Provides a type of firewall by hiding internal IP addresses.
- Enables a company to use more internal IP addresses.

The *private addresses* are reserved addresses not allocated to any specific organization. Since these private addresses cannot be assigned to global addresses used on the Internet and are not routable on the Internet, you must use a NAT gateway or proxy server to convert between private and public addresses. The private network addresses as expressed in RFC 1918:

- 10.0.0.0–10.255.255.255
- 172.16.0.0–172.31.255.255
- 192.168.0.0–192.168.255.255

NAT obscures an internal network's structure by making all traffic appear originated from the NAT device or proxy server. To accomplish this, the NAT device or proxy server uses stateful translation tables to map the "hidden" addresses into a single address and then rewrites the outgoing Internet Protocol (IP) packets on exit so that they appear to originate from the router. As data packets are returned from the Internet, the responding data packets are mapped back to the originating IP address using the entries stored in the translation tables.

IPv6 Networks

As mentioned earlier, the number of public IPv4 addresses are running low. To overcome this problem as well as a few others, IPv6 was developed as the next-generation Internet Protocol version.

IPv6 provides a number of benefits for TCP/IP-based networking connectivity, including:

- Utilizes 128-bit address space to provide addressing for every device on the Internet with a globally unique address.
- Allows for more efficient routing than IPv4.
- Supports automatic configuration.
- Offers enhanced security to protect against address and port scanning attacks and utilizes IPSec to protect IPv6 traffic.

Since the IPv6 uses 128 bits, the addresses are usually divided into groups of 16 bits, written as 4 hex digits. Hex digits include 0, 1, 2, 3, 4, 5, 6, 7, 8, 9, A, B, C, D, E, and F. Colons separate the groups. An example of an address would be:

FE80:0000:0000:0000:02C3:B2DF:FEA5:E4F1

Similar to the IPv4 addresses, IPv6 are divided into network bits and host address. However, the first 64 bits define the network address, and the second 64 bits define the host address. Therefore, in our example address, FE80:0000:0000:0000 defines the network bits and 02C3:B2DF:FEA5:E4F1 defines the host bits. The network bits are also further divided where 48 bits is used for the network prefix and the next 16 bits is used for subnetting.

To facilitate simplified automatic addressing, the IPv6 subnet size has been standardized and fixed to 64 bits, and the MAC address is used to generate the host bits within the unicast network address or link-local address when stateless autoconfiguration is used.

With IPv6, you still have unicast and multicast addressing. However, unicast addressing can be divided into:

- **Global unicast address:** Public addresses that are globally routable and reachable on the IPv6 portion of the Internet.
- **Link-local addresses:** Private non-routable addresses confined to a single subnet. They are used by hosts when communicating with neighboring hosts on the same link but can also be used in creating temporary networks, for conferences or meetings, or in setting up a permanent small LAN. Routers will process packets destined to a link-local address, but they will not forward them to other links.
- **Unique local addresses:** Meant for private addressing, with the addition of being unique, so that joining two subnets does not cause address collisions.

You may also have an anycast address, which is an address that is assigned to multiple computers. When IPv6 addresses communication to an anycast address, only the closest host responds. You typically use this for locating services or the nearest router.

Default Gateway

A *default gateway* is a device, usually a router, which connects the local network to other networks. When you need to communicate with a host on another subnet, you forward all packets to the default gateway.

The default gateway allows a host to communicate with remote hosts. Every time a host needs to send packets, it will first determine if the host is local (same subnet), or if it is remote it has to go through a router to get to the remote host. The router will then determine the best way to get the remote subnet and forwards the packets toward the remote subnet.

To determine if the destination address is local or remote, it will look at the network bits of both the sending and destination hosts. If the network bits are the same, it will assume the destination host is local and send the packets directly to the local host. If the network bits are different, it will assume the destination host is remote and send the packets to the default gateway.

For example, you have the following:

> Sending host address: 10.10.57.3
> Sending host subnet mask: 255.255.255.0
> Destination host address: 10.10.89.37

By isolating the network address for the host, you have 10.10.57.0. By isolating the network address for the destination host address, you have 10.10.89.0. Since they are different, the packet will be sent to the default gateway and the router will determine the best way to get there.

Of course, if the subnet mask is wrong, the host might misidentify a host as being local or remote. If the default gateway is wrong, packets may not be able to leave the local subnet.

Name Resolution

In today's networks, you assign logical addresses such as IP addressing. Unfortunately, these addresses tend to be hard to remember, especially with the newer more complicated IPv6 addresses. Therefore, you need to use some form of naming service that will allow you to translate logical names, which are easier to remember, to those logical addresses.

There are two types of names to translate. The first ones are host names, which reside in the Domain Name System and are the same names used with the Internet. When you type a name of a Web site or server that is on the Internet, such as www.microsoft.com or cnn.com, you are specifying a domain/host name. The other name is your computer name, also known as the NetBIOS name. If you are on a corporate network or your home network, the host name is usually the computer name.

HOSTS AND LHMOSTS FILES

Early TCP/IP networks used hosts (used with domain/host names associated with DNS) and lmhosts (used with NetBIOS/Computer names associated with WINS) files, which were text files that would list a name and its associated IP address. However, every time you needed to add or modify a name and address, you would have to modify the text file on every computer that needed to know the address. For larger organizations, this was very inefficient because it could include hundreds if not thousands of computers and the text files could become quite large.

In Windows, both of these files are located in the C:\Windows\system32\drivers\etc folder. The hosts file (see Figure A-1) can be edited and is ready to use. The lmhosts.sam is a sample file and it will have to be copied as lmhosts without the .sam filename extension.

Figure A-1

A sample host file

```
# Copyright (c) 1993-1999 Microsoft Corp.
#
# This is a sample HOSTS file used by Microsoft TCP/IP for Windows.
#
# This file contains the mappings of IP addresses to host names. Each
# entry should be kept on an individual line. The IP address should
# be placed in the first column followed by the corresponding host name.
# The IP address and the host name should be separated by at least one
# space.
#
# Additionally, comments (such as these) may be inserted on individual
# lines or following the machine name denoted by a '#' symbol.
#
# For example:
#
#   102.54.94.97    rhino.acme.com    # source server
#   38.25.63.10     x.acme.com        # x client host

127.0.0.1         localhost
204.52.32.33      acme.com
192.168.3.12      webserver
192.1.68.3.12     webserver.acme.com
```

Although the hosts and lmhosts files are considered legacy methods for naming resolution, they can still come in handy when troubleshooting or testing because name resolution will check these two files before contacting naming servers. For example, you just installed a new server but you do not want to make it available to everyone else. You can add an entry in your local hosts file so that when your computer resolves a certain name it will resolve to the IP address of the new server. This keeps you from changing the DNS entry, which would affect all users on your organization's network until you are ready.

DOMAIN NAME SERVICE

Besides becoming the standard for the Internet, *Domain Name Service (DNS)*, is a hierarchical client/server-based distributed database management system that translates domain/hosts names to an IP address. In other words, although you may have a DNS server (or several servers), sometimes referred to as name servers, to provide naming resolution for your organization, all of the DNS servers on the Internet are linked together to provide worldwide naming resolution while allowing your to manage the DNS for you organization.

The top of the tree is known as the root domain. Below the root domain, you will find top-level domains such as .com, .edu, .org, and .net and two letter country codes such as .uk, .ca, and .us. Below the top-level domains, you will find the registered variable name that corresponds to their organization or other registered name. The second-level domain name must be registered by an authorized party such as networksolutions.com or godaddy.com.

For example, microsoft.com is registered to the Microsoft Corporation. When you search for it, will first contact the .com DNS servers to determine the name server for microsoft.com. It will then contact the microsoft.com DNS servers to determine the address that is assigned to microsoft.com. Larger organizations may subdivide their DNS name space into subdomains, such as technet.microsoft.com, msdn.microsoft.com, or social.microsoft.com.

A host name is a name assigned to a specific computer within a domain or subdomain to identify the TCP/IP host. Multiple host names can be assigned to the same IP address although only one name can be assigned to a physical computer or virtual computer.

A fully qualified domain name (FQDN) describes the exact position of a host within the DNS hierarchy. Examples of full names include:

> www.microsoft.com
>
> technet.microsoft.com
>
> server1.sales.microsoft.com

WINDOWS INTERNET NAME SERVICE

Another name resolution technology is *Windows Internet Name Service (WINS)*, which translates from NetBIOS (computer name) to specify a network resource. Since the growth of the Internet and the scalability of DNS, WINS is considered a legacy system.

A WINS sever contains a database of IP addresses and NetBIOS names that update dynamically. Unfortunately, WINS is not a hierarchy system like DNS so it is only good for your organization and was made only for Windows operating systems. Typically, other network devices and services cannot register with a WINS server. Therefore, you would have to add static entries for these devices if you want name resolution using WINS.

When you share a directory, drive, or printer on a PC running Microsoft Windows or Linux machines running Samba, you would access the resource by using the Universal Naming Convention (UNC), also known as Uniform Naming Convention to specify the location of the resources. Traditionally, UNC use the following format:

> \\computername\sharednamed\optionalpathname

For example, to access the shared directory on a computer called server1, you would type the following name:

> \\server1\data

However, DNS has become more popular so you can also use host names with the UNC. For example, you could use:

> \\Server1.microsoft.com\data

Index